A Composite View to the Past

A methodological integration
of zooarchaeology and archaeological
geophysics at the Magdalenian site of
Verberie le Buisson-Campin

Jason Thompson

BAR International Series 2623
2014

Published in 2016 by
BAR Publishing, Oxford

BAR International Series 2623

A Composite View to the Past

ISBN 978 1 4073 1258 3

BAR Publishing is the trading name of British Archaeological Reports (Oxford) Ltd.
British Archaeological Reports was first incorporated in 1974 to publish the BAR
Series, International and British. In 1992 Hadrian Books Ltd became part of the BAR
group. This volume was originally published by Archaeopress in conjunction with
British Archaeological Reports (Oxford) Ltd / Hadrian Books Ltd, the Series principal
publisher, in 2014. This present volume is published by BAR Publishing, 2016.

Printed in England

BAR
PUBLISHING

BAR titles are available from:

BAR Publishing
122 Banbury Rd, Oxford, OX2 7BP, UK
EMAIL   info@barpublishing.com
PHONE   +44 (0)1865 310431
FAX   +44 (0)1865 316916
www.barpublishing.com

Contents

List of Figures

Chapter 1 Introduction

Debates of alleged human modernity and archaism have dominated much of the recent Eurasian Paleolithic archaeological literature. Most debate has tended to proceed through the overt position and relative disposition of various interesting theoretical questions, such as "When did Modernity arrive in Europe?", or "Which Pleistocene human chronospecies brought Modernity to Europe?", or even, "Were Neanderthals modern?" Some even ask, "Were Neanderthals human?" The evidences on which such debates have occurred have tended to consist of data derived from artifact seriations and various attribute analyses of lithic technology, and, especially since the late 1980s and 1990s, upon mitochondrial DNA and other (unfortunately non-comprehensive) genetic studies. These debates have also tended to serve as either lumping or splitting devices, emphasizing continuity or disparity between Neanderthals and anatomically modern humans (hereinafter AMH), allegedly echoed and evinced in broad Paleolithic technological categories of Middle and Upper (or, rather, Middle vs. Upper, appositively).

The traditional assumption was that behavior (at least as visible in lithic technology) correlated precisely with hominin morphology, such that archaic *Homo sapiens* (or *Homo antecessor* or *Homo heidelbergensis*) was understood to exhibit a certain specific finite range of functional "archaic" behaviors, among which was the construction of Acheulean bifaces; Neanderthals expressed Neanderthal behaviors, expressed in Mousterian lithics; Cro-Magnons engaged in Cro-Magnon behaviors, encapsulated in Upper Paleolithic technologies (Bordes 1969; Binford and Binford 1966, 1968; Mellars 1970, 1973). Such arguments tend to invert the architect's familiar refrain that form follows function. Indeed, given the lengths to which many archaeologists and paleoanthropologists have gone to argue against conspecificity between "archaic" and "modern" humans, it would seem some assume that function follows form. Some also allege that the functions of Lower or Middle Paleolithic artifacts existed completely independently of form or even intentional manufacture (Rolland and Dibble 1990; Tattersall 1995). To some degree, analyses of human subsistence organization have begun recently to figure into such debates, and have been treated to an ideational developmental trajectory similar to that observed in the lithic perspectives above (Hensilwood and Marean 2003) although currently to a lesser degree than studies based purely upon lithic analyses.

The main question posed here is, simply, what is modern subsistence, or, to change slightly our analytical perspective, what constitutes subsistence modernity? For example, in terms of lithic technology, the traditional view has been to see modernity in various African Middle Stone Age (hereinafter MSA) or Eurasian Upper Paleolithic (hereinafter EAUP) stone tool industries from northeast Africa, the Near East, Anatolia, and Europe, typified by allegedly standardized blade blank production, tool construction on blade blanks, particularities in core preparation and treatment, and the presence of variously-shaped microlithic tool components and armatures, defined against the presumed or observed lack of such materials in earlier industries. With regard to morphological or genetic modernity, decades of animated literary focus have sought to define modernity as the present state of contemporary human morphology in opposition to that observed in the current paleontological inventory of Neanderthals and other forms of "archaic" Eurasian humans, with postulated genetic continuity between contemporary and prehistoric AMH human populations extending back into MSA or Eurasian Middle Paleolithic times. This, of course, is the great Out of Africa vs. Regional Continuity debate. Just how much the dynamics of this debate will be subject to revision pending recovery of additional human fossil or archaeological material is a very open question.

Yet, to return to the question posed above, what is modern subsistence? For in fact, this seemingly innocuous question is itself composed of many others. IS there such a thing as modern subsistence? What qualities characterize subsistence modernity? What definitions can apply? Is there in fact a modernity package, or trait list, that we can use heuristically in application to an understanding of modern subsistence (Henshilwood and Marean 2003)? If there is a modernity package, who decides what should be placed in it, or should there be multiple packages? How wide are the temporal ranges of modern subsistence, its geographic ranges, its ranges of technological *accoutrements*? For how long has subsistence modernity existed, where, and with what other material associations? How wide is the modern subsistence behavioral range? How, or perhaps even, *can* an impression of subsistence modernity be used to inform us about non-modern subsistence? In other words, does an understanding of what something may not be or is not actually tell us what something may be or is? How, how much, and why? What is the nature of modern subsistence in evolutionary terms? Are we to see subsistence modernity more in biological/naturalistic terms of ecological niches and trophic levels, or morphologically and specific (i.e., as a species-based phenomenon)? Should we view it as the crossing of some cognitive threshold or presumed cerebral encephalization barrier? Are all or none of these interrogatory items relevant?

An even more crucial question and problem would be that of how to test archaeologically for modernity in subsistence behaviors. For an answer to that question would involve again treatments of temporality, subsistence technology, behavior, geography, environment, ecological niche, niche cohorts (peers, competitors, guilds), cognition, and, to some extent, physical morphology and presumed genetic and evolutionary continuities and disparities. This is all the more challenging when such a test is applied at the level of one archaeological site, in this case, at one well known site from the Magdalenian of the Paris Basin (hereinafter MPB), northeastern France: Verberie le Buisson Campin (the bush camp of Verberie, hereinafter VBC). Whereas a more exhaustive description of VBC will follow below, some points must be addressed now, in relation to testing the relative subsistence modernity of this MPB site. Estimating or testing subsistence modernity in the MPB actually describes a process of interrogating human evolutionary adaptations to the Late Pleistocene and tardiglacial of the Paris Basin from the content and configuration of available archaeological faunal data from VBC, since zooarchaeology and faunal analysis represents a means for directly testing such (Enloe 1983; Enloe 1993).

What, however, do we mean by "available" data? At VBC, available faunal data are composed of excavated archaeofauna. As we shall see below, however, estimating the content and configuration of VBC fauna will also involve expanding our definition of "available". For recent surveys at VBC suggest that the site itself may in fact be larger than previously thought, covering a larger area of a Pleistocene point bar terrace of the Oise River than that indicated by excavation alone. Furthermore, IF the site is appreciably larger than those areas which have been excavated and retired, and contains additional deposits of archaeological material, then by definition previous analyses of VBC archaeological material are incomplete. This would mean that some part of the VBC faunal inventory is also incomplete simply because the site has not yet been retired. So, at this juncture, we can now see the outlines of a problem just beginning to emerge, involving how to estimate and interpret archaeological material content, configuration, scale, and orientation in possibly unexcavated areas, as well as how to incorporate such data into currently available datasets. Solving this problem will occupy much of our focus below.

The form of the present study will consist of the following. We will investigate in Chapter One the anthropological/ archaeological concept of Modernity, and seek to gain relevant awareness of what this rather vague construct actually entails, of when it occurs/occurred, where the phenomenon occurred, and of which hominin species may reliably be understood to have enacted it. We may, in fact, regard Chapters One and Two as a joint or complementary exercise in providing and establishing the cognitive context of the present study. We will then turn to an examination of Behavioral/Cognitive Modernity (hereinafter BCM), consisting of an analysis of this concept's emergence in the archaeological literature. We shall also seek to learn about the nature of evidence used in discussing BCM, both as this material exists in its own right, and also as it pertains to the broader anthropological origins debate

concerning the comparative evolutionary dispositions of AMHs and Neanderthals. This, in turn, leads us to what has been termed the "modernity package" (Henshilwood and Marean 2003), or a set or list of traits or characteristics within archaeological materials that are presumed to be indicative of BCM, serving as proxies for cognition, anatomic morphology, and neurology (virtually by default since other 'modernistic' explications are often refuted). Blade lithic technology, for example, is regarded as a virtual *fossil directeur* of modernity. Do blades = modernity? Does modern cognition = blades? Do blades = other modernity proxies in the modernity package?

We will likewise examine the chronological nature of modernity. Was the advent of, or transition to, modernity a gradualistic or a punctuated phenomenon? It may also be that the chronological onset of modernity occurred differently in different times and places, in mosaic or "kaleidoscope" ways (Pettitt 2007). We will also describe a means of "seeing" modernity, involving assessing whether there exists certain complementarities of modernities, as in asking if the MSA modernity = EAUP modernity, or whether both are or aren't commensurate with Australian modernity. We may now ask the philosophical question of whether an understanding of archaeological phenomena is more a matter of what is seen, how it is seen, or some combination thereof. That avenue leads us finally to an inquiry into the dynamics of subsistence modernity, discussing observed changes in subsistence technology and ancillary changes in prehistoric diet breadth, geography, altitude, seasonality, and prey species. This will be done in application to the EAUP lithic technological sequence, with special attention devoted to the Magdalenian.

Yet, by what means can we see modernity, or, indeed, dynamic human agency in static archaeological phenomena, in general? We shall in Chapter Two discuss archaeological models and analogies as some of our primary means for seeing and studying subsistence modernity amongst Paleolithic hunter-gatherers. An examination will then ensue of the development of archaeological and ethnoarchaeological analogies and models, especially as developed during the 1960s and 1970s, moving from the Man the Hunter Conferences (Lee and Devore 1968) to the "tyranny of the ethnographic record", in ignorance of temporal, geographic, environmental, and biological particularistic differences between contemporary and past hunter-gatherers (Wobst 1978). We will see also that despite some confusion in the literature, archaeological/ethnoarchaeological subsistence models and analogies are not at all the same things, even though they do often seek to explain aspects of the same anthropogenic phenomena. Analogies, for example, involve estimates of similarity or comparability based upon observation and/or documentation. Models are more schematized descriptions of systems. We might, therefore, suggest, according to the familiar theme of archaeological method and theory, that whereas models are actually more theoretical constructs, analogies are more methodologically-based. What, if anything, bridges the two, and how is this relevant to analyses of Paleolithic subsistence?

Binford's (1967; 1968; 1981; 2001) significant formulations of Middle-Range Theory (hereinafter MRT) can serve to negotiate between analogical and model-based archaeological reasoning. At one level, MRT comprises a cognitive toolkit, composed of both theoretical and methodological components, for inferring past causal processes explanatory of observed archaeological patterning. One of the primary demonstrations of MRT has involved the methodological use of archaeofaunas in zooarchaeological studies to test hypotheses of past human subsistence, especially the development during the 1980s, 1990s, and 2000s, of increasingly elaborate, sophisticated, and explanatorily powerful techniques for using prehistoric animal bones and their structural, chemical, and physical properties to identify anthropogenic conditioning and patterning of the zooarchaeological record. We will also seek to understand the familiar logistical vs. foraging poles of the subsistence spectrum.

Having established the subjects of our focus, and the tools we will use to see them, Chapter Two will also outline some of the presumed dynamics and social contexts of Paleolithic logistical subsistence, especially regarding its physical, economic, and possibly cognitive bases. Logistical subsistence involves an active posture, in relation to more passive foraging strategies, suggestive of augmented and elaborated roles of information awareness, especially observation and reconnaissance in order to synthesize information for predictive purposes. Additional topics will include discussion of possible material correlates of elaborated information gathering, recording, synthesis, and predictive transmission. Chapter Two will conclude with treatments of Magdalenian culture, and its consistency in material expression across space and time. This consistency may in fact be suggestive or illustrative of intensified social identification and group identity, perhaps indicated by intensified group integration and risk-pooling. We will estimate Magdalenian economic "value" through possible indices of preferences, expressed archaeologically as particularities of prey carcass selectivity and carcass disposition. This involves a critique of optimal-foraging models based upon their (often radically) non-anthropological biological bases in favor of an anthropological, human-behavioral model of Paleolithic risk-management. The assumption here is that anthropological models should be used to abstract the dynamics of human cultural systems.

Whereas Chapters One and Two established the cognitive context of the present study, Chapter Three details its methodology and physical setting. We begin with descriptions of VBC as an open-air MPB site on a Pleistocene point bar terrace of the Oise River, with multiple components and multiple occupation surfaces (Audouze and Enloe 1997). Perhaps three hundred to four hundred square meters of the site have been excavated, which represents a very small percentage of the total area represented by the point bar. Radiocarbon age estimates of the site range between 13.3 ky and 10.6 ky (Enloe and David 1997:55). The discussion turns next to a basic treatment of the Paris Basin, as well as the general depositional/sedimentological characteristics of the Late Pleistocene Oise River. What sorts of physical, post-depositional processes impacted the site? What anthropogenic conditioning is present? We will investigate the activities of mild bioturbation on sediment, and of density-mediated bone destruction, root vermiculation, and mechanical weathering on archaeofauna. This is a search for patterning.

What we may further say of anthropogenic conditioning of the archaeofauna at VBC will require a good impression of complementarity/disparity between faunal data from multiple loci at VBC. This will also be discussed further in Chapter Three in terms of describing a methodological comparison and contrast between the faunal content, structure, and configuration of two datasets from VBC Secteurs 190 and 202 Level II.22. We will note a lack of taxonomic diversity in the fauna, as well as palimpsest deposition of redundant data. We will investigate the faunal configuration and spatial structure through an analysis of skeletal element spatial distribution. If, however, we suggest that only a small area of the site has been tested directly through excavation, we have to note the incompleteness of the total archaeological sample from VBC as well as to note again that it may in fact be much larger than excavations suggest.

If the site is in fact larger, then barring excavation of the entirety of the Pleistocene point bar on which it sits the archaeological inventory of VBC will always be incomplete. In other words, our analysis of its material inventory and distribution (content and configuration) is by definition incomplete. This is another very large and interesting problem. If we cannot directly sample archaeological content through excavation of the total area, can we at least estimate unexcavated archaeological configuration by some other means? Are there ways to sample the configuration of unexcavated archaeological materials? Chapter Three further proposes geophysical survey as a means of gaining such impressions, in particular ground-penetrating radar, since it offers highly accurate data both vertically in profile and horizontally in plan map view. Chapter Four provides the present study's detailed analysis of faunal content and structure. Chapter Five describes an elaborate, multifaceted experimental methodology with imagery and results for determining the degree to which ground-penetrating radar can be used to image the scale, configuration, and orientation of small-scale subsurface materials in 1) a completely artificial sandbox setting and 2) a "natural" sedimentological context similar to that at VBC. Chapter Six describes the practical application of a ground-penetrating radar survey at VBC, as well as imagery and results correlated with direct content-testing undertaken during excavations at VBC in 2008 and 2009. Chapters Seven and Eight expound upon possible summaries and conclusions based upon the analyses of content and configuration, as well as provide recommendations for future research and a personal afterward.

Chapter 2 Tracking Modernity: What is it?

In Anthropological usage, "Modernity" is a connotative term, indicating a generally Westernist, post-Enlightenment philosophical perspective that developed especially during the periods of European colonization, the Industrial Revolution, and the early 20th Century (Appadurai 1996; Comaroff and Comaroff 1999; Kahn 2001). It is noteworthy that Anthropology developed as an academic discipline during the same timeframe. Linked closely with the Modernity perspective is the somewhat broader behavioral-cultural movement or trend of "modernism", which symbiotically both generates and is generated by experiential modernity, consisting of shifting sets of norms, styles, and habits to large degrees mediated (if not 'controlled') by governmental, military, media, and corporate entities (Habermas 1987). It may therefore be easiest to describe Modernity as a paradigmatic tradition, used to experience, describe, and provide some basic structural sense to our "normal" contemporary physical reality. Although Modernity and modernism are not of necessity perfectly commensurate with Westernism and a sense of Euroamerican ethnocentrism, the complex socio-economic, academic, and historic interlinkages between Westernist and Modernist thought cannot be overstated.

Within the Modernist perspective, and utilizing "its" own modernist proclivities, the primary Anthropological paradigm during the same timeframe has been evolutionary in nature, seeking and producing explanations of human biology, culture, reality, and origins in terms of change over time, using a variant (i.e., geologic time) of the familiar rectilinear timeframe imposed by the popular monotheistic religious traditions (Bamforth 2002; Kahn 2001).

The Westernist consciousness in which our Anthropological tradition developed has over the same timeframe participated in, caused, and variously otherwise experienced profound social changes. As a result, Modernity, modernism, and Anthropology are to a large degree *defined by* sensitivity to changes, especially time-sensitive, diachronic changes. This comfort with the concept of change, in terms of socio-economics, history, and science, has contributed in no small measure to a tendency to construct a modern "now" in relation to present-day immediacy, discontinuous with an archaic "then". If "then" was no different experientially, materially, or historically than "now" then ideological constructions of a rectilinear timeframe become meaningless. Obviously "now" is something other than "then", according to the Modernity paradigm, and if they weren't different, then rendering distinctions between the two would be nonsense. Since the 1990s, a peculiar behavioristic offshoot, termed "behavioral modernity", has also entered the archaeological literature, focused primarily on the documentation of specific material instances of "modern human" uniqueness as defined against the backdrop of a very incompletely known but allegedly "archaic" past.

Behavioral Modernity?

There are four basic issues pertaining to a discussion of behavioral modernity, three of which relate to objective categories of periodicity, locality, and identity; the fourth issue involves the actual archaeological material that is appraised to be "behaviorally modern", on which the previous three are themselves based. A fundamental question of modernity's periodicity would be simply when did it first occur and how long did its developmental process last? The two primary models in the literature contrast with respect to this timing, with one seeing the process as relatively late Pleistocene and sudden in nature (Klein 1994, 1995, 2001; Mellars 1995, 1996, 1999), and the other as a more continuous, synthetic process beginning in the Middle Pleistocene and lasting through the Eurasian Upper Paleolithic and African Late Stone Age (Henshilwood and Marean 2003; McBrearty and Brooks 2000; McCall 2006). One may also cogently query the presumed locality of modernity's emergence. Was modernity confined to an initial florescence only in South Africa with subsequent later diffusions to the Levant and the rest of Eurasia (Klein 1994, 1995, 2001; Mellars 1995, 1996. 1999), or did it unfold as continuous expressions of a more gradual process with dispersed geographies (Barker et al. 2007; Bar-Yosef and Kuhn 1999; Habgood and Franklin 2008; McBrearty and Brooks 2000)? Finally, in terms of identity, which hominid actors accomplished behavioral modernity? In South Africa, modernity proxies are typically associated with Anatomically Modern Humans (hereinafter AMH) (McBrearty and Brooks 2000; Mellars 1999), while Eurasian Middle and Upper Paleolithic archaeological sites often present rather ambiguous associations between hominids and material in different areas at much different times (Barker et al. 2007; Habgood and Franklin 2008; Pettitt 2007; Zilhao et al. 2006).

The fourth basic issue relating to behavioral modernity concerns the nature of the evidence for modernity itself, namely the material of the human fossil and archaeological records and the interpretations rendered from them. The material itself is nothing new, of course, consisting of the same art objects, bones, stone tools, human remains, and associated landscape features (i.e., "sites") that have traditionally served as the main focus of Old World prehistorians. What are new are subjective recapitulations of older interpretations of the material combined with much newer inputs from other disciplines (genetics and chemistry, via the African Eve hypothesis) that have resulted in the assembly of a "package" (or theory and trait list), supposedly visible archaeologically and paleontologically that can be used to "spot" behavioral modernity in different times and places (Habgood and Franklin 2008; Pettitt 2007). This trait list or "package" is composed of human morphology, art, personal adornment and presumed body modifications, blade-based lithic technology, bone, wood, and other organic technology, socio-demographic elaboration and population growth, and economic intensification (Habgood and Franklin 2008; McBrearty and Brooks 2000). The ubiquity, or lack thereof, of any of the "package" phenomena in isolation or in tandem seem to depend just as much upon where and when one samples as it does upon which Upper Pleistocene hominid species is sampled. Pettitt (2007:759) introduces a "kaleidoscope" metaphor to convey this impression of modernity as a cumulative but irregular set of separately variable, interacting regional trajectories, with no one particular regional variant (including the South African Middle Stone Age) serving as "the" central driver.

There is also an inherent tension between the description and identification of the behavioral modernity "package" on the one hand (i.e., allegedly modern human behavior and its various material correlates) through the use of its own conceptual definitions within the archaeological literature on the other. For example, without reference to any authorities in particular, various (sometimes even isolated) technological characteristics of modernity (lithic blade technology for example) are often held to be self-evident and auto-referential proxies of modern human cognition *and even other modernity characteristics* (i.e., blades = art, recognizable kinship networks, etc.); modern human cognition is then often invoked as a necessary and sufficient causal mechanism for the appearance of art and lithic blade technologies and everything else presumed to be in the modernity package.

This has the effect of devolving the discussion into a chicken and egg scenario. On the one hand we have chickens, while on the other we have eggs. We know that chickens hatch from eggs. Yet, it becomes a much dicier proposition "to explain" the presence of certain archaeological Culture A-type eggs through appeal to Culture A-type chickens *lacking any evidence at all at a site of the past chickens themselves*, which approximates numerous archaeologically demonstrable scenarios from many regions that present archaeological materials in the absence of associated human remains. This is all the dicier if we suppose that Culture A-type eggs may be indistinguishable from other kinds of eggs, especially if found in broken form. Furthermore, a much wider epistemological gap has to be crossed in order to postulate the past existence of entire families of "modern", networking and hierarchically-ranked and logistically-organized Culture A-type chickens at a site merely on the basis of the shapes and sizes of undiagnostic eggshell fragments.

Origins Models

The current "state of the state" regarding paleoanthropology and Paleolithic archaeology could be quite accurately described as a *détente* between two basic orthodoxies that explain some, but not all, of the human evidence in the archaeological and fossil records. Previous research and advanced training seem to indicate the methods whereby individuals choose a side in the divided camps. An influential synthetic and quasi-diffusionary model of human modernity obtained after Cann et al. (1987) published a pivotal paper, describing a hypothetical Middle Pleistocene genetic bottleneck event that truncated mtDNA diversity amongst ancient human populations. According to this interpretation, the population bottleneck eliminated most mtDNA lineages from the Pleistocene human gene pool, such that subsequent anatomically modern populations feature a low diversity of mtDNA that originated from a single anatomically modern African woman approximately 200 kya. This Recent Out of Africa model (hereinafter ROA) also implies that "modern humans" diverged evolutionarily from all earlier possible common ancestors perhaps as long ago as 400 to 800 kya based on a subjective reading of a figurative molecular clock, with AMH emigrating to all portions of the planet and replacing, outcompeting, killing, or otherwise negatively impacting regional anatomically archaic humans (Cann et al. 1987; Stringer and Andrews 1988; Tattersall 1995; Vigilant et al. 1991). Regardless of what the fossil or archaeological record indicates, for many the genetic data indicated a wave of advancing anatomical modernity from Africa that swamped the indigenous human populations of Eurasia by virtue of the possession of "behavioral modernity" (some would even question the label of 'human' for earlier populations). The sheer volume of publications by molecular anthropologists, paleoanthropologists, and Paleolithic archaeologists in many cases immediately subsequent to the publication of Cann et al. (1987) indicates, however, that many of the ancillary ideas that were subsequently worked into the synthetic ROA model must have existed alongside it or prior to it, but perhaps lacked a convenient genetic buttress that the mitochondrial DNA studies tended to indicate.

In opposition to the ROA model would be the Multiregional Model (hereinafter MRM) (Wolpoff and Caspari 1996, 1997). According to this orthodoxy, the retention in various regional *Homo* populations of a mosaic suite of purely anatomical symplesiomorphies (general cranial robusticity, lack of mental eminence, supraorbital morphology, sexual dimorphism) indicates long periods of continual gene flow between regional populations of conspecific humans spread across Africa and Eurasia (Hawks and Wolfpoff 2003). The implication is that gene flow would perhaps also be implicative of cultural/behavioral interaction. It would appear that one recent discovery in particular, that of the Siberian Denisova hominins (Reich et al. 2010), substantially buttresses the MRM, with the demonstration that as much as 4% to 6% of the genome of contemporary Melanesians is shared with this isolated Siberian population although no shared lineage with Neanderthals is noted. The Denisova hominid represents a previously unknown genetic signature of human populations in association with Middle Paleolithic technology only hinted at in the prior comparative morphology of human remains from eastern Eurasia and Australasia (Hawks and Wolpoff 2003). Whereas Cann et al. (1987) and Krings et al. (1997) explicitly removed Neanderthals from "modern" human ancestry, troubles with timing of the "molecular clock" (Templeton 1993), publication of the Denisova hominin find, and the demonstration that Neanderthals did in fact contribute DNA to contemporary Eurasian populations (Green et al. 2010), among other technical analyses, have weakened the ROA position regarding no Neanderthal contribution to the contemporary genome. This softening of positions related purely to genetic data may in fact explain some of the recent emphasis on possible behavioral segregation between archaics and moderns.

Much of the selected archaeological evidence (such as it is) that is frequently mobilized in favor of the ROA model (UP blades vs. MP flakes, the supposed absence of art objects in Neanderthal contexts) has been described above. It may be pertinent, however, to note that archaeological evidence marshaled in support of the ROA human origins model is in many cases based upon a selective use of mainly cave-derived archaeological data, focused upon lithic technological characteristics and absence of evidence for "archaic" art. It is noteworthy that this selective use of technological data can be interpreted to support the notion of Eurasian archaic replacement by AMH but is ultimately inconclusive. Subsistence data, however, tend to paint a much subtler vista of a variable, diachronic suite of gradual adaptations at variance with the starkness of the lithic technological record. Subsistence analyses of some European cave-derived fauna (i.e., Enloe 1993, Stiner and Kuhn 2006) suggest the continuation of "archaic" foraging behaviors amongst UP anatomical moderns and impressions of more "modern" use of small animal prey amongst Neanderthals. Analyses of fauna from some open-air sites also strongly suggest "modern" effective large mammal hunting behavior amongst archaic populations in Europe (David and Farizy 1994; Scott 1980; Thieme 1996).

Evaluating the Modernity Models

Evaluations of the modernity models (gradual vs. sudden, widespread vs. restricted) appear to be related to the differential importance or focus placed upon particular aspects—lithics, art/adornment, etc.—of the modernity package. If one views changes in lithic technology, proportions of blades, microliths and estimations of standardization, as primary foci, then a generally gradualistic model seems to be employed (Barker et al. 2007; McBrearty and Brooks 2000; McCall 2006). If art, adornment, and other proxy indices of allegedly symbolic cognition are deemed more illustrative of modernity, then a more punctuated, Late Pleistocene emergence is seemingly

invoked (Klein 2000; Mellars 1999). Henshilwood and Marean (2003) appear to adopt a third middle-range position, whereby changes to the subsistence base, including the incorporation of new species, periodization, elaboration and intensification of use, and (presumably) altered social roles and archaeological manifestations thereof, are perhaps less biased indices of modernity. The presumption is that "modern" subsistence organization may also be reflective of "modern" social organization, and that both should have clear material correlates in the archaeological record (Davidson 2010).

The Behavioral Modernity Construct: Drilling Down

One of the crucial debates in the literature concerns either how to apply or not to apply the conceptual buzzphrase above, "behavioral modernity" (= behaviorally modern), to particular archaeological cultures (Bird and O'Connell 2006; Clark et al. 2003; Henshilwood et al. 2009; Henshilwood and Marean 2003; Mellars 1999, 2004, 2006a; White et al. 2003). As with modernism above, the paradigm used seems to be premised upon a conception of primary disjunction between "behavioral modernity" and its implicit precursor of behavioral non-modernity, almost a "then" contrasted by a figurative "now". As above, some of the most pertinent questions regarding "behavioral modernity" are also the most basic: What is it? We've tried to answer that. When, where and how do we see it? We've tried to answer that, basically in the archaeology of the Late Pleistocene Old World. Henshilwood and Marean (2003:628) provided a handy if lengthy archaeological topical trait list, similar in most respects to Habgood's and Franklin's (2008) "package" above with some other inclusions: intentional burial of the dead along with art, ornamentation and decoration, symbolic use of ochre, worked bone and antler, blade-based lithic technology, standardization of artifact types and artifact diversity, complex hearth construction, organized use of domestic space used as proxy indices of expanded exchange networks, effective large-mammal exploitation, seasonally focused (logistical) mobility/subsistence strategies, use of harsh environments, and fishing/fowling strategies, all of which are often held indirectly and even quite directly to suggest essentially modern linguistic and cognitive capabilities.

The aforementioned trait list does not, however, actually provide much clarification since it is immediately obvious that most, if not all, of the above archaeological traits used to define behavioral modernity involve the employment of rather subjective if not romantic adjectival qualifiers such as "intentional", "symbolic", "standardization", "complex", "organized", "effective", "harsh", etc. as well as issues of archaeological visibility. This very subjectivity in descriptors affixed to the primary terms used to "define" behavioral modernity is itself illustrative of both theoretical and methodological subjectivity in archaeological appraisals of it. Behavioral modernity is therefore something of a moving target. It's hard to "hit" it, apparently, but before it can even be hit it has to be seen. How do we see it? Is it a matter of what we see or how we see? It will be obvious that many of the traits used to define behavioral modernity equate rather well with many of those used to describe the African Middle and Late Stone Age and Eurasian Upper Paleolithic; this is unsurprising since these traits developed within and are defined according to those literary traditions, and are freely used by many scholars in reference to other materials from those and even other areas. At its base, then, we may note that "behavioral modernity" refers to a suite of archaeologically visible material attributes, such as technological sophistication, art, evidence for various forms of specialization, and geographic expansion. We may ask, however, if all of us mean all the same things when we use it. Furthermore, do we know that behaviors which result in art or language production are also associated with the production of blades and microliths, with "complex" hearths, or with "effective" large mammal exploitation? And is it perhaps likewise unknown whether "archaic" behaviors such as Acheulean bifacial thinning and Levallois core reduction have ever been involved in the production of art or language? (It would likewise be quite interesting if and when gender scholars set about analyzing the subject matter and portrayal within Paleolithic art objects, which have restricted subject matter at best. And who is alleged to have been the artists?)

Much of the complexity involved with behavioralizing modernity (notwithstanding the familiar difficulty in analyzing human behavior generally, or in estimating 'modernity' specifically) relates to imprecision in the construction of the very phrase "behavioral modernity". Some sense of the oddness of the phrase can be gained by inverting the word order in it and switching nouns and adjectives. This is not merely a word-game, since we do not investigate "modern behaviorality". First, how can events of possibly 100,000 years ago or even much more in any way be even rhetorically "modern"? Which things do humans consciously do that aren't somehow "behavioral"? We might then note that the use of the phrase behavioral modernity is in reality an attempt to organize conceptually a very broad array of paleoanthropological and archaeological data and method/theory into a useful heuristic for delineating presumed differences between our anthropological conceptions of beings behaviorally "Similar to ourselves" and " the Other", in this case the discursively obvious Other category being behaviorally "non-modern" or even a different species of hominin altogether (else why make the distinction?). One can also discern rather a dismissive tone in some of the more pessimistic discussions of possible "archaic" kinds of modernity (Tattersall 1995, 2000). In many cases, it is simply assumed that Middle Pleistocene or "archaic" humans equal archaic, as opposed to "modern", behavior.

In temporal terms, by assigning the modifier "behavioral" to modernity it can then be discussed independently of particular regional chronologies, allowing comparisons/contrasts between materials thought to be of similar "behavioral modernity", regardless of their actual chronological ages. In other words, the behavioral modernity concept is itself a large (and growing) analogical and taxonomic structure, building on contrasts and comparisons between datasets, between fossil assemblages, fossil hominid populations or even individuals, and between conceptual rubrics from different places, concerning different times, that nonetheless appear to have some things in common. It links some fossil humans with putative behaviors from various time periods that are presumed to have resulted in the formation of portions of the archaeological record through similar behavioral processes. But who actually "does" (or in this case 'did') behavioral modernity? Was this really answered? Do precise identifications of agency even matter if we can just understand some aspects of the developmental trajectories that were followed, since we are discussing *behavior* as opposed to genetics?

In attempting to elucidate the phrase behavioral modernity and the identities of its actual users or authors, it may be useful to juxtapose the adjective "Behavioral" with that of "Cognitive" (Bednarik 2008), indicating Culture, in a cultural ecological sense (even despite the current passé connotations for Culture among some social scholars). The phrase "cognitive modernity" may serve to highlight the ultimate (extrasomatic) sources (thought and culture) of the postulated modern attributes more accurately than "behavioral". Answering the "who did it?" question then becomes a process, as above, of linkage. The linkage is between paleoanthropologically- or paleontologically-defined chronospecies (anatomically modern humans or early modern humans, hereinafter AMH or EMH) and a suite of "modern" cultural/behavioral attributes (often defined on the basis of archaeological visibility) extrapolated onto the hominids. Which human chronospecies "did it"? McBrearty and Brooks (2000:481,485), in their gigantic synthetic-summary treatise, suggest that a common highly mobile late Pleistocene African culprit--anatomically or early modern *Homo sapiens* or AMH/EMH--was "the" author of behavioral modernity, as well as giving the "when", about 160 kya in South Africa. Others see evidence that even Neanderthals were capable of modernity (Zilhao et al. 2006). But there is a clear trend towards equating modernity with AMH. The assumption upon which this is based is that AMH behaved essentially in "modern" ways, by which we mean similar to ourselves, or at least in ways sensible or understandable to us, recognizable or perceptible. One problem in framing the issue as "behavioral modernity" is that it seems to hedge, as though the behavior either may or may not result from human cognition (but probably didn't, wink-wink, nudge-nudge) in archaic contexts, whereas it *must* relate thereto for moderns. Does this imply that there is no necessity to discuss cognition or culture in relation to archaics?

Recent North African fossil evidence (White et al. 2003) and the publishing of a multitude of South African archaeological material have continued the trend toward attributing the origination and elaboration/diffusion of behavioral modernity specifically to EMH, with an overt appeal made to an evolutionary "neuropsychological" African origins model (Bar Yosef-Mayer et al. 2009; Clark et al. 2003; d'Errico et al. 2001; Henshilwood et al. 2004, 2009; Klein 2000; Lycett and von Cramon-Taubabel 2008; Mellars 2006a, 2006b). On the one hand, we have a key conceptual corpus and academic tradition developed in relation to the intensely studied Eurasian Paleolithic; on the other hand, we have a newer body of data and fossil material from Africa indicating connections between the two. Unfortunately for many European contexts, we have abundant lithic and subsistence (faunal) data lacking secure associations with human fossils. The Denisova material (unknown and archaic human DNA lineage with MP technology and evidence of contemporary genetic affinities) vastly complicates matters. Assessing behaviorally modern visibility is therefore of necessity often based completely upon lithic and/or faunal analyses in many contexts. This is not, however, to imply that interpretations of more complete archaeological samples present an unambiguous "picture". This is especially true in terms of complex spatial organization, the existence of which appears to be rather problematic to demonstrate in many contexts. Active current debate involves this transition, especially regarding the nature of the Chatelperronian or Perigordian lithic industries associated with Neanderthals, for instance at Arcy-sur-Cure and St. Cesaire (David et al. 2009). For much of Africa, the Levant, and Europe, however, we lack reliable indices of technological authorship in the form of associated human materials.

It is therefore entirely plausible to criticize the modernity package concept and models, at least as they are used in relation to sites lacking clear hominid associations with lithic material, especially when they are based solitarily upon cave-derived lithic criteria. Moreover, even when "behaviorally modern" hominins are well-documented in association with archaeological materials, there is a tendency to see what one wishes in the human fossils themselves, as in defining the familiar Qafzeh 9 hominin (generally without reference to other human fossils *from the same assemblage*) as an example of "anatomically modern" (Brace 1995, 2005). If Qafzeh 9 is in fact "anatomically modern", what does this say about the other hominins in the rest of that very sample, or of the nearby Kebara hominins? Few attempts have been made to claim a modern pedigree for Kebara Neanderthals, for example. Some would choose either to change the subject or even to ignore the possible "modern" morphological or behavioral characteristics of such "nonsymbolic, nondeclarative" hominins even if they are used as "the best yardstick we have by which to judge our own uniqueness" (Tattersall 1995:289). We should note again the choice of words: nonsymbolic, nondeclarative, uniqueness and *judge*: not "prove", or "demonstrate" or "investigate", but "judge". In other words, to opine, about *us* and our "uniqueness" against the metric of the Other.

The "behavioral modernity" debate over the previous decade traces also to the essential cessation of attempts

to link "modern" archaeological material culture with morphological or anatomical modernity. Since basic human body plans have changed little in the past 200 ky, and since it has become clear that multiple presumed species are associated with MSA/Middle Paleolithic technology in different areas the focus of discussion has shifted to purely extrasomatic behavioral foci, even to implicit attempts at "finding" the first examples of art, symbols, or even language in the MSA (Henshilwood and Marean 2003). Instead of investigating ranges of human behavior, attempts are made to elevate certain interpretations of Late Pleistocene South African archaeology through the competitive demonstration and documentation of a series of material/cultural "firsts" that has been conflated with the Out of Africa hypothesis. The debate, such as it is, has taken the form of an apparent quest for the "first" blades, for the "first" art, for the "first" "effective large mammal exploitation", symbolic behavior, spoken syntactic language, and complex spatial organization (Henshilwood and Marean 2003).

Much to the contrary, Brace (1995, 2005) has often (and often abruptly) noted that the general long-term trend toward reduced human morphological robusticity indicates relaxation of natural selective pressures due to human occupancy of a cultural as opposed to ecological niche, although his interpretations have seemed to fall out of fashion recently. The net effect of the behavioral focus in the recent archaeological literature seems to be a contemporary overt overemphasis of selected (mainly non-European) archaeological materials (especially art, symbolism, adornment) that may be related more to the dynamics of contemporary academic economics (journal publishing and faculty tenuring), research funding, and the awarding of book contracts than to a measured appraisal of the actual adaptive and evolutionary significance of what are essentially trivial frequencies of such materials even in the African archaeological record (consider, for example, the number of handaxes and MSA flake artifacts vs. the number of "art" objects) (see Bouzouggara et al. 2007; d'Errico 2003; d'Errico et al. 2001, 2003; Henshilwood et al. 2003; Henshilwood and Marean 2003).

Finally, even the very language used breathlessly to describe the allegedly "first" or "earliest" art objects (such as the scratched ochre pieces from Blombos Cave) betrays the use of connotative terminology to convey personal, subjective assessments that are quite at variance with what we know about the alterative processes of material diagenesis and taphonomy as things enter first the archaeological then geological records. Do we know that the famous Blombos ochres were scratched all at once? Would a stepwise or cumulative *chaine operatoire* in making these items really indicate modern cognitive faculties? How do we know they were etched all at once? Do we actually know the complete morphological, stylistic, and behavioral ranges that early art objects should exhibit? Have similar efforts been expended by geologists and paleontologists in quest of "the first" clam or brachiopod? Just how likely do we really suppose it would be that we will ever find "the first art object" given the dynamics of taphonomy and diagenesis? Moreover, should we be truly confident that we would identify it even if found? How valid are conclusions drawn from isolated samples?

In two regions with secure associations between hominids and archaeological materials, South Africa and Australia, we find completely different chronologies, patterns of time-successive adaptation, and technological change. For the South African MSA, McBrearty and Brooks (2000:530) note the following diachronic technological trajectory: blades, grindstones, pigments and lithic points by 250 ky; use of aquatic resources, long-distance exchange, mining, and bone tools by 100 ky; microliths and presumed composite tools by 75 ky; beads and body art, adornment by 50 ky. For Late Pleistocene Australia, Habgood and Franklin (2008:211) note a different trajectory: pigments, grindstones, and ground-stone tools by 50 ky; long-distance trade, burials, use of aquatic resources by 40 ky; art and adornment by 40 ky; bone tools present by 25 ky; lithic points and microliths among the last items to appear in the toolkit at about 5 ky. Lithic blades appear not to be present in the earliest Australian lithic assemblages (Davidson 2010), while Australian microliths are absent until the very end of the Paleolithic (Habgood and Franklin 2008). With respect to microlith manufacture, while "standardized" blade and microlith production (microliths produced on blade segments) are very strongly associated in South African material from Klasies River Mouth (McCall 2006), South Asian microliths appear to have been manufactured on flakes and lack geometric forms, indicating rather a divergent approach (Misra, in comments to James and Petraglia 2005:S21).

The Australian example suggests that some fairly diagnostic elements of the modernity package from Africa were lost en route or were perhaps never developed, within a very distinct regional variant that essentially inverted the MSA order and trajectory of technological development. It is by no means clear then that African modernity = Australian modernity. In Australia, blades and microliths were not even present in the first iterations of the AMH technological repertoire, whereas these are treated as virtual *fossils directeurs* for the MSA, and held to indicate the material panoply of other modernity proxies. This is an interesting problem. For on the one hand the modernity package is used at least partially to explain how AMHs allegedly "replaced" Neanderthals in Europe (i.e., possession of 'superior technology'), while for AMHs moving into a previously unoccupied Australian landmass the generally best-attested diagnostic elements of it are absent, at least during the earliest periods. Did the absence of archaic hominids somehow obviate the need for blade-based lithic technology and microliths? The relatively late development of bone technology in Australia also becomes all the more puzzling since perhaps one might expect bone or composite tools to fill the gaps left by the blades and microliths. The Australian sample therefore generates a number of stimulating questions. Did the Australian modernity package "devolve"? Do the earliest

Australian inhabitants represent an example of non-modern adaptation to influx of modern technology? Two phenomena do, however, seem to loom as potential avenues of productive research: 1) the unfamiliarity of Australian fauna to human predation, based upon 2) the absence of archaic human occupations. It could be that the complete modernity package was simply unnecessary for Australian subsistence. This also potentially warns us against overuse of technological data in studying subsistence; tools are merely implements used to accomplish tasks, whereas subsistence behaviors represent much wider ranges of phenomena.

There is, however, a slightly different question than the ones posed above that we might ask, one that is perhaps even more basic, but more difficult to answer succinctly. Which recognizable human socio-cognitive attributes actually underlie the diagnostic material criteria of behavioral modernity, and how do we recognize them archaeologically in subsistence organization? In other words, how does a presumably "behaviorally modern" archaeological culture, such as the Magdalenian, modernistically manifest itself in terms of subsistence, and what patterns might we seek to recognize that are illustrative of modernity? Instead of looking at technological styles and trends, how might we see modernity in subsistence? If evidence for consistency/standardization, intensification, and systematization indicate definitively "modern" technological trends, such as blade and microlith manufacture in the African MSA (McCall 2006), then evidence for systematic, intensified, or standardized subsistence behavior might also evince modernity. We might also note that subsistence organization may be a better index of modernity in that it represents actual adaptations as opposed to changes in stylistic trends known to affect lithic reduction, art, adornment, and probably all material modernity indices to some extent. Are there subsistence behaviors indicative of modernity that might also fail to express lithic technological indices? Which ones? Should we regard such potential phenomena as analogies of unwitnessed fallen trees in a forest, or of Schrodinger's cat? If a modernistic subsistence behavior didn't leave accompanying traces in recognized UP styles of lithic technology, would it be still modernistic? If there are no standardized modernistic blades or microliths found, does that mean modern subsistence didn't happen?

It may be pertinent to recall that what actually underlies "behavioral modernity" is unquestionably a combination of human cognition and Culture, in the cultural-ecological sense, as the primary human mechanism for adapting to the environment (Steward 1955). Attempts to define and recognize "modernity" in a prehistoric human-behavioral sense are therefore also at least partially attempts to define and identify aspects of that which is culturally "not Other", in other words, to some extent, to identify behaviors familiar or at least sensible to ourselves. Or, if not actually familiar, we seek to find evidence for some thought process or processes visible in the archaeological record that indicates the development of cognition that we can classify as being recognizably "human". Cognitive processes constitute and underlie, therefore, a considerable portion of attributes held as markers of modernity. Yet, in archaeology, few things are so simple. Human cognition is not actually visible in the archaeological record. What are visible are some material correlates of cognition, and not the thoughts themselves, of course. So we must keep digging. It seems reasonable that two places to investigate, where visible archaeologically, would be evidence for subsistence evaluation and subsistence risk-management. How are prey species and food sources evaluated in comparison to one another in terms of composition, nutrition, or utility, in terms of comparative/ differential availability and tolerated ranges of conditions and geographic emplacement? What spatial phenomena might be associated? And how did "behaviorally modern" peoples deal with variable subsistence risks associated with those things?

Did the suite of behavioral modularity that we term modernity develop uniformly and commensurately from an essentially finite time period, or did this development take place gradually, in a mosaic, piecemeal fashion? Adherents to the view of a late African emergence and diffusion appear to stress an interpretation of sudden, full emergence (Grine and Henshilwood 2000, 2001; Renfrew 2008). In this view, the entire set of modernity traits developed once at a finite point from which it was then later spread. Others see the advent of modernity as a gradual, mosaic process, or even one of discontinuous starts and stops (Bar-Yosef and Kuhn 1999; Brace 2005; d'Errico and Nowell 2000; Pradel 1966). In this view, different modernity traits arose independently of one another and at different places and times. In point of fact, it is also entirely possible that the advents of modernity took place independently in different areas and were *unrelated as historical events* (emphasis mine) (Brace 2005; Wolpoff and Caspari 1996).

The European Paleolithic Era describes that period of time during which humans manufactured, and survived primarily through the use of, stone tool technologies in Pleistocene Europe. The word "Paleolithic" itself, in the Greek, means roughly "of or pertaining to (the) Old Stone" age: palaioV = palaeos = ancient or old, liqoV = lithos = stone, plus an -ik- ic- adjectival suffix (Liddell and Scott 1889). In archaeological usage, the term Paleolithic generally refers to any number of deliberately manufactured lithic industries ascribed to an immense interval of time, on virtually all non-polar terrestrial landmasses, between about 2.5 million to 10,000 years ago. There exist regional categories of Paleolithic archaeological and paleontological material, specified on a regional basis: i.e., the European Paleolithic, the Paleolithic of Australia, etc. The Paleolithic is also commonly broken into chrono-stratigraphic subdivisions, of Lower, Middle, and Upper, which refer to material attributes common to each temporal interval. In African contexts, the Paleolithic is termed the Stone Age, which is itself also divided into Lower, Middle, and Later periods quite commensurate chronologically with the Lower, Middle, and Upper Paleolithic.

The European archaeological record has also generally been abstracted according to the following evolutionary scheme: the European Lower Paleolithic, or Acheulean (from ~500 ky to ~120 ky) was succeeded in time and space by the Middle Paleolithic, synonymous with the Mousterian in Europe (from ~120 ky to ~40 ky), which was in turn followed by the UP (~40 ky to ~10 ky) (Bilsborough 1992; Blades 1999; Bordes and de Sonneville-Bordes 1970; Mellars 1999, 2006a; Straus 1995). Breuil and Peyrony significantly refined material understandings of the Middle and Upper Paleolithic, while much contemporary research has been focused on resolving issues relating to the incorporation of hominid macroevolution into their archaeological constructs (Blades 1999; Dibble and McPherron 2006; Monnier 2006). The evolutionary paradigm underlying studies of the Paleolithic is therefore self-evident, a subject to which we will return below.

The underpinnings of all serious appraisals of the European Paleolithic involve clear evolutionary outlines (Harrold 2000; Sackett 1986, 1991). Two popular heuristics invoked to explain Near Eastern and European UP evolution are the Multiregional Continuity (Frayer et al. 1993) and the "Out of Africa" replacement (Cann et al. 1987; Stoneking and Cann 1989) models. Both have clear epistemic derivations from the macroevolutionary penumbras of Phyletic Gradualism (in the case of the Multiregional model) (Weidenreich 1939) and (pertaining to the recent Out of Africa model) Punctuated Equilibria (Gould and Eldredge 1977). A newer third, more synthetic European model proposed by Trinkaus and Higham et al. (2006), blends various aspects of the Multirgeional and Replacement models into a cohesive alternative, severing the questionable conflation of hominid macroevolution and lithic typology.

We might also ask, why all the fuss about "behavioral modernity" in the first place? Much of the debate relates to how Paleolithic Archaeology and Paleoanthropology are currently and jointly involved in what is the latest reappraisal of much of the human fossil and archaeological records. More will certainly follow this one if the archaeological literature is a reliable guide. Yet, much of the debate has shifted from assessments of morphological modernity to the new, improved behavioral synthesis almost in spite of anatomical modernity (Hublin 2009; Rightmire 2009; Tattersall 2009). Recent demonstrations of human taxonomic uncertainty (Middle to Late Pleistocene existence of multiple coeval species, such as at Denisova and Flores) have been combined with demonstration of considerable ancient human genetic diversity (i.e, Denisova hominin again, and more complete Neanderthal genome) (Krause et al. 2010; Martinón-Torres et al. 2011). These new developments have also forced redefinition and reattribution of several specimens from the early human fossil record. This taxonomic and genetic diversity is, however, unaccompanied in much of the Eurasian Middle Paleolithic with unique lithic technological accoutrements, suggesting the use of similar or identical technology for much of the Middle to Late Pleistocene by at least three human lineages (anatomical moderns, Neanderthal, and the Denisova population). The obstinate but recurrent attempts made to force lithic technology to fit preconceptions of hominin taxonomy are pervasive in the literature, it being easy to demonstrate broad stylistic and typological trends (especially from cave-derived sequences), but are unlikely to end the debate.

For most of Europe, the UP and MP are abridged stratigraphically and chronologically by transitional lithic industries that exhibit features common to both the earlier and later material, yet portray enough differences to allow at least some researchers to posit separate transitional categories. This is significant in itself, especially insofar as the two dominant models explaining Quaternary hominid evolution (Recent Out of Africa Replacement circa 200 ky and Multiregional Continuity models) jointly cite the same material as evidence for their respective positions (recent total replacement of archaic hominids by modern humans without genetic admixture vs. multiregional, mosaic continuity between archaics and moderns with genetic and cultural admixture). Since Neanderthals are quite strongly associated with Mousterian MP lithic assemblages in Europe, and since Upper Paleolithic industries are often held to be of modern human fabrication, any evidence of "transitional" industries (i.e., presumed technological continuity) abridging the MP and UP is of crucial importance, one logical consequence being that some degree of acculturation or biological admixture may have occurred between Neanderthals and moderns. Some, however, suggest that transitional lithic technological categories be discarded as observer-biased mistakes, products of post-depositionally disturbed site stratigraphies, or site-specific recoveries of differential stages of the same lithic reduction sequences (Dibble and McPherron 2006; Rolland and Dibble 1990). Yet, without reliable indices concerning the biological identities of the makers of any given lithic industry, we must question the salience of any macroevolutionary generalizations if based primarily upon lithic typologies. The latter is a serious point, perhaps in need of some clarification.

The Allegory of the Hammer and the Nail Gun (Thompson 2012)

Let us assume that a distant future archaeologist lacking any knowledge of hammers, nails, and nail guns visited and surveyed a site. In the course of these activities, our prehistorian finds two implements of unquestionable intentional manufacture: one, a rusty Bostitch hammerhead, the wooden handle having long since rotted without a trace, and the other, the articulated metallic and synthetic components of a Bostitch electromagnetic nail gun, whose various perishable components have also completely disintegrated, leaving no residues. There were no human remains associated with these artifacts, and no other material associations. Just the two isolated artifacts, found at the same elevation of the same site. Although the "complex" nail gun was found at the same elevation

as the rusty, old hammerhead, the archaeologist assumes that they understand the apparently differential artifact functions and is thereby secure in assigning an earlier date to the more "primitive" hammerhead. But given what we know about our own material culture, would such an assumption be necessarily warranted or correct? Lacking any material associations, would the archaeologist attribute the simple hammer and the complex nail gun to manufacture by the same *species*, in this case humans? On the basis of what criteria would the archaeologist even conclude a shared manufacturer in such a scenario? On the basis if what data from the site could they conclude the functional identity between both tools (i.e., to drive nails), perhaps knowing nothing about construction practices? Would they understand the possible comparative economic significance represented by the cheaper hammer and the pricier nail gun (rich vs. poor contractor competing for jobs), or that whereas the hammer might have belonged to a solitary, self-employed contractor the nail gun might have belonged to a large, national traveling *crew* of multiple contractors? Lacking evidence of either nails or ancillary perishable technology it is doubtful anyone without *a priori* awareness of these implements would even recognize a similarity of function, to say nothing of manufacturer identity. Though mere allegory the above serves as a potentially ominous warning for much of what currently passes for archaeological systematics and interpretation as based upon presumptions of Middle and Upper Paleolithic stone tool technology given our distant level of awareness. The demonstration of blades in Middle and even Lower Paleolithic contexts, and the location of bifaces and flakes at Upper Paleolithic sites might be indicative of much more behavioral continuity than is currently fashionable to suggest (Bar-Yosef and Kuhn 1999).

Whereas complete reviews of the origins models are precluded here, one would make some very basic observations from one's own replication knapping experiences. Insofar as lithic technology relates to hominid biology and evolution, one sees no justification for advocating a replacement model of modern human origins or the MP to UP transition based purely upon lithic technology. Presumed efficiency in lithic reduction, especially among UP industries, relates to the predictable, controllable blade blank morphology and numerosity per core volume/shape in blade-based strategies, not a strict stylistic adherence to blade templates (Audouze 1987:194). This apparent "efficiency", however, is contingent upon extensive core preparation, with time inputs and raw material shapes and volumes as constraining factors. In other words, blades (and by extension UP industries) are not in themselves *de facto* indices of technical superiority or even relative knapping "skill". In one's opinion and experience, Levallois flake and blade production methods are qualitatively and quantitatively more difficult to master, and require greater inputs of time and raw material to produce predictably. The Levallois learning curve entails much ancillary information; yet, the likes of linguistic ability and learning ability are commonly attributed only to UP industries (Tattersall 1995). The blade core preparation techniques are, however, once mastered, much more resource- and time-efficient and less labor-intensive for systematic blank production after extensive core preparation. This suggests that blade technologies may represent adaptation to the limits imposed *by* particular raw material sizes and volumes as opposed to imposing a Levallois, MP style *upon* a given core. If that is correct then perhaps we should simply ask *why* "anatomically modern" humans failed to fashion blades earlier than they did.

European Upper Paleolithic

The European Upper Paleolithic (UP) has been traditionally viewed as the evolutionary, chronological, and geographic cultural/material successor to the regional Middle Paleolithic (MP), with major issues in the topical literature relating to: 1) the stratigraphic, chronological, functional, and stylistic differences between MP and UP lithic reduction sequences, toolkits, and individual tool items, including the behaviors that resulted in their manufacture; and 2) the taxonomic and cultural/behavioral activities of both of two morphologically distinct hominins (Neanderthals and supposedly 'anatomically modern humans') extant at the time of the UP's inception in Europe at approximately 40 ky (Adler et al. 2006; Anikovich 1992; Bar-Yosef and Kuhn 1999; Bilsborough 1992; Blades 1999; Bordes 1961,1971; Bordes and de Sonneville-Bordes 1970; Cachel 1987; Cachel et al. 1997; Clark 1994; d'Errico et al 2003; de Sonneville-Bordes 1963; Ellwood et al. 2001; Grayson and Delpech 1997; Harrold 2000; Laville and Rigaud 1973; Klein 2000; Kuhn and Stiner 1998, 2006; Lahr and Foley 1998; Lindly et al. 1990; Marks 1983; Mellars 2005, 2006; Soffer et al. 2000; Stiner and Kuhn 1998; Stiner et al. 2000; Straus 1991, 1999, 2005; Svoboda 1994a, 1994b; Zilhao 2006; Zilhao and d'Errico 1999). Comprised of cultural- and chrono-stratigraphic (culture-historical) constituents such as the Chatelperronian, Aurignacian, Gravettian, Solutrean, and Magdalenian, the European UP also represents well-documented large-scale changes, or pattern alterations, in paleoclimates and paleoenvironments, hominid biology and culture, human and prey species' geography, and demography (Baryshnikov and Hoffecker 1994; Bleed 2006; Bocquet-Appel 2000; Bocquet-Appel et al. 2005; de Beaune 2004; Dobson and Geelhoed 2001; Enloe 1993; Grayson and Delpech 1997, 2001; Harrold 2000; Henry et al. 2004; Hoffecker 1999; Mellars 2003; Mulder et al. 2006; Stiner 2002a; Straus 2006). The Magdalenian is the terminal European UP lithic industry, and it occurred during the post-Late Glacial Maximum/terminal Pleistocene period, a "transitional" lithic industry spanning times transitional between full glacial and contemporary Holocene conditions.

Characteristics of the European Upper Paleolithic

The European Upper Paleolithic is primarily defined against the preceding Lower and Middle Paleolithic, and the subsequent Mesolithic/Epipaleolithic, by presence/ absence and compositional attributes of UP lithic assemblages. "Typical" attributes of the European UP consist of: 1) an apparent shift from Mousterian flake-based tool blanks to 'standardized' blade blanks, struck from multiple platform, prismatic cores as opposed to flakes drawn from discoid or Levallois cores; 2) increased relative frequencies of endscrapers, burins, and borers, multiple tools (fashioned on more than one section of the same piece); and 3) composite tool technology, including barbed harpoons with cordage loops, broadhead bone/ antler points with microlithic blade inserts, netting, basketry, and other organic components (Bar-Yosef and Kuhn 1999; Blades 1999; Bordes 1971; de Sonneville-Bordes 1963; Harrold 2000; Hoffecker 2005; Mellars 2006; Soffer et al. 2000; Straus 1995). Accompanying the UP lithic industries were developments in organic technology such as clothing, basketry, and ropes, nets, and snares, (Soffer et al. 2000) and a profusion of cave and mobiliary art objects and styles that are generally absent in the Lower and Middle Paleolithic (Bar-Yosef and Kuhn 1999; Bilsborough 1992; d'Errico et al. 2003; Straus 1995, 1999).

Whereas the above refers to generalized UP attributes, more specific, stylistic and subjective characteristics of the individual culture-historical UP subdivisions, such as those typical of the Aurignacian, serve further to subdivide the UP. For example, Perigordian and Chatelperronian backed points frequently feature "abupt" retouch; Aurignacian scrapers are generally fashioned on "thicker" blades or laminar flakes, and contain higher percentages of split base and beveled base bone points than Magdalenian assemblages; the Solutrean is typified by elongate, bifacially-flaked foliate tools with flat, parallel retouch; Magdalenian assemblages feature barbed harpoons and smaller, thinner, and "more standardized" blade tool blanks (Audouze 1987; Bar-Yosef and Kuhn 1999; Blades 1999; Bordes 1971; de Sonneville-Bordes 1963; Harrold 2000; Laville and Rigaud 1973; Mellars 2006a).

General characteristics of the separate UP lithic traditions are as follows: The initial European UP industry, the Aurignacian, is composed of relatively thick blades and scrapers, with wide, heavy retouch, and numerous split-base bone points, with blades struck from prismatic cores; Chatelperronian industries feature abrupt retouch on tools with retention of some Mousterian tool types (mainly side scrapers), and diagnostic implements such as Noailles burins (dihedral) and tanged Font-Robert points, with very sparse frequencies of bone implements, and varying frequencies of Gravett points (backed pointed blade or bladelet); the Gravettian industry appears essentially similar to the Aurignacian, except for the appearance of numerous, diagnostic Gravette points (as above); Protomagdalenian industries (known only from Laugerie-Haute and Abri Pataud in Dordogne) contain numerous backed blades and bladelets, with diagnostic burins, endscrapers, borers, and many bone tools; the Solutrean industry, defined on the basis of a particular parallel unifacial and bifacial retouch style on elongated "laurel leaf' points (similar to North American Paleoindian and Archaic points) and both split and beveled-base bone points; the final UP industry, the Magdalenian, is defined by generally smaller and more numerous backed bladelets, diagnostic tool types of burins, endscrapers, borers, piercers, becs (beaks), the initial appearance of geometric microliths, and more numerous and stylistically-varied bone points (beveled-base with some split-base), needles, awls, and barbed harpoons, many with cordage loops for retrieval of projectiles and targets (Benet-Tygel 1944; Bordes 1961; de Sonneville-Bordes 1963; Kidder and Kidder 1936; Laville and Rigaud 1973).

Magdalenian Lithic Technology

The Magdalenian lithic industry has been defined on the basis of morphological and statistical characteristics, according to reduction sequences and diagnostic tool typology (Audouze 1987; Bordes and de Sonneville-Bordes 1970; Harrold 2000; Laville and Rigaud 1973; Schmider 1982; Symens 1986; Straus 1995). It is unquestionably "modern" behaviorally. Most interpretations of UP lithic variability can be reduced to two primary theoretical concepts, where 1) variability is abstracted as indicating successive occupations by different cultures defined by the comparative frequencies of allegedly diagnostic tool types (Bordes 1961, 1971; de Sonneville-Bordes 1963) and 2) lithic variation constructed as functional (task-specific, climatic, or seasonal) differences between lithic industries (Binford 1981; Laville and Rigaud 1973; Schmider 1982). It is possible, if not probable, that both cultural and functional contingencies impacted the development of Magdalenian technology, with equifinality obscuring any direct or specific causality. It may therefore be most productive to discuss causal or operational sequences or chains (chaines operatoire) as opposed to discrete monocausal phenomena.

With respect to the operational chain of manufacturing Magdalenian implements, Audouze (1987:190-192) suggests that the fundamental building block involved a very systematic and deliberate core preparation strategy to initiate striking platforms and to shape the cores for blade extraction. Raw material was reduced and shaped into a roughly symmetrical core (quite similar to a thick bifacial handaxe or a football flattened partially) featuring a frontal crest, serving as the percussive guide for removal of the initial, or crested, blade (lame a crete), determining the removal of subsequent blades (Audouze 1987:191). These cores (often composed of exotic materials) generally consisted of two, opposed striking platforms, with some cores from VBC featuring four opposed platforms, with blade removal from one platform serving as the rejuvenation removal for the opposite platforms (Audouze 1987:191). More expedient cores (generally on local raw materials) involved the placement of one or two platforms (oriented perpendicularly instead of in opposition if multiples), lacking extensive preliminary preparation; these expedient cores produced fewer blades of much shorter lengths (Audouze 1987:191).

While Magdalenian reduction strategies were geared toward blade production, what did the people themselves do with these blade blanks? At VBC, thick, unretouched cortical and partially cortical blades were apparently used to cut meat, as based on microwear studies (Symens 1986). On retouched pieces, Magdalenian tools were often constructed so as to feature multiple tools on the same blade blank, such as truncated, backed blades with unretouched cutting edges, burins and endscrapers on unilaterally backed blades for more task-specific uses (Symens 1986). The diagnostic UP backed bladelets may represent composite sagaie armatures, analogous to contemporary broadhead arrows with razor-edged blades to augment bleeding and shock trauma upon target entry (Audouze 1987:194). Some further impressions of Magdalenian implement functions can be gained from Keeley's (1987, 1991) and Symens' (1986) lithic microwear studies. For identifiable tools, Keeley (1987, 1991) indicates that the primary uses were for butchery and meat-cutting (of reindeer), hide-scraping and other hide-working activities, some cutting and processing of plant materials, and retooling/re-hafting of composite and hafted implements, such as burins, scrapers, and backed bladelets. Symens (1986) also suggests that extensive meat-cutting was a dominant functional application of Magdalenian assemblages, along with bone- and antler-working for the production of sagaie points, harpoons, needles, and other implements.

Production and refining organic artifacts was apparently a major functional concern for Magdalenian populations, while the literature suggests that lithic projectiles decreased in absolute frequency. Burins and bone/antler/ivory tools increase in frequency, variability, and complexity during the Magdalenian, which are indirect indices of the importance organic and composite tool technology played (de Sonneville-Bordes 1963; Kidder and Kidder 1936; Stettler 2000). Burins, both hafted and unhafted, of dihedral, parrot-beak, and micro varieties, were most likely used to engrave or chisel bone, wood, ivory, shell, other stone, etc., for removal of projectile blanks or other tools, and for production of graphic art (de Sonneville-bordes 1963; Keeley 1987, 1991; Stettler 2000; Symens 1986). There is obviously, therefore, a complex dynamic relationship between increasing frequencies and kinds of burins and composite lithic/organic tools in the Magdalenian, coupled with frequency decreases or outright absences of purely lithic projectiles.

MP to UP Transitions and Behavioral Adaptations

No discussion of later UP developments is complete without reference to apparent MP to UP behavioral transitions. The archaeological database suggests that the late MP and earliest UP (Aurignacian) hominid niches in Eurasia were similar with respect to lithic technology, settlement patterning, and subsistence preferences (species selection, seasonality, faunal treatment, habitation sites, and lithic variability) across the crucial transitional period from about 40 ky to 30 ky (Blades 1999; Cachel 1987;

Churchill and Smith 2000; Enloe 1993; Stiner 1994, 2001; Stiner and Kuhn 2006). A general shift in hominid dietary breadth occurred slightly earlier, from about 50 ky to 40 ky (Stiner 1994, 2001; Stiner and Kuhn 2006). This expansion of dietary breadth, also known as "the Broad Spectrum Revolution" (Stiner 2001), involved an increase at numerous archaeological sites in the frequency of smaller prey species with relatively fast reproductive rates, better able than megafaunal mammals to offset human predation through quicker reproductive rebounds. From approximately the late Wurm pleniglacial and especially after the Late Glacial Maximum UP humans also focused increasingly on middle-sized to small ungulates and small herbivores (red deer, reindeer, various antelopes, horse, rabbits, squirrels) and developed increasingly efficient non-lithic technological means (nets, snares, basketry, harpoons) for the reliable capture of smaller, more mobile prey species (Stiner 2001; Stiner and Kuhn 2006).

Associated with the early UP expansion of diet breadth was a clear trend towards the increased acquisition and implementation of dietary fat as a nutritional staple (Cachel 1987; Cachel et al. 1997; Enloe 1993; Speth 1983; Speth and Spielman 1983; Stiner 1994). In high northern latitudes, especially in those areas with highly seasonal variation in the proportions of available dietary fat and carbohydrates, hominid protein ingestion must be limited unless adequate fat is present, relating to complex metabolic interactions of proteins, urea, and digestion (Cachel 1987; Speth 1983; Speth and Spielman 1983; Stiner 1994). Absent adequate dietary fats, protein metabolism becomes increasingly inefficient even with increased protein consumption, and can lead rapidly to somatic starvation and protein deficiencies (Cachel 1987; Speth 1983; Speth and Spielman 1983). Ethnoarchaeological research has demonstrated that fat acquisition guides many of the most basic hunting and post-acquisition prey transportation decisions, as well as labor-intensive post-butchering faunal processing, made by contemporary northern and arctic hunter-gatherers (Binford 1978, 1981; Morin 2007). It appears that the preoccupation with fat acquisition developed during the late MP, in the Mediterranean Basin and in the areas of Southwest France and Cantabrian (northern and eastern) Spain, perhaps in response to changing environmental availabilities of prime-condition megafaunal prey (Cachel 1987; Stiner 1994, 2001; Straus 1999).

After approximately 40 ky, demographic changes in Europe are archaeologically visible. Two major shifts in the distribution of sites occurred across Europe during two periods, from 40 ky to the LGM, and subsequent to the LGM, lasting to the end of the Pleistocene at about 10 ky (Blades 1999; Bocquet-Appel 2000; Bocquet-Appel et al. 2005; Churchill and Smith 2000). From 40 ky, the area of Southwest France (Aquitaine) and Northeast Spain (Cantabria) were essentially permanently occupied, as were other cave and rockshelter sites throughout Central/ Eastern Europe. Variability in population density and site frequency is visible, ranging gradationally from higher in Southwest France to much lower in Northern

France, Germany, and Poland. For the period from the Aurignacian to the LGM, Bocquet-Appel (2000:568) estimates the entire UP European human population in France increased constantly but very slowly, from 5,400 to about 8,900. During the LGM, between 20-18 ky, a population contraction and decrease in UP site frequency occurred, focusing human occupation in Southwest France (Bocquet-Appel 2000; Bocquet-Appel et al. 2005). This decrease in site frequency and area of occupation presumably relates to the advance of the Fenno-Scandian ice sheet and macroenvironmental changes wrought by it. After the LGM, during the late Solutrean and Early Magdalenian from 20 ky to 18 ky, the human population increased, especially somewhat later during a "Magdalenian explosion" in site frequency and types of occupied habitats (from caves and rockshelters to open-air sites), with human individuals perhaps numbering as high as 40,000 across the Magdalenian culture area (Bocquet-Appel 2000:568).

Aurignacian settlement patterns and residential mobility in Southwest France may represent a period of dynamic adaptation based upon seasonal and perhaps larger scale, macroenvironmental forcing (Blades 1999). Climatic deterioration, altered compositions of biotic communities and geographic changes in habitat connectivities (i.e., landscape factors) caused changes in the methods and frequencies of human population interaction (Blades 1999, 2003; Churchill and Smith 2000). The basic Aurignacian trend in Southwest France was toward a diachronic reduction in (seasonal) group mobility as measured by lithic raw material procurement and utilization intensity, with higher mobility in the early Aurignacian and lower mobility in later stages (Blades 1999, 2003). Such a pattern accords well with Bocquet-Appel's (2000) model of gradational population contraction from NE to SW Europe during the Aurignacian, and begins to outline the extremely dynamic contexts within which the subsequent autochthonous regional developments of the Chatelperronian, and later industries, occurred (Bordes 1961; Bordes and de Sonneville-Bordes 1970; Laville and Rigaud 1973). Unfortunately, at the present, the "makers" of the early Aurignacian (i.e., of the incipient European UP) are unknown. Lacking reliable associations between Aurignacian material and human remains, it is extremely difficult to evaluate macroevolutionary models of subsequent archaeological entities through reference to the incipient UP. Whereas we know who made and used Mousterian MP tools in Europe (Neanderthals, based on a distinct lack of associated anatomical moderns), such is not the case with respect to incipient, UP Aurignacian industries and the ways in which they relate to potentially associated Chatelperronian/Perigordian contemporaries or near-contemporaries. The "picture" is therefore rather jumbled and of only vague focus for this crucial transitional period.

The Magdalenian in Europe

As above, the Magdalenian tradition was the terminal European Upper Paleolithic industry, lasting from about 18 ky to 10 ky and was geographically the most widespread

European Late Quaternary cultural entity, with examples from France, Spain, Germany, and Poland (Audouze 1987; Harrold 2000; Jochim et al. 1999; Schmider 1982). Earlier research on Magdalenian hunter-gatherers tended toward the conflation of the Magdalenian into a larger, generic UP "catchall" category based on the presence/absence of diagnostic "type-fossils", such as blades or burins or bone/ antler points (Benet-Tygel 1944; Bordes 1961, 1971; Bordes and de Sonneville-Bordes 1970; Kidder and Kidder 1936), which obscured some of the Magdalenian's uniqueness. Moreover, the near or complete domination of the faunal assemblages at many Magdalenian archaeological sites by single ungulate taxa was traditionally viewed as deliberate and focused economic "specialization" upon the chronic pursuit of particular prey species (Binford 1981, 1984; Schmider 1982), as opposed to indices of seasonally-adjusted and variable, mobile economies. In general, these trends were part of a larger archaeological paradigm viewing the European Upper Paleolithic as representing "progress" over the preceding Lower and Middle periods, a common perspective in 18th and 19th century French archaeology (Straus 1994).

Magdalenian Subsistence and Settlement

Magdalenian hunters of Europe appear to have utilized two general site types as based upon the present state of the data: 1) Rock shelter or cave sites in SW France, Cantabrian Spain, and assorted similar sites in the culture area (i.e., Arcy-sur-Cure in Burgundy), and 2) open-air uplands or fluvial valley sites (Audouze 1987; Audouze and Enloe 1991; Bocquet-Appel et al. 2000; Schmider 1982; Straus 1995). Associated fauna at these sites tends to suggest much more mosaic and variable conditions than at present, including reindeer, wild horse, aurochs, boar, mammoth, red deer, and other European Late Pleistocene animals (Audouze 1987; Benet-Tygel 1944; Enloe 1997, 1999, 2004; Enloe and David 1992, 1997). There is an obvious preponderance of reindeer, however, and it appears that the Magdalenian lifeway was to some degree focused on a seasonal habitation round premised upon reindeer migration (Enloe 1997, 1999; Mellars 2003). When reindeer populations were sparse, migration to offset overgrazing was presumably unnecessary, and the deer could be hunted throughout the year on an encounter basis; higher reindeer populations exhausted food resources and migrated seasonally, using routes that served as key foci for planned, specialized hunting episodes (Audouze and Enloe 1991; Enloe 1999). Magdalenian open-air sites may therefore relate to high group mobility and group fragmentation by bands of hunters during those periods when migrating reindeer could be predictably acquired *en masse*. Such a predictable resource could be processed and stored given suitable planning and divisions of labor (Enloe 1999; Soffer et al. 2000). The caves and rock shelters may have served as ceremonial centers and/or group aggregation sites for wintering. Better understanding of cave art function should clarify these impressions. More intensive study of art production and function amongst indigenous Arctic humans may also

help in gaining understandings of possible causes and mechanisms for cave art development in Europe during the onset of pleniglacial conditions (i.e., as entertainment for residence-bound folks during brutal cold).

A planned emphasis on seasonally variable and migratory reindeer populations would have left Magdalenian hunters to pursue other food items when reindeer herds had left their general vicinities. Barbed harpoons, fish leisters, cordage and basketry, netting, and related technology do indicate alternate prey acquisition, and recovery of botanical items from some sites indicate that olives, various legumes, sloe, pistachio, wild grape, wild oat, triticum wheat, and numerous grasses were in use by Magdalenian times (Aura et al. 2005). In the case of dietary plants, it is likely that much of the harvesting, storage, and processing technology related to their use were themselves composed of perishable materials (i.e., baskets, bags, winnowing sieves, etc.), and so the general absence of these items at Magdalenian sites coupled with the obvious focus on reindeer is not indicative of an unusually meat-intensive diet. Rather, much of the direct evidence of Magdalenian, indeed Paleolithic plant use has simply biodegraded, just as have the ancient plants themselves.

With respect to Magdalenian open-air sites, the Paris Basin figures heavily. In the Paris Basin of France, 50 Magdalenian sites are now known, occurring mainly in fluvial valleys; seven of the sites have defined living floors, five of which have identifiable hearths (Audouze 1987). Two of these sites (Pincevent and Verberie) feature plentiful faunal remains. During the Magdalenian of the Paris Basin (MPB), most open-air fluvial sites were located preferentially near river confluences and abundant flint sources (Audouze 1987). The living floors were oriented around slab-lined hearths of two distinct styles: a flat variety (0-5 cm depth) and basin-shaped (5-20 cm depth), of between 40-80 cm in diameter, beside which were often empty or low artifact density areas of several square meters in area, perhaps indicating the "negative" remains of ephemeral shelter structures (Audouze 1987).

Considering the numerous interpretations and reinterpretations of data derived from stratigraphically complex cave sites (for MSA and Eurasian MP) we should ask whether cave-derived data are really adequate for addressing competitive assessments of "modernity" through subsistence and spatial analysis. Difficulty in caves relates to deposition within them, in terms of constancy of accumulation, spatial restriction and material concentrations. Caves offer fundamentally biased samples of landscape use. Furthermore, if caves really represent residential sites, how well are we informed about non-residential sites associated with them? What behaviors and formation processes do we not see through the focus on caves, especially pertaining to the modernity debate?

Models and analogies developed from long cave stratigraphic sequences generally portray change over time (such as between lithic technological industries) because they exhibit materials deposited over long spans of time. In cases of successive industries in caves, there often exists little evidence that they are causally related. Changes in artifacts relate in many cases to long-term accumulatiom, similar to accumulation of changes in geologic lithostrata. Ephemeral open-air sites offer more snapshot estimates of behavior accumulated over more sensible, human intervals of time as opposed to physical, geological accumulations. Yet, can we even see organized spatial use in cave contexts, given their depositional peculiarities, stratigraphic/accumulation complexities, and the interpretive difficulties they cause? Have caves biased our archaeological view back to the past?

The Allegory of the Cave Bias

The Modernity Debate (archaic vs. modern, Middle vs. Upper Paleolithic, Africa vs. Eurasia) is mainly premised upon selective uses of cave-derived data from Africa (Blombos Cave, Klasies River Mouth), the Levant (Kebara, Qafzeh, Tabun), and Europe (especially if not virtually by definition, the Perigord). This is an obvious bias. To allegorize this:

1. We have (a) given cave site(s), perhaps but not necessarily with indications of lithic technological change over time, with younger material presumably deposited over older. There may or may not also be a general increase in the frequency of the younger in relation to the older material.

2. We then infer that whatever impressions we have for the "older" material should be utterly localized and only related to events and processes *at that cave site.* Even though there may be other nearby MP cave sites just like ours, we know our MP cavefolks didn't really interact with others in nearby or distant caves because they were nonsymbolic, nondeclarative MP hominins (Tattersall 1995). Now, UP occupations are assumed to be multiplicatively associated through time and across space with other UP ones at local, regional, continental, or even transcontinental levels of analysis from perhaps 100 ky because of the ROA model. We "know" this because one technological type is MP and the other is UP and because we can much more easily see *well-preserved* (emphasis mine) open-air UP sites in the archaeological record between the caves. We also know that a selective reading of selected genetic data might ambiguously support our UP assumptions. We do know there were former Lower Paleolithic and Middle Paleolithic sites in many areas, but they were eroded in the remote past. We also fail to ask whether Early Upper Paleolithic open-air site distribution conforms more to that observed for the Middle Paleolithic/MSA or the later Upper Paleolithic. We also fail to ask if the Lower and Middle Paleolithic were also spread by diffusion and invasion as is alleged for the Upper Paleolithic, or even if we should interpret the Upper Paleolithic transition as a set of purely unrelated local phenomena as is assumed for the Lower and Middle Paleolithic. But anyway...

3. We then conveniently overlook the fact that it is really only with the Magdalenian that ephemeral open-air sites actually *seem* to become chronologically and geographically widespread and relatively more frequent in the archaeological record, unquestionably somehow related to gradual increases in demographic density.

4. We also again overlook the facts that in both the Levant and Europe there are untold numbers (many thousands) of Lower and Middle Paleolithic lithics found outside caves, mainly in drainage channels and sand/gravel pits (Mellars 1996). We almost never ask whether these eroded sites mean that there were larger Lower and Middle Paleolithic populations than are commonly assumed. These "archaic" lithics were moved from upslope locations *where they were deposited by people* and were redeposited in downslope catchments, indicating the *former* presence of "archaic" open-air sites inconveniently destroyed by physical geomorphic processes. But we know such sites *used to exist.* We just forget to discuss them because they present profound interpretive difficulties and because they clutter our paradigms.

5. We then forget to ask if we can really infer differences in spatial organization between the Lower, Middle, and Upper Paleolithic from the general paucity of open-air evidence and from biased cave datasets. We do know we lack crucial open-air data for all time periods so sometimes we briefly mention something about the Lower and Middle Paleolithic.

6. We forget to ask if cave spatial data from the Levant and Europe actually indicate *ANY* differential spatial organization or spatial use between the Lower, Middle, and Upper Paleolithic.

7. We forget that most human behavior does not take place in caves. People do not hunt mammoths or gather mussels inside caves.

8. People do not forage for or logistically collect tubers inside caves.

9. People do not normally harvest lithic raw materials inside caves.

10. Actually, beyond occasional painting, eating and sitting, and disposing of the dead, we really don't know *what* people were doing inside caves, yet we just can't help but continually to discuss them.

11. Caves are "behavioral sinks"-- analogous to limestone carbon sinks that concentrate and skew recoverable data over immense spans of time. We need to look much more at open-air sites in order to get wider views of human adaptations accumulated over actual human time spans. Open-air short-term "behavioral sinks" exist in some places, but the field is dominated by cave analyses. This is analogous to investigating the Earth's carbon cycle only by focusing upon big, visible, and sexy end-product carbon sinks such as carbonate outcrops while ignoring the more mundane seawater, atmosphere, and biota that *form* the rocks, because they are harder to sample and interpret.

Even a focus on the most famous reliably dated cave sites, such as Qafzeh, Kebara, Blombos, or Howieson's Poort possibly neglects short-term or stochastic adaptational and spatio-behavioral ranges of variation, since caves can indicate variability that is insensitive to "real time" as it is experienced by humans. Cave deposits are independent of short-term contingency, whereas most human behaviors take place in the short-term immediacy of the "now". Caves' constant material deposition and accumulation processes are conducive to impressions of very long-term behavioral differentiation *because of the protracted manner in which materials accumulate inside caves.* Caves are therefore valuable repositories of diachronic long-term, general data accumulated over long geologic time-scales. Their often more complete sequences are extremely important once we realize the inherent difficulties in using cave sequences to estimate past human behavior over smaller synchronic intervals. Open-air ephemeral sites, however, reflect much more short-term contingencies especially regarding spatial organization and spatial use.

Given the size of the Old World landmasses of Africa, Eurasia, and Australasia (Africa: 11,668,598.7 sq mi; Eurasia: 20,846,000 sq mi; Australia: 2,941,299 sq mi), how much comparative space is actually represented by the aggregate area excavated from inside ALL caves and rock shelters? Have archaeologists *ever* focused a commensurate amount of time to gaining understandings of extra-cave archaeological areas? We must modulate cave-derived inferences with available data from open-air sites for ALL time periods, infrequent and rare as they are. Do we assume that apparent long-term differences in cave-derived Middle Paleolithic technology from different caves fails to exhibit local, regional, or continental variability similar to that alleged for the Upper Paleolithic from cave sites? If so, why? If not, why not? Are Middle and Upper Paleolithic datasets from caves truly comparable given exigencies of the passage of time and differential archaeological visibility, to say nothing of the ways in which earlier archaeological materials were reconfigured by later occupants? Do we know that there were profound functional differences between Middle and Upper Paleolithic assemblages or do we describe assumed functional difference based upon impressions of style and attributes from biased cave samples?

We need to look closer at open-air faunal assemblages to address questions of spatial organization and subsistence. While anatomical modernity used to serve as the focus of the modernity debate, the discussion has now shifted to behavioral/cognitive modernity as the information used in the debate has expanded and as the reference frames have matured. Rare Lower Paleolithic open-air sites such as Clacton-on-Sea, Lehringen, and Schoningen have forcibly demonstrated that many prior impressions of Acheulean and Clactonian technology were quite simply wrong. Inadequacy of modernity definitions abounds, with many of us talking past one another in the rush to publish. Even cave-derived data indicate basic continuities between the Middle and Upper Paleolithic:

1. Occupation of the same places.
2. Use of the same prey species in subsistence.
3. Frequent use of same technologies.

This generalization applies also to open-air datasets where they are available, indicating that both Middle and Upper Paleolithic humans used the same basic kinds of places, the same basic prey species, and frequently the same basic lithic technologies in the courses of living their lives. We should study the variability between the Middle and Upper Paleolithic, but the constant bickering over discontinuity overshadows the continuities. We need to get at space and subsistence for all time periods. We lack good "snapshot" views of most kinds of Lower, Middle, and Upper Paleolithic open-air spatial organization, except in very rare cases, such as Pincevent and Verberie (again, the tardiglacial Magdalenian). The European Upper Paleolithic technological transition also presents sociological/demographic contingencies since we know there was a general increase in demographic density across the Upper Paleolithic, especially after the LGM and Wurm/Wisconsin tardiglacial and the onset of Holocene conditions.

We need to develop methods to "see" both continuity and variability in differential uses of space, subsistence, and spatial organization of Lower, Middle, and Upper Paleolithic sites. If there is evidence of either continuity or discontinuity between Lower, Middle, and Upper Paleolithic in terms of subsistence and spatial organization these should be apparent at preserved open-air sites. We must also use the Upper Paleolithic spatial data we have at our disposal to identify possible indices of Lower and Middle Paleolithic open-air spatial organization. In other words, how can we use what we have to find what we need? Analysis of Lower and Middle Paleolithic sites such as Mauran (David and Farizy 1994), La Crotte de St. Brelade (Scott 1980), Schoningen (Thieme 1996), Lehringen (Movius 1950), Clacton-on-Sea (Wymer and Singer 1970), and La Borde (Jaubert et al.) have indicated greater behavioral complexity for "archaic" humans than many Out of Africanists have tended to discuss. Lower and Middle Paleolithic behavioral indices can then be used to help inform us about Upper Paleolithic behavior at open-air sites.

The Magdalenian and Behavioral Modernity.

In terms of the criteria above, and by virtue of the definitive technological characteristics of the Magdalenian, we can reasonably ask if the Magdalenian was "behaviorally modern". Several of the behaviorally modern criteria appear to be met: the Magdalenian material clearly exhibits blade-based lithic technology, worked bone and antler, and increased artifact diversity and standardization (as compared to earlier Eurasian UP industries), and a diachronic diminution in physical size. This is especially noteworthy in consideration of Sackett's (1977) stylistic diagnostic criteria of expressive coherence and congruence. Magdalenian technology is extremely internally consistent, widespread, and regular. The Magdalenian also features composite implements comprised of multiple pieces of different raw materials, including barbed harpoons with cordage fastenings and fish hooks. The cordage is also indirectly indicative of presumptive net and snare technologies. Harpoons, hooks, and nets seem to satisfy the behavioral modernity criterion of fishing and fowling, and expanded dietary breadths.

The culture area of the Magdalenian, in tardiglacial northwest Europe, and featuring cold-weather fauna such as reindeer and mammoth would seem to fulfill the criterion of harsh environment use. As above, the construction of slab-lined hearths surrounded by putative activity areas

satisfies the criterion of complex hearth construction. The preceding Magdalenian attributes are, however, primarily compositional and/or technological and durable in nature. How would behavioral modernity be visible in terms of Magdalenian subsistence and spatial organization? Henshilwood's and Marean's (2003) criteria give us some hints for where to look, for areas we might search for this presumptive visibility: differential spatial organization, effective large mammal exploitation and seasonally focused subsistence/mobility strategies. Chapter III will now provide a discussion of the actual toolkit we have at our disposal to "see" subsistence modernity, as well as Chapter IV details my proposed methodology for seeing it at a particular site.

Chapter 3 Models and Analogies in Palaeolithic Archaeology

A key concern of any scientific academic discipline is the manner in which new ideas and methods are incorporated into the disciplinary literature and discursive corpus, such that the discipline grows and changes over time – hopefully in such a way that it becomes more, not less, relevant with age, and is increasingly successful in explaining itself and its subject matter. To the extent that such a discipline subjects itself and its central axioms and theories to empirical scrutiny, how are its basic ideas formulated? What methodologies are developed to answer questions posed by its practitioners? How are resilient concepts that remain non-falsified after empirical testing incorporated into the disciplinary corpus? These are fundamental questions besetting any science. With respect to Paleolithic Archaeology, such questions and the answers thereto are extremely important in order to identify, and to maintain, appropriate analytical frames of reference. In other words, what ought Paleolithic archaeologists to know in order to practice their brand of Archaeology?

A reasonable overarching goal of a contemporary theoretically oriented Upper Paleolithic (UP) Archaeology is the production of cumulative (generalized and generalizing) understandings of the human past, to varying degrees free of the constraints of particular time periods or social contexts (Gibbon 1984; Trigger 1989). To the perspective above one would add a basic understanding of the types of contemporary behaviors and processes that can result in material patterns and configurations similar to what is found in the archaeological record, and a humble awareness of physical, non-anthropogenic formative and alterative processes revealed through actualistic and ethnoarchaeological research (Binford 1967, 1977; 1980; 1981; 2001; Chang 1967; Gould 1978; Hodder 1979; Wobst 1978). Lastly, the UP archaeological goal would include inferences of human subsistence organization and its patterned effects, since subsistence represents a direct link between humans end their surrounding environment (Enloe 1993:102-103).

Yet, insofar as it is possible subjectively to detail what Paleolithic archaeologists *should* know, it is incumbent upon us to acknowledge that the archaeological record, especially that of the Paleolithic, is highly biased and incomplete. At best, it is a "static pattern of associations and covariations among things distributed in space" (Binford 1980:4). There is, in other words, a lot we don't, or can't, "know". We must instead suggest or infer. Recoverable data are discontinuous, as are interpretations based upon them. We lack reliable indices (at least in most cases) of putative Paleolithic kinship systems, political functions, and religious beliefs, even at larger group levels of analysis, to say nothing really of smaller groupings or individuals. Many of the utilitarian economic components of

Paleolithic hunting-gathering adaptations are recoverable, in the form of lithic, bone, and antler implements whose forms very graphically indicate probable functions, as are sparse examples of non-utilitarian, "art" items, whether mobiliary or cave art, although indices of their more amorphous sociocultural functions are irrecoverable. Expressed axiomatically, we cannot, however, expect to understand, or explain, the archaeological record merely by studying that record itself, especially in isolation.

Archaeology, as practiced within the anthropological continuum, has inherited as one of its main motivations the study of the Other and the Other's "otherness" (Wobst 1978). This applies especially to the ways in which Archaeology as a discipline attempts to use ethnography and its corollary ethnoarchaeology to fabricate contemporary understandings of past human societies. Yet, understandings of past human societies are obscured by a set of contingent problems that do not often affect contemporary ethnographic research, namely, temporal dislocations between actor and observer, and various configurations of materials and associations whose former direct and proximate causal origins cannot now be subjected to observational analysis. Whereas the contemporary ethnographer can study human actors through direct observation, archaeologists, of course, cannot study their subjects in real-time. One struggles, in fact, to conceptualize a situation of remoter "otherness" than one in which the observing party is alive and the subject of that observation is deceased, as it is in archaeological studies. One tends to construct the issue through an interrogatory appeal to one of the Ancients' (and especially ancient hunter-gatherers') most obvious predictive problems: How to hit a moving target?

Studying Paleolithic Hunter-Gatherers

For with respect to the study and explanation of past hunter-gatherers and their extinct lifeways, we are indeed attempting to hit moving targets. Epistemically, it seems often true that the more archaeologists think they understand the human past in general terms, the less they actually know with relative certainty in specific instances, since the "target" (the past human Other) moves, as functions of time-distance, resolution and analytical scale, research focus (wide or narrow, local vs. regional), and topic (economy, geography, settlement pattern, etc.). To cope with this observational translocation of the target, archaeologists often invoke to some extent the behavior of contemporary observed humans, through analogies, in order to affix possible behavioral causation to archaeological arrangements of material culture (Trigger 1989). Such has been a primary component of virtually all archaeological inquiry since the latter half of the 20th century, mainly in response to a widespread desire among archaeologists to make (or to remake, as it were) Archaeology more scientific and to develop a body of *predictive* theory specific to the discipline (Gibbon 1984).

The explicit theoretical and methodological use of analogy in archaeological reasoning became progressively more common in hunter-gatherer studies of ethnoarchaeology and zooarchaeology, at least since the 1960s (Ascher 1961; Binford 1967; Gibbon 1984; Lee and Devore 1968; Wobst 1978). Most commonly, archaeological analogies have been constructed through the ethnographic and ethnoarchaeological studies of arid regions and polar hunter-gatherers (i.e., the !Kung-San of the Kalahari, the polar Nunamiut and Inuit), occupying rather extreme environments under pressure from agricultural and industrial neighbors (Binford 1978a, 1978b; Lee and Devore 1968; Sahlins 1968; Wiessner 1982, 1983; Wobst 1978). With respect to the present research, much Zooarchaeology and faunal analysis also constitute excellent examples of analogy-based methodological and theoretical applications. Finally, the ethnoarchaeological modeling of past hunter/gatherer subsistence through appeal to the behaviors of contemporary human behaviors has also occupied much of the relevant literature and research. Paleolithic hunter/gatherer archaeology has made especially extensive use of predictive models based upon analogies, and theoretical/simulation models based upon ethnoarchaeology and other, more hypothetical-deductive research.

Analogy and Middle Range Research in Archaeology

Whereas the use of argumentative analogies became a common fixture in the archaeological literature during the 1960s (Ascher 1961, 1962; Binford 1967; Chang 1967), and led to the development of an "analogical interpretive toolkit" through appeal to contemporary hunter/gatherers, (Schuyler 1968), it also became apparent that there are major theoretical problems involved in the use of contemporary analogies as heuristic devices. First, the use of contemporary observed human behaviors as explanatory aids for archaeological investigations is somewhat contradictory, for it begs the question: What connections really exist between contemporary observed behavior and the archaeological record, and what assumptions are involved in presupposing them? Moreover, some of the earliest ethnoarchaeological research concerning analogies with contemporary hunter/gatherers resulted in the rather naïve abstraction of these extant societies (especially the !Kung) as virtual "fossil populations", lacking appreciations of their specific culture histories and the effects imposed upon them by historical agricultural/industrial encroachments (Kelly 1995). Such a perspective subordinates and homogenizes much behavioral variation in favor of constructing artificial (but convenient) theoretical generalizations, ignoring the time-distance and geographic, environmental, biological, and historical contingencies unique to both contemporary and past hunter/gatherers (Gibbon 1984; Kelly 1992).

Wobst (1978) has characterized the above as the "tyranny of the ethnographic record", and advocates the study of past material and behavior through inferential retrodiction and methodologically through hypothetical deductive research. Binford (1981) describes such methodology as Middle Range Theory (MRT) or Middle Range Research, in which the identification of material patterning agencies is back-projected onto inferred past human behavioral processes that operated to condition the material and its observed patterning. To this end, Binford (1981) partially defines MRT through reference to the Paradigm, Theory, and Hypothesis guiding it: The Paradigm is the cognitive frame of reference underlying inferential arguments; Theory refers to a guide for understanding and generalizing about inferential arguments; Hypotheses refer to inferential arguments themselves that are empirically testable. For Binford (1977), scientific archaeology proceeds by testing hypotheses, and pruning those that lose or lack explanatory power from the disciplinary corpus. In many respects, MRT is essentially what Wobst (1978) describes as "retrodicting" inferred behavioral causality on the observed archaeological record. A good contemporary example of such middle range research is subsistence inference through faunal analysis.

Archaeofauna in Ethnoarchaeology and Zooarchaeology

Beginning in the 1960s and 1970s, archaeologists have used the faunal assemblages from archaeological sites as integral, constituent elements of their research programs (Binford 1977, 1978; Frison 1974; Kelly 1995; Olsen 1964; Uerpmann 1973; Yellen 1977). Prior archaeological research had tended to catalog and inventory fauna in site reports or monographs without actually using or integrating the faunal data themselves as explicit research foci. In the 1970s, especially, the use of faunal remains for analyzing past human subsistence entered the literature, and developed generalized research trends that would later burgeon during subsequent decades: faunal quantification, mechanisms of faunal attrition, faunal taphonomy, and faunal demography, as well as ethnographic accounts of faunal use and processing (Binford 1977, 1978a, 1978b; Binford and Bertram 1977; Kelly 1995; Klein 1978; Yellen 1977).

The use of archaeofauna as means for testing explicitly formulated "middle-range" hypotheses concerning human subsistence diversified rapidly in the 1980s. This was especially true regarding the growing sophistication of faunal quantification methods (Grayson 1984; Speth 1983), and the identification and analysis of faunal preservation/alteration processes (Behrensmeyer and Boaz 1980; Binford 1981, 1984; Brain 1980). In some ways, the growing awareness of preservation and quantification biases represented natural outgrowths of the "maturing" discipline of zooarchaeology; i.e., increasing familiarity with fauna and data patterning elicited studies of processes to account for the faunal patterning. Studies were undertaken to "identify" the signature patterns of specific bone taphonomic and physical attrition/alteration processes (Brain 1980; Gifford 1981; Hanson 1980; Hill 1980; Lyman 1984, 1985; O'Connell et al. 1988; Speth 1983). The aging and sexing of archaeofaunal populations also gained in sophistication during the 1980s, and provided crucial information regarding the possible "targeting" and selective planning capacities of human hunters (Grant 1982; Klein et al. 1983; Klein and Cruz-Uribe 1984; Stallibrass 1982).

The 1990s and 2000s have witnessed the further refinement and sophistication of faunal data-gathering and analytical techniques. The growing awareness of faunal patterning biases (the demography of faunal populations, density-mediated destruction, selective element transport, carnivore activity, human behavior, and physical/geologic processes) entered the disciplinary literature, and represent increasingly specialized research themes that obtain even today (Blumenschine et al. 1996; Butler and Lyman 1996; Chase et al. 1994; Enloe 1993,1997, 2004, 2006; Enloe and Turner 2005; Gifford-Gonzalez 1991, 1993; Kent 1993; O'Connor 1996; Pike-Tay 1995; Pike-Tay et al. 2000; Stiner 1991a, 1991b; Stiner et al. 2000). Comparisons/contrasts between carnivore and anthropogenic accumulation and alteration signatures are extremely common (Marean and Spencer 1991; Marean and Frey 1997; Stiner 1991a, 1991b). Of particular interest for the present research are Enloe's (Enloe and David 1992; Enloe 1993, 1997, 2004, 2006) faunal analyses elucidating meat sharing, the calculation and use of faunal element ratios as heuristic devices, and fabric analysis through element spatial positioning.

Ethnoarchaeology mainly affects zooarchaeology through presenting a comparative means for the recognition of variable hunter/gatherer organizational strategies and activities (such as faunal processing), at least insofar as such are visible in the patterning of faunal remains from archaeological sites, linking material with possible conditioning agencies (Binford 1980; Enloe 1993). Contemporary ethnographic accounts of various faunal processing behaviors serve as possible indices for comparable past behaviors, or also as enquiry guides, suggestive of productive methods of interrogating archaeological datasets. Ethnography can therefore influences the research design of archaeological investigations by portraying contemporary examples of possible causative processes, or a baseline for reference. As we shall see below, however, this is based upon assumptions of similitude between inferred causal processes in the past and observed human behavior in the present that may be oversimplified.

Modeling (Paleolithic?) Hunter-Gatherers

Geertz (1973:44) suggests that a critical aspect of science is whether observed phenomena can be made to reveal the speculative causal processes underlying them. Paleolithic archaeology more extensively uses abstractly modeled and simulated analyses of archaeological phenomena (i.e., patterning and associations in lithic and faunal assemblages) to estimate unobserved causal processes. Analogical and system/structural models of hunter/gatherers, based on ethnography and ethnoarchaeology, comprise much of the relevant literature, especially since the Man the Hunter conference (Kelly 1995; Lee and Devore 1968). Table 3.1, below, summarizes some of the more (subjectively) salient models respective of the present research project.

Table 3.1. Subsistence/Settlement Models.			
Author	Model	Derivation	Pub. Date
Mortensen	Circulating/Radiating	theoretical/historical	1972
Wiessner	Population	theory/simulation	1974
Wood	Locational preference	ethnoarchaeology	1978
Hodder	Spatial/material	ethnography	1979
Binford	Foraging/Logistical Coll.	ethnoarchaeology	1980
Odell	Representative sampling	theoretical/statistical	1982
Chang	Fishing foragers	ethnoarchaeology	1988
Rocek	Seasonal economy	ethnoarchaeology	1988
Sullivan	Settlement chronology	ethnoarch./survey	1988
McCartney & Glass	Statistical/simulation	theory/simulation	1990
Headland	Socioeconomic	ethnography	1997
Kolb & Snead	Spatial/material	pedestrian survey	1997
Hewlett et al.	Cognitive	theoretical	2000
Prentiss & Chatters	Historical contigency	theoretical/historical	2003

It may first be useful conceptually to delimit just what it is I mean by the phrase "hunter-gatherer", Paleolithic or otherwise. After the Man the Hunter conference, a "nomadic" hunter-gatherer lifeway entered the literature, consisting of five basic characteristics: 1) egalitarianism, 2) low population density, 3) lack of territoriality, 4) minimum food storage capacities, and 5) flux in band composition (aggregation and dispersion based upon resource availability) (Lee and Devore 1968). According to Isaac (1990), hunter-gatherer is synonymous with the *generalized forager* economic model of subsistence, in which plant foods comprise the majority of caloric input, along with an absence of strict territoriality or defense posturing, and a group population maintained in accordance with available foods. Stiner (2001), however, has described a "broad-spectrum" model of hunter/gatherer adaptation, based on a wide variety of smaller animals that are reproductively more capable of rebounding from human predation, and perhaps inputs of stored, seasonally available plant foods. Furthermore, the term hunter-gatherer can also refer to an anthropological or typological archetype, as opposed to agriculturalists, industrialists, etc. For the purposes of this dissertation, I use the phrase mainly as a heuristic device with economic and anthropological-typological meaning. With respect to past hunter/gatherers, Kelly (1995) also suggests that subsistence and mobility serve as feasible social-organizational research topics, since coarse estimations of them are possible through reference to the archaeological record.

Headland's (1997) socioeconomic and ethnographic construct serves to describe his conception of the post-revisionist Historical-Ecological model of culture change. Its central premise is that the epistemic revisionism of the 1980s and 1990s in Anthropology resulted in the formation, or consolidation, of a new "Historical-Ecological" school of thought relating to hunter/gatherers. Headland (1997) identifies three distinct phases of hunter/gatherer ethnographic/ethnoarchaeological understandings: 1) Pre-1966 "Hobbesian" notions of hunter/gatherer life as short, nasty, and brutish; 2) Post-1966 (Man the Hunter conference) view of purer social egalitarianism and the doctrine of "original affluence" among hunter/gatherers (which is actually also reminiscent of 19th century Romanticist conceptions); and 3) The Revisionism of the 1980s and 1990s which resulted in a "new synthesis" of Julian Steward's culture-ecology and the "New Ethnography's" perspective of historical-ecology. Essentially, this model suggests that any means of analyzing human culture must include the diachronic evolutionary analysis of human ecological settings, abstracting culture change in relation to broader systemic changes.

Binford's (1980) very influential ethnoarchaeological subsistence/settlement model provides a basis for understanding, abstracting, and predicting various relationships between archaeological patterning and human behavioral processes. This model delineates two "poles" (logistical collecting and foraging) of a "foraging spectrum" (Kelly 1995), with which site functions, site types, and human conditioning activities may be partially correlated. Based on his familiar Nunamiut ethnoarchaeological research (1978), Binford's (1980) model has also been used as a template for numerous subsequent hunter/gatherer research designs. Brumbach and Jarvenpa's (1997) use of ethnoarchaeology to study and predict the potential and effects of sexual divisions of labor through spatial organization, and Chang's (1988) ethnoarchaeological model of site formation processes at Northwest Coast fishing contexts are based on Binford's research design. One of the primary research considerations of such studies lies in framing the discussion of the conditions under which we may expect certain configurations of archaeological material to be formed. Likewise, Odell (1982) describes analogical modeling in archaeology as a process of identifying suitable comparisons, in order to provide a structure of ideas for archaeological reasoning. Binford's (1980) and Odell's (1982) models are conceptually very fertile for the generation of new research.

Widely used in Levantine archaeology, Mortensen (1972) proposed a geographic/locational archaeological model similar in many respects to that later proposed by Binford (1980). In Mortensen's (1972) model variable residential mobility is abstracted along a continuum ranging from circulating (higher mobility) to radiating (lower mobility). This is essentially equivalent to Binford's (1980) foraging-logistical collecting spectrum; in both models residential mobility is treated as a dependent variable that scales in relation to other variables such as season or population (Mortensen 1972). Whereas Mortensen's (1972) model has been widely applied in Near Eastern and Levantine Paleolithic contexts to abstract mobility (Coinman 2005; Marks and Freidel 1977; Olszewski and Coinman 1998), Binford's (1980) has been widely applied also, especially in European Paleolithic Contexts (Audouze and Enloe 1991; Blades 1999, 2003; Enloe 1993; Mellars 1989).

Contemporary impressions of past seasonality and material resource distribution also figure into such models. Rocek's (1988) use of ethnoarchaeology to predict occupational seasonality highlights the importance of a judicious use of indirect evidence. In this study, Rocek (1988) uses tree-ring data seasonally to ascribe shifts in the timing of labor investments made by past Navajo settlements. Rocek assumes site location and site functions were actively determined by seasonality, which are demonstrated by covariance between expected and observed seasons of Navajo tree-felling for structural uses. Such indirect evidence also figures heavily in Wood's (1978) optimal location settlement model, which seeks to predict site location. For Wood (1978), subsistence and settlement are based on ecological characteristics of the "site environment" (not quite 'catchment', but quite similar to it), which, according to the model, humans seek to locate and to optimize based on purely rational decisions. In other words, the archaeological predictability of location may be based on contemporary human impressions and awareness of previously advantageous locations, as measured by past resource availability, slope gradients, water drainage, etc.

Whereas many ethnoarchaeological models are based on observations geared toward understandings of material distributions and associated causal behaviors, some also feature more explicitly theoretical/predictive theses. Hewlett et al. (2000) detail an ethnoarchaeological "internal working model" of human relations to describe possible causes and effects of sharing and in-group cohesion. The central assumption and conclusion of Hewlett et al. (2000) is that diachronic in-group social bonding and affection serve to condition group members to share with one another, which is then extrapolated to past human societies to predict some material correlates. In the sense that Hewlett et al. (2000) stresses the (internal) "giving environment" of human social groups, the model echoes Bird-David's (1990) generous nature bank. At one level, this is partially persuasive, in that within-group socialization and conditioning should obviously serve to encourage within-group transfers of resources, and this is archaeologically productive since such sharing has been demonstrated in the archaeological record (Enloe 2003). The pooling of economic risk serves as a theoretical catalyst to the development of sharing, as based upon the rational, perceived (concomitant, individual and collective) benefits of maintaining group productivity and mitigating the effects of various catastrophes, broadly similar to Wiessner (1982) and Winterhalder (1997).

Hewlett et al. (2000) was partially prefigured in the literature by Hodder's (1979) Aftrican (Kenya, Zambia, Sudan, and Nigeria) ethnarchaeological and theoretical model of abstracting in-group and out-group material indices from the archaeological record. For Hodder (1979), increased between-group competitions predict increased uses of material culture as means of maintaining internal social cohesion and the exclusion of "outsiders". Within this model, archaeological material diversity (stylistic, functional, etc.) may indicate internal power relationships and interaction strains between individuals and groups. Such an interpretation obviously implies that material similarity and dissimilarity both have social ramifications. Although this model is not strictly predictive, it does serve to highlight that there may sometimes be more to material stylistic variation than purely form-functional correlations

Wiessner (1974), Sullivan (1988), and Kolb and Snead (1997) produced predictive models premised upon the use and location of space in archaeology. Wiessner (1974) envisioned a linear relationship between human individuals and groups, and the respective amounts of interpersonal space they required for performance of economic functions in their communities. This model was partially theoretically derived, and also resulted from from Kalahari ethnoarchaeology (from !Kung sites and intra-site activity areas), and assumes that, all other things being equal, each human requires a finite and constant amount of interpersonal space, from which rough reconstructions

of community population may be estimated. According to the model, community settlement area is indicative of human population in absolute numbers. Although somewhat simplistic, owing to its early date (in terms of such modeling literature), this construct does indicate the general theoretical position from which many later population estimator models originated. Kolb and Snead (1997) intimate that community spatial organization should be modeled as differing scalar constitutions of human social systems. In their opinion, a community of humans constitutes a geographic "microregion", which is the most common unit of archaeological human settlement encountered at sites (Kolb and Snead 1997). In other words, they suggest that the community-level of human social organization is the most productive level of analysis, since higher resolution family or individual groupings are difficult or impossible to ascertain archaeologically in most contexts.

Human and artifact populations also provide axes of modeling interest. Prentiss and Chatters (2003) describe a theoretical evolutionary model based on Northwest Coast (US) ethnoarchaeology. Seeking to explain the manner in which material cultures enter, occupy, and leave the archaeological record, the model's principal hypothesis is that styles and forms (and by extension, cultures themselves) first enter the record, diversify, and are then decimated and exit it through interaction with more competitive or dominant cultures and styles (Prentiss and Chatters 2003). As a means of explaining some of the "battleship curves" that result from frequency plots of artifact styles, this is an extremely persuasive construct. It is not, however, obvious that the model can be used to explain the contingent disappearances of all cultures and styles from the archaeological record.

We must, however, devote some time to another type of model used in archaeology and especially ethnoarchaeology: the Optimal Foraging models.

Optimum-based Models

A major peripheral research track into modeling hunter/gatherers was taken by researchers investigating "optimal foraging" and "central place" models (Hawkes et al 1982). These models were developed in Biology, and were only subsequently retooled and reworked in order to fit them into archaeological discourse (Aronson and Givnish 1983; Hawkes et al. 1982). Optimal foraging models construct consumer behavior such that various chronic instances of resource acquisition (i.e., hunting, plant gathering, etc.) are designed and enacted "optimally', according to rigorous cost/benefit calculations that seek to maximize efficiency (Hawkes et al. 1982). These models likewise assume that hunting and foraging forays are made from a central locus that is emplaced with an "efficient" sense of centrality, to "maximize" available resources by strict central location (Aronson and Givnish 1983). In both cases, these models are premised upon some basic assumptions, or discursive epithets, such as optimal, central, maximum, efficiency, and so forth, that indicate their contemporary economic biases. A further assumption these models make relates to the presumed diachronic operational effects of natural selection to strengthen trends toward centrality and optimization (Aronson and Givnish 1983; Hawkes et al. 1982).

The discursive usages of terms such as "maximal" and "optimal" are clues to the biases inherent to the models making use of them, especially those pertaining to conceptions of behavioral or cognitive modernity. Contemporary conceptions of "maximal" and "optimal" are rather constrained by the socio-economic historical particularities of the people that developed the models (mainly American anthropological archaeologists). Moreover, hunter-gatherer cost/benefit calculations are presumably quite stochastically and situationally variable, especially when the sample is widened to include past hunter/gatherers. The consideration of mosaic, geographically and seasonally highly variable Pleistocene environments also suggests that many Paleolithic hunter/gatherers lack definitive contemporary analogs, such that the past behaviors may not be adequately modeled through simple analogical references to the present (Wobst 1978). Such maximal and optimal conceptual models should therefore be used with a great deal of caution and disclosure of potential caveats.

It would be prudent to examine some assumptions with respect to behavioral-cognitive modernity respective of the dynamics of a logistical subsistence posture. Many of the items in the behavioral modernity package, such as burial of the dead for example, are modified by adjectives such as "intentional". Does this imply that a behaviorally or cognitively modern person might intentionally bury the dead whereas premodern people didn't? Does this mean premodern humans absolutely did not bury their dead, and yet if they did, would the burials have been unintentional or stochastic? How should this be modeled? Accidental or spontaneous inhumation would seem terribly nebulous hypotheticals to test but these are literally implicit. In the interest of reducing confusion and imprecision, one would replace the more romantic epithets used to describe behavioral modernity (intentional symbolic burial of the dead, for example) with the much simper "systematic" and/or "consistent". One will therefore attempt to discuss behavioral-cognitive modernity in this analysis in terms of the archaeological visibility of systematized subsistence attributes. This is especially important with regard to models, analogies, hypotheses, and even theory. Without an emic ethnography of Magdalenian subsistence, we will not be in a position to assess its "efficiency". But we should certainly be able to assess whether or not Magdalenian subsistence strategies were expressed systematically, coherently and consistently.

Issues in Paleolithic Hunter-Gatherer Researc

With respect to the literature reviewed above, there are certain major theoretical issues that arise and recur, due to shifting but often convergent research trends, presumed methodological innovations, and varying topical concerns. These recurrent theoretical issues are partly epistemological or philosophical in nature, and yet derive also from divergent methodological preferences and their effects; I will argue that this conceptual duality (i.e., on the one hand theoretical, on the other hand methodological) constitutes one of the more intractable problems for Paleolithic hunter-gatherer researchers to solve. For example, in the crude abstract, attempts to solve theoretical research problems tend to raise additional methodological issues; likewise, attempts at refining methodologies often lead to further interpretive complications based on their variable relevance to anthropological and archaeological theory (such as they are). For the purposes of this paper, I will confine myself to issues relevant to UP hunter-gatherer research.

One of the, if not "the", primary conceptual, theoretical, and methodological problem(s) in Paleolithic hunter/gatherer research involves philosophical complications in the use of argumentative analogies with contemporary hunter/gatherers to explain past human behavior. As above, at least since the 1960s and the Man the Hunter conference (in 1966), various ethnographic accounts of contemporary observed hunter/gatherer behavior have been extrapolated to the material residue and spatial associations of Paleolithic hunter/gatherer sites in order to "explain" them. Above, I referred also to cognitive difficulties in assessing the degree to which (if at all) *any* contemporary hunter/gatherer cultures can really serve as valid analogies for extinct UP hunters. According to Wobst (1978), it is probable that a wider range of variability existed between past hunter-gatherer populations than we can observe or document today. This means that, apart from the problem of choosing allegedly appropriate explanatory analogies, we also have no real means with which to test our certainty that any given extinct hunter/gatherer entity actually *has* modern analogies. For instance, whereas it is entirely possible to document apparent similarities in the spatial patterning of lithic knapping debris between past and contemporary occupations, we have to *assume* that the patterns themselves derive from commensurate causal processes since we can't observe the actual real-time formation of the past one. Any statements made regarding past human behavior should therefore be couched in terms clearly indicative of the assumptions on which they are ultimately premised, and offered as potential explanations, as opposed to probabilistic ones.

At a more purely "analogical" level, however, it may be useful to document the types and applications of analogies used most frequently in the archaeological literature before addressing the theoretical complexities involved in their explanatory use. Ascher's (1961) treatment of analogy in archaeological reasoning set the general trend for the types of analogies typically used in archaeology. Ascher (1961) described two primary types or categories into which essentially all analogies used by archaeologists fall: 1) direct historical analogies, and 2) bounded analogies.

In direct historical analogies, there exists some degree of historical continuity between the ethnographic and the archaeological cases under consideration. With respect to bounded analogies, no direct historical relations are posited between the ethnographic and the archaeological cases. Stahl (1993) provides extremely useful criteria for further distinguishing between which of the two analogical categories to employ, by means of a rigorous use of ethnographic source criticism. Stahl (1993) suggests that archaeologists use a "taphonomic assessment" of ethnographic biases in order to find good ethnograohic analogs. The implication is that we as archaeologists need better to understand the "formation processes" of contemporary ethnographic accounts before using them as heuristic devices in archaeological explanations, which is a valuable perspective.

The difficulty with analogical appropriateness also has Anthropological significance, at least in terms of Boas and his tremendous influence on the discipline. One of Boas' (1940) main contributions to Anthropological thought was that of the neutral and particular cross-cultural analysis of various differences and similarities between human groups. There are however many complications involved with the use of comparisons between extinct human populations in archaeology. For example, at the observational level it is true that similar technologies can be found throughout the UP; lithic blades, for instance, are documented in some Middle Paleolithic (MP) and many UP contexts (Bar-Yosef and Kuhn 1999). Few would argue today, however, that the nearly ubiquitous presence of blades in MP and UP lithic assemblages relates by necessity to shared evolutionary and historical contingencies at the level of individual cultures. Instead, it is quite possible if not probable that the manufacture and use of blades as lithic implements originated independently, at different times, in different geographic areas, among different cultures (or even species, in the case of UP Europe and the Levant), for different or similar reasons. Moreover, with respect to similarities in spatial artifact patterning, similarities between artifact styles from separate regions, or similarities in the treatment of faunal species at archaeological sites, it is likewise inadvisable to assert a necessary commonality in causation as may be suggested by the use of contemporary explanatory analogs. Discussions of archaeological causation are themselves complex matters, as below.

A failure to observe uncritically the many potential causes of various archaeological phenomena (equifinality) can result in gross overgeneralizations and outright incorrect conclusions. Although there exists an interesting and informative micro-literature in archaeology relating to science philosophy and archaeological causal explications, there is not space or time herein for a comprehensive treatment thereof. Let it suffice to say that with respect to archaeological causality, it is necessary to be aware of multiple simultaneous causal possibilities for virtually any archaeological phenomenon. First, there is the possibility that a given singular phenomenon (i.e., a past culture, an artifact, a site) derives from multiple causes (multi-causality). Examples of presumably multi-causal archaeological phenomena can be found in large-scale events such as pyramid construction and the development of state-level organizations in Ancient Egypt, the hominid evolutionary effects of Quaternary glaciations, and at smaller scales such the origins of Southwestern French Paleolithic cave art, the development of basketry, and so forth, all of which presumably share multiple, discontinuous causes. Second, there is also the possibility that multiple archaeological phenomena (i.e., the collocation of and spatial associations between a retouched flake, an unretouched blade, and animal bones) can be regarded as the multiple effects of a common cause (human meat processing). This dualistic tension underlies virtually every archaeological explanation in the literature, and serves as a generator of intense debate. It is, however, prudent clearly to distinguish between analogs and models before progressing.

Archaeological Models vs. Argumentative Analogies

The Random House Unabridged Dictionary (2006) defines *analogy* as follows:

1. a similarity between like features of two things, on which a comparison may be based: *the analogy between the heart and a pump.*
2. Similarity or comparability: *I see no analogy between your problem and mine.*
3. *Biology.* an analogous relationship.
4. *Linguistics.*
   a. the process by which words or phrases are created or re-formed according to existing patterns in the language, as when *shoon* was re-formed as *shoes,* when *-ize* is added to nouns like *winter* to form verbs, or when a child says *foots* for *feet.*
   b. a form resulting from such a process.
5. *Logic.* a form of reasoning in which one thing is inferred to be similar to another thing in a certain respect, on the basis of the known similarity between the things in other respects.

The same resource provides the following definitions for *model*:

1. A small object, usually built to scale, that represents in detail another, often larger object.
2. Model
   a. A preliminary work or construction that serves as a plan from which a final product is to be made: *a clay model ready for casting.*
   b. Such a work or construction used in testing or perfecting a final product: *a test model of a solar-powered vehicle.*
3. A schematic description of a system, theory, or phenomenon that accounts for its known or inferred properties and may be used for further study of its characteristics: *a model of generative grammar; a model of an atom; an economic model.*

4. A style or design of an item: *My car is last year's model.*
5. One serving as an example to be imitated or compared: *a model of decorum.* See Synonyms at ideal.
6. One that serves as the subject for an artist, especially a person employed to pose for a painter, sculptor, or photographer.
7. A person employed to display merchandise, such as clothing or cosmetics.
8. *Zoology* An animal whose appearance is copied by a mimic.

I provide the definitions above for both *analogy* and for *model* because much of the relevant archaeological literature treats them similarly, as though models constituted analogies, and *vice versa.* This is not the case. Models can be formulated based upon strong analogies between phenomena, and analogies can be drawn between models, but they are not at all equivalent terminologically or functionally. In archaeology, it is common to use the logical definition of analogy, as in an archaeological inference based upon perceptible similarities between things. Archaeological usages of models, however, tend to stress graphic and logical schematics of inferred systemic processes, or abstract simplifications of systems used for their demonstrative explanatory values (or, simply, heuristics). Archaeological models of Paleolithic hunter/gatherers can be regarded as analogous to other systemic models yet again such do not constitute formal logical analogies. Analogies are based on comparisons, while models (as we're using the term) are based upon abstractions of systemic processes, and we have described above some of the tensions inherent in attempting to find and model Paleolithic hunter/gatherer analogies.

Subsistence/Settlement Models

Models, as used in Paleolithic archaeology, are schematic heuristic devices used to explain and to predict various selective aspects of human behavior. In many cases, the models themselves are generalizations based upon ethnographic research, and generally seek to explain the incorporation of human systems into surrounding environments and other frameworks (Kelly 1995). Yet, besides a series of contingent, documentary observations, what actually goes into the formulation of these models that is specific to archaeology? To be blunt, whereas one may find these models to be efficient means with which to discuss archaeologically visible aspects of these extinct human systems, there are limitations involved in their application, especially considering Wobst's (1978) "tyranny of the ethnographic record". Not all past behaviors are archaeologically visible, not all past behaviors have contemporary analogs, and few ethnographic hunter/gatherer subsistence models were actually designed for archaeological use. We will hereby confine remarks to those models that feature explicit archaeological applications.

Kelly's (1995:112-115) extremely valuable comparative work on hunter-gatherer adaptations notes the following types of data as means to distinguish between individual settlement/subsistence systems and models as based upon ethnographic documentation: residential mobility, available food biomass within immediate area (ill-defined), distance traveled, total area occupied (at a site), and periodized mobility (how many days the group is moving during an annual cycle). The (uniformitarianist) assumption that selective pressures operate (and assumedly operated in the past) to some degree in conditioning variable residential mobility between hunter/gatherer groups allows the retrodiction of inferences into the past (Kelly 1995; Wobst 1978). Residential mobility can be understood as means of adapting to the local environment, and variable residential mobility as a means of distinguishing somewhat between differing behaviors and groups (Binford 1980; Kelly 1995; Mortensen 1972). Since estimates and effects of mobility are archaeologically visible, contingent upon certain assumptions (to which we will turn below), it is also archaeologically highly relevant.

Binford's (1980) and Mortensen's (1972) models, both premised upon periodically variable residential mobility as a means of describing human subsistence/settlement spectrums, serve as explanatory and predictive devices used by many archaeologists, working in many areas, to correlate hunter/gatherer activities and material at sites. To review and summarize their models, both Binford (1980) and Mortensen (1972) abstract residential mobility as a dependent variable that fluxes in response to independent variables such as seasonality, resource distribution, time, and many others, along a spectrum of hunter/gatherer residential possibilities (i.e., circulating and radiating, or foraging and logistical collecting). The specific descriptive terminology applied to any given cultural unit (i.e., circulating or logistical collecting) is not, in fact, the point; the overarching point is rather the use of independent variables (weather, resources, etc.) as a means of estimating and predicting value fluxes in the dependent variable of residential mobility. Herein lies the real predictive and retrodictive value associated with the archaeological use of these models, once allowances are made for underlying assumptions. This allows the models to be formatted as theories, with implications for testable hypotheses. For much of the past 20 years or so, an uncomfortable assumption has been to link "archaic" Middle Paleolithic subsistence to the foraging/radiating strategy, and Upper Paleolithic subsistence with logistical collecting/circulating modes, more by convention and argumentative symmetry than by any substantive demonstrative linkage between them.

Yet, beneath the bones, as it were, of Binford's (1980) and Mortensen's (1972) subsistence/settlement models, are presumptions regarding the past operation of uniformitarianist processes of human behavior. We must assume, for instance, that hunter/gatherer human groups undergo changes in the location of their primary residence for similar, rational and understandable purposes, regardless of whether they lived in the past or in the present. We assume that past humans needed to eat, needed shelter, socialization, and companionship just as contemporary hunter/gatherers do. We must make such assumptions because there is no acceptable philosophical alternative. There is simply no way to escape uniformitarian assumptions about past human systems unless and until we are able somehow directly to observe or sample them in real-time. This is unavoidable at present. If we do not invoke such assumptions as based on contemporary human behavior, then we are left with only educated or uneducated guesses regarding the activities of past cultures.

Middle Range Theory, Material, and People

Middle-range theory (MRT) and Middle-Range Research (MRR), as above, were presented as means of conducting methodical (and methodological) hypothetical-deductive archaeological research, preferably, rigorously-oriented around stated theoretical axes and particular research designs (Binford 1980, 1981; Wobst 1978). The goal of such applications was to develop sound methodologies for explaining the material patterning found in the archaeological record through inferences, experimentation, and analogy to contemporary observed behaviors. This is an obvious goal, for quite often the only thing one has with respect to the archaeological record *is* material, and so means of extracting data and inferring causality must be developed for it. This very material, however, whether artifactual, spatial, associational, etc., also contains unspecified amounts of non-material or social conditioning (Wiessner 1982). Therefore, another way of phrasing the goal of MRT and MRR is to recast the objective as the search for and analysis of behavioral correlates of material patterning.

For example, Binford's (1980) model describes resource-level organization and residential mobility geared toward resource acquisition. With regard to human subsistence and settlement, however, there are clearly social factors that also serve to provide structure to the material patterning in the archaeological record. This suggests that while items such as site location and site type may be based on organization to (a) particular resource(s), other considerations, such as internal site structure, exchange patterns, stylistic material variation, etc., are the results of personal interaction (at interpersonal, intragroup, and intergroup levels). Specifically, whereas organization to specific material resources could govern or affect site placements due to geographic frequencies and distributions, much of the actual material patterning within the site parameters would reflect organization around persons and the social relations of production (Wiessner 1982:176). Yet, there are perhaps other means of visualizing both the behavioral and material/spatial aspects of social relations and physical activity.

Boundary Theory as a Means of Abstracting Archaeological Social Space

There is no necessary distinction between social and physical roles or social and physical space. This is also

true of the spatial patterning, content, configuration, and social conditioning of material at archaeological sites. For example, apparent spatial boundaries in material patterning within sites can also refer to and coincide with social role and functional boundaries (Kooyman 2006). In environmental terms, spatial and social boundaries are created and maintained between entities in order to simplify, and to order, the environment, such that ideational "fences" are created around geographic areas, events, people, ideas, behaviors, etc. (Ashworth et al. 2000:474). As a theoretical postulate, we may couch such behavioral and physical boundaries in the following terms: most human behavior takes place within a given spatial area and may leave behind certain material correlates in the archaeological record. At the hypothetical level, we can further test whether we can find patterned evidence of behavioral and/or spatial boundaries in the archaeological record and in which associations and configurations.

Kooyman (2006) has provided a model of social space constructed as patterned spatial differentiation in the loci of behavior at archaeological sites. Such spaces are conceptualized by variability in the locational flexibility and spatial permeability to intrusion or encroachment of individual activity areas. Such spaces may be reflected in the boundaries between activity areas at sites, conforming to a simplified scheme of permeability versus impermeability (Kooyman 2006). Areas of permeable space could relate to such activities as exchange, negotiation, or other forms of communicative behavior. Such would be difficult at most archaeological sites to document reliably. However, areas of fundamentally impermeable behavior, such as primary butchering areas or kill sites, can theoretically be expected to occur outside or away from other areas (Kooyman 2006). Sound reasons for the existence of impermeable behavioral space theoretically exist at hunter/gatherer sites, both contemporary and archaeological, such as minimizing sanitary concerns due to butchering and evisceration (i.e., leaked intestinal contents and sanitary concerns at a residential locus), or the prevention of microlithic and smaller knapping products from entering the food supply through contamination. One would expect such impermeable areas to feature material indices of ideational and spatial boundaries, perhaps observable in material distributions (for example, tight clusters of artifacts, areas of little or no artifact concentration, etc.). Kooyman (2006) suggests further that permeable areas would feature gradational infiltration of material from other areas and emigration of material to other areas, while impermeable roles and spaces would be much more obviously delimited. Yet, material and space are not the only things pertinent to subsistence, especially logistically oriented subsistence.

Paleolithic Logistical Subsistence: the Original Information Age?

Most archaeological subsistence models are based upon economic and physical bases. There are, however, cognitive factors that underlie many of the routine activities taking place within any economic system, having to do not with materials but with thoughts. A logistical strategy based upon episodic fluctuations in resource availability and/or mammal prey species migration must also place extremely high values upon *information* and data. The entire logistical posture is at its base an *active* strategy as opposed to a *passive* foraging-by-encounter one. The consumption of information, the predictive capacity of the system as based upon past experience and transmission thereof, indicates an entirely different situational awareness in contrast to more passive organizations. Undertaking a logistical strategy also implicitly indicates some capacity for perceiving, tracking, processing, and recording/memorializing basic subsistence data from past experiences and incorporating or transforming the past experience into *predictive* information. The gathering of such experience and data also suggest the possibility of reconnaissance and intelligence-gathering activities. Reconnaissance would likewise involve a sequential, multi-step process of observation, communication, evaluations, and predictive actuation and planning, including labor organization for accomplishing tasks. Logistical subsistence may also require high mobility in order to acquire the sorts of information necessary to undertake it. It certainly tends to increase encounter rates with prey and with other human groups, facilitating exchanges of information and resources (Grove 2010).

Information as Commodity?

Given the presumed mobility of Magdalenian hunter-gatherers, the roles played by information and intelligence may change in terms of function and importance. Foraging within a familiar landscape would presumably present generally familiar risks. This may prove untrue in unfamiliar landscape settings, where entirely new sets of risks and perils, in perhaps different proportions and combinations, could be encountered. Information about such risks, and about the landscape environment itself, would obviously be of significant value. Controlling the access to and distribution of such intelligence and information might offer powerful incentives for the mnemonic or graphic capacity to store it for future use. In this sense information itself becomes commoditized in its own right, and the ability to acquire it and make use of it becomes pivotal. Such data could relate locations and abundance of prey species, material resources, geographic and geologic features, pertinent landmarks, etc. The point being that access to useable data with currency would be an unquestionably valuable asset, especially if this access was predictable. Yet, how might we "see" this in archaeological materials? Seeing it would probably entail not a direct example, of course, but examples of potentially related secondary phenomena indicative of informational/symbolic awareness.

Art might be one such secondary occurrence illustrative of either a new or diversified approach to information consumption and distribution. Marlowe (2005) suggests that territorial defense of hunting ranges can play significant

roles in hunter-gatherer societies, and perhaps more so in those societies in which hunting plays proportionately greater roles in subsistence. Economic diversification, in this case relating to the incorporation of a wider dietary base, can therefore be seen as a risk-mitigation strategy (or, the more foods on which one relies, the less likely it is that shortages of any one food class causing wider economic disruption). Moreover, a widening of the economic base, for example, to include fishing and the use of other aquatic resources, tends to decrease group mobility and increase local sedentism, which also increases concern for defending local territorial integrity (Marlowe 2005). In such situations, the productive locality (and the defense against encroachment thereon) becomes increasingly important. If concern for defending various "home" ranges of land motivated Magdalenian populations in Southwest France, for example, immobile and eye-catching cave art may have served at least partially as means of indicating group "ownership" of the caves and rockshelters in the area, many or most of which are located in close proximity to the Dordogne, Vezere, and other rivers perhaps formerly important for salmon fishing as well as hunting.

Magdalenian Human Environments: the Human Context

Changing landscape and climate conditions typified the areas occupied during the Magdalenian, and clearly impacted the lifeways of the people themselves. Magdalenian hunters occupied generally cold landscapes with patchy upland vegetation and gallery forests in fluvial valleys, during the Wurm tardiglacial and the onset of Holocene conditions (Audouze 1987; Aura et al. 2005; Coope and Elias 2000; Jochim et al. 1999; Weniger 1989). In fact, the literature suggests that one overarching theme in contemporary research relates to the successful and pervasive adaptation of Magdalenian cultures to a very wide variety of localized habitats, from river valleys, to upland plains, coastal zones and mountainous regions, with seasonal periodic alterations of these local habitats (Aura et al. 2005; Jochim et al. 1999). Where minor differences in the expression of Magdalenian material culture are noted, these differences tend to segregate into categories of faunal prey species representation, settlement patterning, and the presence/absence of certain artistic styles and objects (Weniger 1989). In other words, the Magdalenian is the Magdalenian, regardless of when it occurs or where it is found geographically. Whereas environmental change had effects on the human populations during these times, it is evident that demographic and population "pressures" and other social factors played causal roles in the Magdalenian's development and material expression.

The social climate of the Magdalenian can be summarized as a tight social integration, revealed by a remarkably consistent expression of material culture over a geographically diverse and widespread area (Jochim et al. 1999; Soffer et al. 2000; Straus 1995). Material representation of this social integrity can be seen in a number of ways in the Magdalenian, perhaps most fundamentally in the apparent in-group sharing of meat during the occupancy of some sites (Binford 1984; Bird and Bird 1997; Enloe and David 1992). One way to view the use of sharing is as a form of risk-pooling, or insurance, with understood mutual and individual benefits, as contingencies or risk mitigation strategies to offset resource or labor shortages and other stochastic or unpredictable mishaps. Meat-sharing and other forms of Paleolithic economic redistribution may be abstracted as means of mitigating both individual and collective failures, or insurance against catastrophic contingencies by spreading risk across wider and variable human abilities, directly analogous to contemporary, institutional risk-pooling by private-sector and governmental entities. Food-sharing can be seen as analogous to paying a premium for an insurance policy. One hunts (or otherwise gathers, collects, forages, etc.) and, if successful, provides a "deposit" (premium) or contribution of a resource to the group or subdivision of it, against which occasional withdrawals or "claims" can be made to offset bad luck, unforeseen accidents, etc. One could argue that a very basic component of this risk-pooling is an innovation or elaboration of material "product" valuation processes, stemming from *active* subsistence orientation and posturing with goal-based predictable or postulated intended results (food surplus for storage and wintering).

The entire subsistence orientation and posturing of the Paris Basin Magdalenian indicates systematization. For the MPB, there appear to be three systematized site-functional types:

1. Systematic tool- or blank-production sites such as Etiolles, with flat, central hearths, near high quality flint sources with sparse fauna in river valleys;
2. Logistical hunting camps such as VBC and Pincevent, also near fluvial channels, with abundant fauna and tools indicative of hide-working and butchery, with hollowed, stone slab hearths;
3. Plateau sites, such as Ville-St.-Jacques, with abundant tools and fauna, away from river valleys (Audouze and Enloe 1991:64).

Sites with diverse fauna and tool types are interpreted as summering/wintering sites, while sites with abundant but taxonomically restricted faunal assemblages are interpreted as autumn logistical sites staged to intercept migrating reindeer (Audouze and Enloe 1991). Aside from the planning and intentionality generally stressed in the literature for UP subsistence, other, more abstract, concepts are also at least indirectly but logically indicated: specific time- and seasonal-senses or accounting to differentiate subtle seasonal transitions; the "logistics" of collocating a specific labor pool of experienced scouts and hunters, knappers, and butchers, strong and healthy enough to work rapidly and intensively in punctuated bursts over short durations (weeks). Despite a few tantalizing clues here and there, for the European UP it is only during the Magdalenian that any suggestion of systematized and punctuated labor arrangements is really

visible archaeologically. One could, in fact, argue that the repeating pattern of relatively small and brief occupations at least at VBC strongly implies a highly focused labor pool, partitioned for some period of time from larger social groupings

Value Metrics: Modeling Magdalenian "Value"

In portraying Magdalenian economic specialization in terms of diversification and elaboration, it is incumbent upon one to provide some basic model, or at least a general outline, of possible economic evaluations therein. With respect to Magdalenian economic "diversification", this refers to a continuation of the "broad spectrum revolution" referenced above for the Middle and early Upper Paleolithic, but with even wider geographic, temporal, and altitude ranges of targeted fauna and flora, as well as technological means of exploiting even greater species diversities. In other words, we are considering new variations on preexisting economic themes. In a more diversified Magdalenian economy, establishing the potential "value" of prey species and raw material items vis a vis other materials and items, or even time, would be a fundamental concern. This evaluation methodology might involve coordination or balancing, between item "cost" and item "benefit". Such cost/benefit calculations may by no means indicate a Paleolithic capitalist mentality. Rather, by widening the resource and technological bases available or preferable for human exploitation and simply bringing more things into the realm of economic possibility would arguably place natural demands on available time and energy. The more things one must consider, the less time and particular focus one may have to devote to minute specifics. How do we ourselves handle expanded tasks and restricted time? Generally, we adapt by prioritizing both time and task, by evaluation. A rudimentary and discontinuous sense of Magdalenian "value" should be visible in systematic and consistent expressions of certain subsistence trends (prey choice, seasonality, etc.).

The (admittedly oversimplified for clarity and brevity) sequential chaine operatoire of such a putative strategy would involve 1) the identification and evaluation of economic inputs (initial; evaluation of prey items or raw materials to be hunted, gathered, collected, etc. and the cognitive processes involved); 2) actual item acquisition (through the expenditures of time, effort, energy, as well as varying amounts of social capital); 3) conversion of acquired materials (food, flint, antler, etc.) into products (i.e., 'processing'); 4) product evaluation (distinct from initial evaluation, instead perhaps estimating added value); and 5) the distribution, consumption or storage of products. In my model, conversion refers to the process of converting a food item or raw material into an actual product. Products can be then consumed directly, stored as is, or modified into subsequent products, stored and distributed again, etc. (adding "value" with each processing step involved).

In any cost/benefit calculation, a very basic metric is simply establishing input "values". What is "value"?

Both costs and benefits can be measured in terms of value. We could discuss value in terms of presumed benefit or material volume per some vague unit of energy, effort, social capital, all three, or yet more abstract dynamics. The main point being that value, and impressions thereof, probably range along a continuum of short term to long term presumed or expected benefits. There would presumably be different value metrics for different purposes, for variable human group sizes, during different seasons, and so forth. Presumed benefit (profit) could be based on a putative "income", or the more or less finite nutritive value of a food item, or the more continuous possible social or symbolic value of symbolic capital. This would resemble a continuum ranging between functional vs. structural value, with "fixed" (raw material units) and variable "expenses" (energy, expended time, effort).

Without getting even vaguer, how might we "measure" value? This is difficult, but we could perhaps state that "value" scales with costs and risks, in acquisition, storage, and distribution, suggesting that value at the time of acquisition may not be at all similar to assessed value later in the economic process, after various layers of additional value may have been added to something. In economics and business, (at least in the private insurance industry), value assessments often treat costs/benefits as equals in zero-sum equations, which are themselves treated as rudimentary predictive models. Such simplistic models generally focus on presumed advantages to large but specific groups of humans (i.e., all male drivers in a geographic area between the ages of 16 and 21), as opposed to small groups or even individual consumers. Moreover, despite the fact that population unquestionably increased in Europe during the tardiglacial, and especially during the Magdalenian, we are still considering small groups of human in comparison to population densities with which most of us are familiar, perhaps in the common 25 to 500 member sizes (Kelly 1995).

Given the abstract but visible differences between the technological and artistic traditions of the Magdalenian and the preceding Upper Paleolithic, much economic diversification may have involved elaboration of concepts and thought modalities amongst the people themselves in relation to food and material technological innovations. I.e., we can propose a concept of economic "profit" was perhaps in use by people during the Magdalenian. Profit could be calculated individually, collectively, or also on product-bases (per item profits vs. per person/per group profits). Profits are, however, generally at least partially cost-based, by which I mean based in real-time, real-world quantities, such as acquisition costs, caloric expense, personal and/or group risk, etc. To clarify, whereas most hominids (perhaps all higher primates in general) likely had some capacity to understand basic costs/benefits in at least some personal or symbolic terms, perhaps by the Upper Paleolithic we can discuss humans as being mutually self-aware. And if we can discuss people as being mutually self-aware, we can perhaps conjecture a degree of mutual group awareness as well, wherein the good of the

individual reinforces and is reinforced by the sustenance of the group. Profit may therefore also be defined partially as a risk-mitigation device, wherein pooled individual and collective mutual "profits" (similar or equivalent to larger-scale institutionalized surplus production) are intentionally pursued "just in case" as a form of insurance. Investments were made in food, materials, but especially people and information, not in truly personal property.

We should also clarify that by "profit" this does not mean personal, acquisitive profit in contemporary capitalistic material terms. The goal was more likely group social maintenance, by means of collective risk-pooling and sharing. In this model, in the context of a broad-spectrum hunter-gatherer band, able parties pay a premium of food or other products into the collective pool as able, with a deliberate focus on overestimating what will be needed. Storable materials would be cached; more perishable materials would be distributed and consumed more immediately. The profits, in such a model, are not to be viewed as individual enrichment, but as a shared social maintenance policy, to address stochastic shortfalls through the allowance of claims made against the group profit/surplus. In essence, the model details the comparative valuation of material, since the costs/benefits of obtaining anything are not fixed, and indeed often covary and scale in proportion to one another.

There are also discursive advantages to the concept of Magdalenian profit-based economic metrics. Such may be relatively easy to calculate and accurate for many things, and could deal with generally known quantities (the average shape, mass, or volume of a given unit of flint, or the caloric content of horse meat). There are, however, potential disadvantages in that cost-basing is only a point-estimate of actual value, perhaps only tangentially related to socially-proscribed material or product evaluations. Due to the inherent complexity of human economic systems, there is also a tendency to describe or to discuss economies as single products (burins), or single species (horse and reindeer) to the potential obscurity or drastic oversimplification of larger Magdalenian economies (although these are certainly not restricted merely to the Magdalenian). For the purposes of this study, we can discuss profit-based economic metrics according to the schematic in Figure 3.1. below.

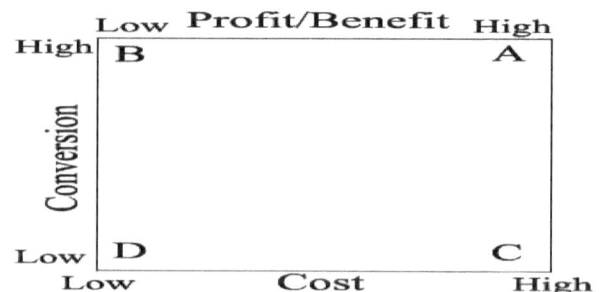

FIGURE 3.1. CONVERSION COST/BENEFIT SCHEMATIC.

Figure 3.1 above indicates some of the complexity within economic valuations. Cost refers to acquisition value; Conversion refers to processing value; Profit/benefit refers to the relative advantage conferred by a given product, item, etc. Although the figure above uses Conversion as the left axis, we could substitute acquisition value, acquisition cost, risk, or any other presumptive variable we should like, and the general operation of the model will be similar. Products can be low cost, require high conversions (high processing inputs) and may be low in terms of perceived profitability. Likewise, a high cost item with a high conversion value may still be a "high profit" product. At this point, one might reasonably ask, "But what intrinsic value do flints or reindeer portions actually have?" And this is a difficulty, for we cannot provide a finite answer. As with so many aspects of anthropology, the answer would contain the phrase "it depends" or some variation thereof. Value is context-dependent, subject to contingency, on case-by-case bases. Regardless of the actual caloric value of a piece of meat, or the Btu value of a piece of wood, in a human economy social factors play large roles in valuation. So that there is a basic, or elemental value to things, and yet also subjective, cultural values, be they sticks or marketable commodities, material profit opportunities or items of symbolic import.

How might evidence of such evaluation be manifest in the archaeological record? It should be evident in patterned subsistence behavior, such as is present at VBC. Furthermore, patterned repetitive evidence of a subsistence focus on particular faunal resources during particular times would offer strong support for the comparative valuation model. Evidence for this model could be found at sites showing a particular emphasis on faunal or material selectivity in areas with overlapping habitats of different game species and numerous available resources. For example, with respect to the Magdalenian, there appear to be two zooarchaeological camps (Enloe personal communication). On the one hand is the horse camp, proposing that horse hunting was the primary Magdalenian subsistence focus; on the other hand is the reindeer camp, abstracting Magdalenian subsistence as a quest for caribou. If both horse and reindeer were locally available at an ephemeral site, at Verberie, for example, strong evidence for a preponderance of either could indicate the comparative valuation of both species.

Value differences in prey species may also be age-mediated when based upon single species prey. For example, with respect to reindeer acquisition at Verberie, Enloe and David (1997) have argued persuasively for an autumn interception of aggregated herds. This seasonal interception was timed for maximal age cohort aggregation in the reindeer herds. Whereas the aggregate *Rangifer* herds would have been at their prime dietary state of nutritive value (Enloe and David 1997:63) there would be variation in the nutrient value *between* age classes. Younger to prime-age animals would presumably have much higher proportions and qualities of fat in their marrow and meat, offering much more balanced nutrition, while geriatric individuals

would have lower comparative nutritive values. Perhaps relatively easier to acquire, elder animals would also be suffering the effects of degenerative diseases and organic failures.

What archaeological effects would age-mediated carcass selectivity have at a site? We would expect some tangible difference, in terms of spatial location and treatment. Older carcasses would have lower somatic fat stores in all body parts, tougher meat, and lower quality marrow. During the fall reindeer intercept, one might expect older carcasses to be consumed more on-site, serving as a main food staple during a seasonal hunt. Older carcasses would be processed for transport perhaps primarily as an adjunct to the acquired young and prime-age carcasses. Abundant hunts might allow for less transport of low-value geriatric carcasses and parts; less successful hunts might require the addition of more geriatric carcasses despite their lower nutritive value. Since young and prime-age animals would be in better nutritional states, their transport costs would be lower while those for older animals would be higher (in both caloric and social capital terms). The younger carcasses may be transported off-site much more frequently than the geriatric specimens. Per Kooyman's concept of impermeable social space (2006), age carcass classes would presumably be separated spatially at sites, especially regarding on-site consumption and off-site transport preparations. Obviously, maintenance of future prey population viability would also be a concern. In leaner years, older animals might be taken and transported at higher rates simply to maintain a breeding herd's future viability, in essence trading some nutritional security in the short-term for more in the long-term. This brings us to the possibility of Paleolithic risk-management.

Paleolithic Risk-Management?

Contemporary actuaries and assorted other risk-management personnel conceptualize "risk" as simply the possibility of or exposure to the possibility of injury, illness, economic loss, failure to complete contractual obligations, etc. There is also obviously subsistence or behavioral risk, consisting of similar exposures to possibilities of injury, illness, loss, and failure to acquire food. Subsistence risk in the past would also come with additional individual and socio-cultural ramifications, echoing into socioeconomics, politics, religion, etc. Things presenting specific dangers (i.e., tornadoes) are termed perils in risk-management parlance, and the term could apply to past humans as well. In terms of Paleolithic risk, the main point for us is that extreme Darwinian cultural and genetic risks were probably inherent in social (and humans are social animals) animal-based subsistence strategies, simply due to much lower human population densities, hence smaller collective risk-pools. A wrong choice, an accident, or dumb bad luck could result in starvation and extinction of self, peer cohorts, local bands, entire regional kinship networks, or even larger population units depending upon contingency, and degree of social integration (and entire non-filial exchange networks if contagious pathogens were involved). Such conjecture hardly captures all the variance of past potential risks, and even individual perils, it must be noted.

Paleolithic risk was not a minor inconvenience as risks are often experienced today, since in the past there were no separate and professionally institutionalized risk-pools and risk-management structures to mitigate poor decisions or misfortune. We are accustomed to such things. It may be that Paleolithic human risk-management strategies arose for creating *de novo* social risk pools intentionally and productively to spread risk across multiple parties, perhaps even multiple societies (just as in contemporary insurance the bigger the risk pool, the less risk any one individual or individual area assumes since risk decreases as a statistical probability according to its dispersion)—once an appropriate demographic density was attained. This is a mathematic function. It's intuitive. But *why*? And how did such things occur during what we can assume about the lived contingencies of human subsistence experiences, and what can this tell us about subsistence modernity? And what might this imply about precedent (Lower to Mid-Pleistocene) human subsistence risk-mitigation strategies?

Given the often stark morphological differences observed between Neanderthals (or indeed, "archaic" Eurasian hominins in general) and AMHs in Pleistocene Europe, according to our contemporary evaluation of potential, past subsistence risks we can question some things about the presumed physical costs and benefits associated with robust and gracile human physiques in terms of performing subsistence tasks. Which morphology was actually exposed to greater subsistence risk? If they were intrinsically unequal in terms of basic subsistence, as Tattersall (1995) suggests, then we might be able to see this archaeologically in terms of risk-exposure. Such is often implied, at least, in our recent literature (i.e., Tattersall 1995, but by no means limited to that), for better or worse, and are hence fair game for analysis even if the emphasis is on interpretation as opposed to experience. And this is independent of assumed measures of comparative cognition. We should recall that actual lived experience counts for far more than interpretation in contemporary institutional risk-pooling. That's why our auto premiums rise even when we ourselves had no accidents; if our premiums rise while we had none we can assume some of our contemporaries *did* have accidents.

It's like this: big muscles are metabolically expensive. Yet, biomechanically, a Neanderthal or "archaic" physique allows one functionally to accomplish many things physically that would be much more difficult if not impossible to do lacking adequate musculature and/ or time-intensive technology or adequate peer cohorts. Such a physique also reduces individual risk exposure. One benefit to a metabolically expensive, robust physique would be that it allows for rapid, expedient acquisition and transport of products such as firewood through the brute force breakage and carrying of heavy tree limbs and fallen trees at an individual level. Breaking branches if not

entire trees and carrying them to hearths was obviously the primary means of processing firewood in remote antiquity, prior to the invention of axes and saws and wedges and transport technology, in solo or ensemble. Anyone that has tried to accomplish these tasks lacking appropriate sawing or hacking or splitting or transport technology will be immediately aware of the advantage that extreme functional musculature provides. One moves the largest possible piece of wood to the fire as one is able, where the wood is then reduced in size by breakage, or by whatever means are available, again, as one is physically able. Some are physically more able than others regardless of an activity's presumed symbolic content.

Another advantage to a robust physique, related to the wood anecdote above, would be that possession of high musculoskeletal rugosity serves effectively to weaponize the entire general environment. If a branch, or a rock, can be thrown at a potential prey target or competitor, then so much the better if it can be thrown at a prey target or competitor with relatively greater sheer power. Any kinetic energy within a projected missile will multiply by the amount of mechanical force driving it (ergo the development of atlatls). This holds true even for contemporary ballistic projectiles, *regardless of a projectile's cross-sectional area* (emphasis mine), of which police and private handgun owner/operators are acutely aware (sometimes it's even better if the projectile is not particularly pointed because greater bluntness transfers more inertial, impactive stopping power per unit area cross-sectionally). Anyone could probably throw a rock or a branch at a charging cave bear with enough power to get its attention assuming one's throwing accuracy is adequate to hit such a moving target. Yet, the raw physical ability to throw a large enough rock or branch hard enough to injure or disable the charging cave bear would provide the individual with that ability a distinct advantage in more potential contingencies than can scarcely be imagined. The social value of such abilities if expressed and multiplied communally would be incalculable. Moreover, robust bones resist breakage. Thick muscle pads the bones during impacts. A heavy frame provides more tackling inertia and resists dislocation. The preceding has profound implications for understanding the contingent individual and social realities in which actual, physical subsistence risks occur experientially in terms of hunting quadrupedal hoofed mammals to say nothing of mammoths, and these should be a greater part of our focus as pertains to behavioral or anatomical modernity in the venues of both individual and social awareness.

If one lacks the brute force capability to manipulate one's environment biomechanically to the extent that "archaic" humans likely could, especially assuming much lower population densities, then social or technological factors probably play a large part actively in assessing subsistence risks and either acting on them or abstaining from them in past human hunting-gathering communities. At least such is the implicit assumption within the ROA model for increasing musculoskeletal gracility, even if not expressed explicitly. While hunting, for example, especially when pursuing a hit and injured target specimen still at large, the contemporary hunter shooting bullets or arrows from long distances (especially with large fauna) will take special care to avoid a direct approach on the possibly flailing beast in solo, unless it is so gravely disabled that a solitary approach on it carries negligible costs in terms of bodily injury. Furthermore, when dismembering or transporting a large felled quarry, the hunter will likely only perform perfunctory tasks even on an expired target, knowing that transport of a carcass might require the participation of others in a social cohort to render any processing economically relevant. We don't frequently speak of such things. I would submit that one reason we don't often speak of such things is directly related to the fact that few paleoanthropologists and archaeologists either hunt or routinely carry heavy burdens over long distances. And yet there is so much to be learned merely through performance of such mundane tasks. It is the social, collective value we are discussing here. For very few of us are able to accomplish anything without peers. Do we imagine that this is a recent synapomorphy? Is collaboration really a recent cladistic trait separating us from our origins, given what we know of non-human primates?

Unfortunately, we will likely never know much about individual past risk-management decisions. Such things don't fossilize particularly well. How were specific risks evaluated at the individual level? How were perils thereby evaluated? Again, risk is just the possibility of or exposure to a loss, while a peril is an actual cause of a loss. What were the decision-making processes, and are contemporary hunter-gatherers even a suitable analog? To answer such questions archaeologists should focus some attention to developing informed perspectives regarding the basic process of social as opposed to individual risk-management, and that one of the first principles of such developments ought to be a rethinking of the contemporary capitalist economic understandings of individualized concepts such as "optimal" or "optimized", especially when attempting useful formulations of quantified models. We should also ask how ranges of subsistence behaviors can be affected by both individual and collective physical (if not athletic) ability and by the ranges of ability expressed by the potential targets of such implicitly predatory behaviors. One seriously doubts that Neanderthals developed their physiques simply by a stupid, obstinate determination to keep doing things "their way" (Tattersall 1995). And it is in this comparative assessment of ranges of subsistence behavior that we broach the subject of contemporary economic models, premised upon contemporary assumptions.

For especially the models of foraging optimality (or 'optimal foraging theory'), for example, are premised upon a set of assumptions regarding animal (mollusks, insects, fish, birds, reptilian and mammal quadrupeds) behaviors that are basically untenable in application to humans for three reasons: 1) most of these models assume that Darwinian "fitness" (another of the terms perhaps to discard or seriously revise in application to humans

in a cultural ecological niche) is based upon *heritable* (emphases mine) subsistence behavior conferring adaptive advantages that are constructed according to contemporary profit/loss calculations; 2) that offspring produced would exhibit the same subsistence behaviors as parents, *for the same reasons* (adaptive advantage); and 3) that the relationship (mathematical) between genetic fitness and subsistence is *known* (Abrams 1982; Andersson 1978, 1981; Aronson and Givnish 1983; Bond 1980; Charnov 1976; Cowie 1977; Davies 1977; Heller 1980; Hodges 1981; Krebs 1978; Lehman 1976; Lewis 1982; Lewontin 1979; McNair 1979; McNamara 1982; Morrison 1978; Norberg 1977; Ollason 1980; Pulliam 1974; Pyke 1982, 1984; Richards 1983; Schluter 1981; Taghon 1981; Turner 1982; Zimmerman 1981). It is also worth noting that biologists can observe their subjects of study, in the individual and the aggregate whereas the archaeologists may not. We know better.

Finally, it's probably not accidental that optimal foraging models were normally based and developed (especially during the 1980s when first incorporated into archaeology) upon analyses of behaviorally simple and non-social animals whose behaviors are highly amenable to quantification and linear modeling. People don't really quantify particularly well. And why is this? It is not the case that people are simply too complex to model, especially in subsistence terms. Eating is after all a very basic human somatic requirement. The difficulty in quantifying humans relates to interpreting precise socio-cognitive causal factors and yet also to the metaphoric image of water ripples spreading from multiple locations in a pool, mutually reinforcing extant ripples and even generating additional, new ripples in unpredictable ways. We're not really studying individual activity in the archaeological record; we're usually analyzing the material after effects of multiple party *interactivities*. Human behavioral group dynamics conditioned the record much more than any individual behaviors. Social roles play large factors in this modeling complexity, whether individually, inter-individually, or at intra-group and intergroup levels of analysis. Optimal/optimizing models posit a false dichotomy between maximum optimal (efficient?) production and the otherwise imperfect. This leaves an enormous continuum or range of excluded possibilities and opportunities, and misses the point that suboptimal production can be offset through social organization and pursuit of additional strategies.

One of the concepts current amongst professional actuaries and other risk-management professionals is that of risk coherence (Babbill and Merrell 2005; Dhaene et al. 2008; Golubin 2006; Hamada and Valdez 2008; Laury and McInnes 2003). To some degree, we all use estimates of risk coherence in our daily lives. Is the risk coherent, meaning is it consistent or variable in nature (i.e., do its parameters remain basically quasi-static or do they fluctuate, meaning constant or variable risk measures)? Awareness of risk coherence then leads to the generation of additional questions: Is the risk understood, do people understand what it actually entails? Are the potential costs of action/inaction commensurate or unequal? Are the potential benefits of action/inaction commensurate or unequal? Such are not posed merely as rhetorical questions, for consciously or not people generally must answer them in the process of managing risks, whether within institutionalized systems or the most egalitarian society. For the opposite of risk management is basically risk ignorance, and while some societies are certainly less risk-prone than others, there are probably few who simply ignore perils and the risks they present.

Kuznar (2001:433) presents a very cogent risk heuristic (Figure 3.2 below), the "sigmoid utility curve", to express a continuum of Andean people ranging from risk-averse to risk-prone (also described by status, which is at least partially misleading, though informative). Risk-prone people are abstracted by the convex portion of the curve from the origin to the inflection, where the risk of losing, p, is undertaken because the potential profit b > potential loss a. Risk-averse people are modeled by the concave portion of the graph form the inflection to the end point, where risk of losing, p, is avoided because the potential debit c > profit d. In this model, risk is tolerated with opportunity for attaining some degree of "profit", which can be actual production of benefits in greater frequency than previously, or attainment of commensurate benefits under low-risk scenarios. Lack of profit opportunity in this model results in lack of tolerance for risks. In other words, to pursue "profit" or surplus production to offset potential future shortfalls, risks *must* be perceived, analyzed, understood, and managed.

Sharing as Risk-Management = Insurance

Several works suggest that since reliance on meat-intensive diets (i.e., hunting) is inherently risky, one mechanism to reduce the amplitude or variability of such subsistence risk is through sharing (Grove 2010; Kaplan and Hill 1985; Kaplan et al. 1985). Although controlling for numerous external subsistence risks is difficult for any economic strategy (external risks = things beyond one's direct control, i.e., weather, meteorites, interpersonal violence, etc.), one inherent internal subsistence risk for hunters is simply variable hunting performance. Sharing and redistribution of hunted meat is one mechanism to alleviate interpersonal hunter performance variance (Grove 2010). A capacity for sharing in many species appears to manifest under certain conditions, expressed as basic models: kinship selection (when value and hence cost of a given item is lower for the giver than the receiver); tolerated theft (contests over resources are won by the party to whom the value of the resource is higher and the cost of competition to the loser is greater); reciprocity (where there are mutual costs and benefits for giver and receiver, but the benefits for both outweigh the costs); and cooperative acquisition (such as in social carnivory, where the cost of not reciprocating is higher in terms of future acquisitions than sharing) (Kaplan and Hill 1985; Kaplan et al. 1985). The anthropological concept of reciprocity, however, was largely developed according to a strict natural selective model for reciprocal *selective* behaviors (emphasis mine) as opposed to social selective factors (Trivers 1971).

There are other, human-behavioral models and systems of understanding that are based on people as opposed to lower order animals or obscure mathematic models. The insurance industry has a very long history—a long *human* history—of conceptualizing, managing, mitigating, and reducing economic risk. There are many degrees of separation between human risk management (which is, after all, human behavior) and between behavioral models premised upon the observation and detailed description of the feeding activities of echinoderms or snails, for example. Furthermore, the insurance industry has long known that *most* people follow *most* traffic rules *most* of the time, and promulgates essentially Boasian, *emic* understandings for why these facts are so: perceived benefits to self *and* others in the avoidance of driving risks. Are *emic* perspectives of optimal sea urchin foraging even rhetorically valid, let alone ontologically possible? If we can understand that most people follow most traffic laws most of the time, and that they do so for reasons of both individual and mutual benefit, it becomes much less a stretch to understand that this is essentially the same as perceived individual and mutual benefit to the participation in collectively beneficial subsistence behaviors. It is reciprocity.

Summary

At the beginning of this chapter was posed the question, what ought Paleolithic archaeologists to know in order to practice their brand of Archaeology? Three general goals were outlined: 1) A cumulative knowledge of the human past free of particularized historical constraints; 2) A basic knowledge of behavior and its material correlates as found in the archaeological record; and 3) An understanding of

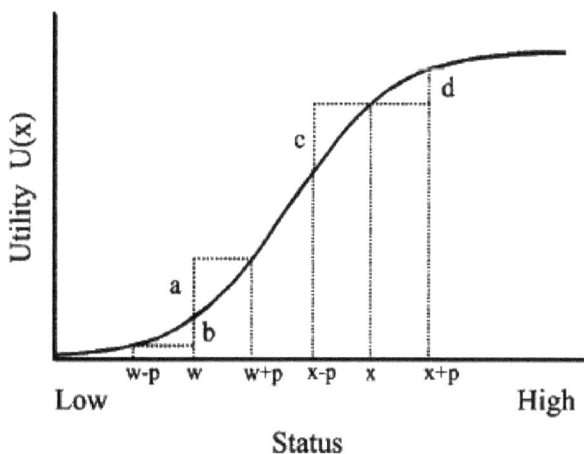

FIGURE 3.2. THE SIGMOID UTILITY CURVE (FROM KUZNAR 2001:433, FIGURE 1).

hunter-gatherer subsistence and settlement organization. It was an unstated given that Paleolithic humans lived as hunter-gatherers, and I am personally aware of no viable alternatives to that generalization. An implicit aspect of the entire discussion has been that since we cannot hope to know everything about how the archaeological record came to be the way it's observed it therefore follows that a very judicious use of ethnographic and ethnoarchaeological analogies and models must be included in order to relate potential causes with observed material effect.

The discussion then shifted to the archaeological uses of argumentative analogies between the present and the past, and various methodological means with which to associate human behavior and material correlates (middle range theory or MRT and middle range research or MRR). Zooarchaeology and ethnoarchaeology were proposed as viable instances of hypothetico-deductive research utilizing MRT and MRR. In essence, the goal of engaging in MRT and MRR was to establish reliable means of interpolating cause and effect and mitigating between past human behavior and its associated material correlates as they are observed in the archaeological record. Faunal quantification, ethnoarchaeological analogies, and the construction and use of various archaeological models were described as examples of MRT and MRR to be found in the contemporary archaeological literature. Given the subject matter and the treatment, I did not feel it necessary explicitly to expose my obvious evolutionist and logical positivist biases. Metaphorically, MRT represents a set of methodological and epistemological tools with which we try to infer a bear from its spoor, with which we attempt analyses of long-smeared, remnant fingerprints from the human past.

With respect to the ethnographic/ethnoarchaeological analogies and the models themselves, it was first noted that analogies and models are not the same things. Whereas some confusion may be found in the archaeological literature relating to the distinctions between them, such are in fact relatively basic. In archaeological currency, analogies are based upon comparisons between things, while models are heuristic abstractions of things associated by various interactive processes. Also posited was a relatively succinct definition of the very concept of hunter-gatherer as used in the literature reviewed. I think the most salient ethnographic and ethnoarchaeological contributions to Paleolithic archaeology are the subsistence analogies and models themselves, as well as the perception of their utility in application as heuristics.

Relevant theoretical and methodological issues were also reviewed. It was suggested that these issues have remained more or less constant through the history of Paleolithic hunter/gatherer archaeological thought and reasoning. The "appropriate" uses to which argumentative analogies are put were discussed. It was questioned whether analogies are actually usable in this fashion. It was also questioned whether they can really be avoided in archaeological discourse. One productive means with which to analyze analogies was suggested as the "taphonomy of analogies", or as awareness of the formation processes through which analogies pass. The huge epistemic issues of archaeological causation and equifinality were developed and discussed. For example, virtually any archaeological phenomenon can be regarded through two simultaneous causal perspectives, namely, multicausality and multiple effects of common causes, both of which contribute to interpretive difficulties through the concept of equifinality. Although somewhat cliché, it will be through further methodological and experimental refinement that interpretive complexities from equifinal process can be mitigated. Archetypal ethnoarchaeological and more theoretical-archaeological subsistence and settlement models were discussed, including a review of those that are subjectively noted to be extremely influential in the contemporary literature. It was also suggested that since MRT and MRR do not by necessity obviate socio-behavioral considerations, the potential use of boundary theory in spatial analysis was suggested. A possible model was proposed for abstracting some aspects of the Magdalenian material economy in terms of evaluation and valuating materials and products from a humanistic and sensible risk-management perspective.

Given the above, and returning to the earlier theme, the means with which to hit the moving target of Paleolithic hunter-gatherer social behaviors are available, given the explicit expression of caveats and certain admissions against interest. For example, with respect to most Paleolithic archaeological sites, we have incomplete and redundant data. We irrecoverably lack many indices of crucial importance to estimating Paleolithic hunter/gatherer social organization. Furthermore, for those data classes that we do have or can recover, we have numerous redundancies, in the form of lithics, fauna, and spatial configurations, in many cases directly superimposed one atop another. It seems a given that there is no one-size-fits-all approach to Paleolithic archaeology, and where possible multiple datasets should be analyzed and compared. In Chapter III is proposed a methodology for doing so at Verberie le Buisson Campin, using fauna from two different areas and geophysical surveys.

Chapter 4 Methodology

What are available data?" By this I do not mean only, "What data are available?" but also, "What do we MEAN by 'available' data?" This is an extension of a question I first asked of the Upper Paleolithic (Magdalenian) site Verberie le Buisson Campin. For at Verberie, three decades of excavation have produced a material inventory of thousands of pieces of animal bone, stone tools, and fire-cracked rock. What these thirty-plus years of excavation did not accomplish, however, was a systematic, comprehensive subsurface test of the entire Verberie site. So my question above actually leads to another: What do we MEAN by available data, and how may we gain access to it? How can we comprehensively test the subsurface content (the archaeological material inventory itself) and configuration (spatial aspects of the material inventory, including distribution, scale, shapes, and orientation) of a site?

VBC is an Upper Paleolithic, multi-component archaeological site in the northern Picardie department of France featuring outstanding spatial integrity in archaeological content and configuration (Enloe 2010). The site has also produced one of the most extensive Magdalenian open-air faunal assemblages in Europe (Enloe 2010). Radiocarbon and thermoluminescence age estimates range between 13,300 +/- 850 to 10,640 +/- 180, placing the site within the Magdalenian of the Paris Basin (hereinafter MPB) (Audouze 1987; Enloe and David 1997:55). The site is located in an agricultural field of approximately 7.2 ha, on a Pleistocene point bar terrace on the south bank of the Oise River (Figure 1) (Enloe and Audouze 2010). The point bar terrace occupies about 25,000 m². Approximately 600 m² have been excavated since 1975, representing at least five (and possibly more) separate occupation surfaces (Audouze 1987; Audouze and Enloe 1997; Enloe 1997:96; Enloe and David 1997:55). The excavated total only represents about 2.5% of the point bar terrace. Faunal analyses have suggested that the site can be understood as an ephemeral, temporary Fall/Winter hunting camp for intercepting caribou during the annual rutting season prior to their seasonal migrations (Enloe and David 1997). Lithic use-wear analysis indicates that tool manufacture, meat-cutting, and hide-working were primary site activities (Audouze 1987; Enloe 2010; Symens 1986).

Excavations at the nearby MPB site of Pincevent have revealed substantial information of Magdalenian human adaptation to the Late Pleistocene and tardiglacial of the Paris Basin. At Pincevent, a suite of technical analyses have demonstrated the presence of multiple, interacting household features, organized around stone-lined hearths

of between 50 and 70 cm in diameter (Audouze 1987; Bodu 2010; Enloe 2010). Pincevent's scale and the presence of multiple redundant households attest to its protracted, long-term occupation by complete domestic units, or a population of family groups (Bodu 2010; Enloe 2010). Refits between faunal remains, lithics, and fire-cracked rocks indicate the interactivity and contemporaneity of these households (Enloe 2010). Demonstrations of domestic organization at Pincevent also led to questions regarding the possibility of similar domestic organization at VBC (Enloe 2010). Was VBC occupied like Pincevent, by a population of family groups? Or was VBC occupied by a subset of such populations, specialized for the performance of particular tasks? These questions outline the basis of test implications: if VBC was like Pincevent, we should find multiple, interacting households organized around hearths. The key is therefore the location of possible intact unexcavated archaeological materials consisting of the hearths themselves, but also of other materials distributed around them in space.

Although VBC has been extraordinarily productive and informative for analyses of Magdalenian subsistence organization, the excavated sample consists of less than perhaps 2.5% of the site surface area available for human exploitation during the Pleistocene. (Enloe 2007; Thompson in press). This presents a rather vexing interpretive problem since whereas VBC represents one of the largest Magdalenian archaeological datasets in the world (Bodu 2010; Enloe and Audouze 2010) conclusions based upon analyses of its content and material inventory derive from what is potentially a very incomplete sample. Moreover, if the site is in fact larger than previously known, then barring excavation of the entirety of the Pleistocene point bar on which it sits the archaeological inventory of VBC will also always be to some degree incomplete. Similarly, analyses of its material inventory and distribution (content and configuration) would also be incomplete. This is another very large and interesting problem since VBC represents a crucial dataset for understanding human adaptations in northern Europe during presumably large-scale environmental changes over the terminal Pleistocene. If we cannot directly sample archaeological content through excavation of the total area, can we at least estimate unexcavated archaeological configuration by some other means? Are there ways to sample the configuration of unexcavated archaeological materials?

A ground-penetrating radar (GPR) survey was undertaken at VBC in 2006, under the auspices of the Centre Nationale de Reserche Scientifique (CNRS) and the University of

Iowa (Enloe et al. 2007). Although this survey was a very large undertaking, it was not a comprehensive, systematic survey of the entire point bar or site area. Among several research agendas were prospection for unexcavated materials, basic feasibility-testing of ground-penetrating radar in a Paleolithic context, and the development of methodologies for applying near-surface geophysics to prospection for very small-scale archaeological materials and features. The 2006 radar survey at VBC was not simply for identifying promising locations to excavate. An explicit aspect of the research design was to try to use ground-penetrating radar as a tool for the evaluation of archaeological material scale and configuration in order to address issues of demography and domesticity at VBC.

The entire gpr project in 2006 was done in such a way as to focus on understanding the past, geared toward cultural issues of demography and domesticity. Such cultural foci are expected to become primary research topics in geophysical archaeology (Conyers 2010; Conyers and Leckebusch 2010). The 2006 radar project at VBC had an overt cultural/behavioral framing, yet it was intended to sample only those areas nearest several hearths and associated activity areas based on the probability of unexcavated archaeological material and, in one case, known *in situ* material 9Enloe 2007; Enloe et al. 2007).

Moreover, the 2006 VBC radar survey at Verberie has already contributed methodologically to developing high-resolution methods for geophysical survey at open-air Paleolithic sites (Thompson in press; Thompson and Storey 2010). For at VBC in 2006 we had first to learn how to walk, so to speak, to learn how to identify radar reflections from unexcavated archaeological material at an open-air site, and to differentiate them from radar reflections from sediment disturbances caused by prior excavation exposures and other subsurface phenomena. At VBC, the reflections from many sources were superficially very similar, and subsequent research has led to the development of reliable methods for discriminating between buried materials. Since we can now reliably spot archaeology at VBC, we can now propose to radar the entire enormous point bar terrace on which the site sits. This is one of the most important Magdalenian sites in the world, and a comprehensive radar survey of the entire site would constitute a magnificent materiospatial database. The geophysics should actually be seen as an accompaniment to excavation, not as a replacement, since it will only be through excavation that actual material content can be tested.

There are still numerous questions that remain concerning Verberie, that are essentially unanswerable barring a comprehensive radar survey. In one 20 m² sector of the site, *secteur* 190, there was no indication of any palimpsest, multiple, deflated occupation surfaces, while there were such discrete, individual surfaces in the nearby sectors 201 and 202 (Audouze personal communication; Audouze and Enloe 1997). In other words, in some areas of the site multiple, redundant occupation surfaces have

been recovered separated by thin layers of sterile sediment that are completely absent from others. Does the apparent redundancy of palimpsest occupation surfaces extend beyond the excavated areas into unexcavated areas of the site, or different areas of the Pleistocene point bar terrace? Is there perhaps an entirely different occupation sequence in unexcavated areas, or multiple differing sequences? Perhaps different areas of the site were used differently, perhaps very differently, but this can be neither established nor refuted with such a small area of the site sampled.

Verberie's Physical Setting and Physiography

Verberie le Buisson Campin (VBC) is located in the Paris Basin (PB), which is a large sedimentary basin in northeast France, in which the contemporary city of Paris is situated in the center (Audouze 1987:183-184). Uplands surround the PB; the Ardennes to the northeast, the Vosges to the east, the Morvan to the southwest, and the Massif Central to the south (Aoudouze 1987:183). Figure 4.1 below provides a general spatial overview of this craton. The small town of Verberie is located near the confluence of the Oise and Aisne rivers at Compiegne. The Paris Basin itself formed during Permo-Triassic times, as an epicratonic, Peritethyan low (or, a topographic low near the Tethys Sea), and it features three primary lithologies: Lower Triassic sandstones, Middle Triassic chalks, and Upper Triassic (Keuper) limestones (Bourquin et al. 1997:670). The carbonate sedimentary rocks of the Middle and Upper Triassic formation in the PB contain numerous deposits of high quality flint, mainly in the valleys formed by fluvial incision into the bedrocks. The dendritic river drainage system is dominated by the River Seine, flowing east to west (Audouze 1987).

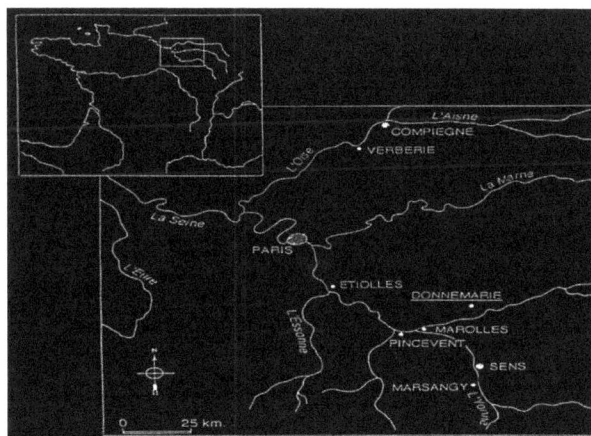

FIGURE 4.1. THE PARIS BASIN.

About 12.5 ky, the Oise River underwent a transition from a braided to a meandering stream channel, accompanied by decrease in both sediment and water discharge and channel incision (Pastre et al. 2002). As the earlier Pleniglacial riverine deposits (sands and gravels) were supplied by cryoclasty and absence of vegetation, the transition in channel morphology probably marks the lapse of full glacial conditions and the onset of Holocene climates (Pastre et al. 2002). The VBC archaeological deposits occur in a matrix of homogenized, very fine calcareous sandy silt deposited during a general aggradational phase that occurred across many river channels in northern France, marking the transition to the Holocene (Cordier et al. 2005; Pastre et al. 2002). Since VBC archaeological materials do not occur in the coarse cryoclastic gravel and sands underlying the silts, it's clear the site was occupied during milder climatic conditions. The change in river channel morphology, decreased sediment discharge, and the occurrence of archaeological occupations probably coincides with the return of browse vegetation to the area, consolidating slopes.

The site of VBC is located on the south (cut) bank of the Oise Rivera tributary of the Seine, upon a presumably Pleistocene terrace remnant, northeast of the town of Verberie, west of the town La Croix-St. Ouen. The site is situated within a contemporary agricultural field, the planting of which is done on a crop rotation basis. Figures 4.2. and 4.3 below provide a regional view of the VBC setting. Figure 4.4., below provides a schematic plan view of the site, while Figure 4.5., below highlights the locations of VBC Secteur 190 and Secteur 202. Images of the material and distribution are provided in Figures 4.6, 4.7, and 4.8 below. Figures 4.9 and 4.10 below show selected faunal items from VBC.

Site and Material Taphonomy at VBC

Although the archaeological material at VBC possesses a very high degree of internal integrity in the original spatial contexts and associations, it may be most prudent to conceive of the Pleistocene sediments containing them to be reworked (removal of extremely fine sediment) to some indefinite degree, mainly though the agency of downward water percolation and earthworm and insect bioturbation (Audouze and Enloe 1997). The positions of most "large" artifacts (larger than 1-2 cm) appear to be quite secure, based upon the strikes and dips or flatly oriented objects; there is also no apparent directional alignment of elongated artifacts as would be expected through the directional fluvial sorting of material with long axes left parallel to the direction of water flow (Audouze and Enloe 1997; Enloe 2006). Whereas burrowing animals would have had a major effect upon artifact distributions (Morin 2006), few burrow traces have been noted at VBC. Few artifacts at VBC were oriented vertically (although I am aware of some exceptions having worked multiple seasons at the site). As the archaeological units are covered with nearly half a meter of overburden, they have been protected against *most* invasive agricultural intrusions from plowing and furrowing. The lack of plow scars directly through most of the Pleistocene sediment indicates a general absence of such mechanical destruction.

Since the removal of the finest sediments from the matrix appears to be the most pervasive post-depositional disturbance at VBC what might be some possible effects of this conditioning agent? Intuitively, what was involved was essentially a volumetric reduction in sediment from the site, as fine sediment was percolated and/or "eaten" or burrowed out from interstitial spaces between coarser sediment and the archaeological inventory. The main effect of such volumetric reduction in fine sediment would be the compaction of the remainder. In a recent application of archaeological experimentation, Andrews (2006) noted that the primary effect of such compaction is a general reduction in the orientation angles of artifacts at sites, with the intensity of this effect varying logically as a function of the time period during which sediment and artifacts are exposed to the process.

FIGURE 4.2. VBC REGION (FROM GOOGLE EARTH).

FIGURE 4.3. VBC SHOWING TERRACE REMNANT (FROM GOOGLE EARTH).

It is by no means certain that we should regard such effects at VBC in a purely post-depositional light, however, as we consider that the main depositional mechanism at VBC was likely low-energy slack-water overbank deposits of silt and fine sand (Audouze and Enloe 1997). It may be the case that much of the removal of fine sediment through downward water percolation occurred syndepositionally, as an effect of the successive gentle overbank flooding of the site. Vermin activity likewise probably occurred syndepositionally, and may have increased in frequency as a function of general climatic amelioration during the waxing Holocene conditions. Regardless of syndepositional and postdepositional disturbances at VBC, at least five distinct occupations of the site have been discerned on the basis of subsurface elevations (Audouze and Enloe 1997). Plotted in profile, these occupations can be seen to undulate gently, perhaps indicating the approximate past surfaces at the site (Audouze and Enloe 1997:199, Figure 1). An absence of frost-wedges, frost-heaves, and gentle slope gradients unconducive to the promotion of gelifluction effectively negate cryoturbation as a serious taphonomic agent at VBC.

Bone Taphonomic Agencies at VBC

In order to account for the bone condition at VBC, a consideration of bone taphonomic agencies and effects is in order. A voluminous (perhaps overly so) literature has accumulated regarding multivariate physical, diachronic bone destruction that treats bone attrition from a variety of causalities (weathering, carnivory, physical geologic processes, and human agencies) as dependent variables that covary as a function of the independent variable, bone density (Andrews, 1995; Binford and Bertram 1977; Butler and Lyman 1996; Chase et al. 1994; Conard et al. 2008; Grayson 1984; Ioannidou 2003; Kent 1993; Lam et al. 1999, 2005; Lyman 1994; Marean and Assefa 1999; Morin 2007b; Munson and Garniwiecz 2003; Olszewski 2004; Rogers 2000; Yellen 1977). While informative and methodologically interesting, these often technical methods for analyzing bone deterioration due to differential bone density have frequently been used (perhaps better to note, 'misused') to explain away much anthropogenic conditioning of faunal assemblages, even at sites with well-established associations between fauna and lithics. Furthermore, there are certainly other properties that affect variable bone survivorship at archaeological sites.

The chemical and structural compositions both of bone itself and the sediment matrices (soil chemistry or pH) in which bone is deposited also play large roles in bone attrition, as does microbial activity (Behrensmeyer et al. 2000; Briggs et al. 1999; Child 1995; Jackes et al. 2001; Locock et al. 1992; Turner-Walker et al. 2002). In site contexts in which flooding and inundation are known to occur (such as a riverbank), water interacts with suites of interrelated chemical and microbial diagenetic processes that generally serve to attack internal bone structure at the molecular level. Quite apart from density-mediated physical attrition, such molecular degradation has to do instead with the biodegradable nature of bone as an organic chemical entity. Such agencies are often lumped together in the catchall category of "bone weathering". The mere presence of water, however, is not generally sufficient to destroy organic archaeological remains as is obvious from the well known collection of human "bog bodies" from temperate Holocene northern Europe. In those situations, anoxic conditions and the presence of tannic compounds have served to preserve bones and soft tissues to a very

high degree. Moreover, at one level, bone tissue that has lost its collagen is basically just a carbonate salt (calcium hydroxyapatite). The presumptive effects of bone deposition in highly acidic sedimentary contexts (forests and rainforests, for example) should result in rapid bone deterioration and generally poor preservation; in highly alkaline environments bones are often well-preserved and mineralized.

With respect to the above non-anthropogenic taphonomic agencies, what may we say about the conditioning effects they would be expected to produce at VBC? If substantial bone destruction had resulted merely from density-mediated attrition or biological processes, what effects would be manifest in the bones themselves? I would argue that bone attrition due to biodegradation has been relatively minor at VBC. Bone weathering and decay has certainly occurred. However, one attribute of the bones from VBC is quite telling. On many specimens, biotic effects are visible in terms of plant root vermiculation, where acids form the roots of plants have touched the bones and left root traces behind through acidic decomposition. Not all bones from VBC show this vermiculation. Generally, the top sides (towards the surface) of bones show this root etching whereas the bottoms do not. Bones in upper levels show more root etches than do those from lower levels. Since not all bones at VBC have been so affected, we can at least presume that vegetation cover at the site was either too sparse or too intermittent to develop root networks sufficient completely to destroy the bones. Pedogenic conditions likewise seem not to have been acidic enough to destroy bone, as many specimens feature very high states of preservation (as attested by the presence of small articulation surfaces and nutrient foramina in many long bones). Fluvial activity appears not to have preferentially sorted and oriented long bones (Enloe 2006). For VBC, human agency seems most directly implicated in bone taphonomy.

Anthropogenic Bone Taphonomic Agencies

If human agency is claimed as the main bone conditioning agent at VBC, what are the visible effects in terms of bone condition at the site? There are a number of visible effects suggestive of anthropogenic bone destruction at VBC. Unfortunately, one of the most direct indices of human conditioning at VBC, cutmarks and chop marks associated with butchery, appear to be altered or obliterated by root vermiculation. Few cutmarks or chop marks were noted in the samples from VBC 190 and II.22. Many have been presumably destroyed by root activity although some are present. Moreover, the presence of burned bone in my samples from VBC indicates some cooking occurred at the site. Grease-boiling of smashed epiphyses is also indicated (Enloe 1997). Nicholson (1992) demonstrated that cooking and/or boiling of bone severely degrades its ability to withstand attritional agencies, to such degree that such specimens may be virtually absent from site inventories. Marrow-cracking of long bones not only disaggregates them; it also exposes greater internal and external surfaces areas to the activities of physiochemical destructive agencies. For the bone tissues of small species of mammals, birds, and fish, cooking and burning may effectively destroy most or even any evidence thereof from presence in an archaeological assemblage.

Structure of Faunal Assemblages at VBC

In consideration of the above, we may cogently ask: so what IS present in terms of faunal samples at VBC? For research conducted to date, including the present study, there is a large majority (nearly 99%) of reindeer for all assemblages at VBC (David and Enloe 1992; Enloe1994, 1997). Isolated specimens of horse, mammoth, and various microfauna are also present (Audouze 1987). The two samples for this study are confined to reindeer remains from two 20 m² secteurs on the coordinate grid plane (Figures 4.4 and 4.5 below), VBC 190 and 202 Level II.22. There are some methodological and epistemological difficulties in comparing/contrasting the fauna form VBC 190 and 202 II.22. As will be explained in greater detail below, these assemblages were excavated in very different ways, with provenance information recorded differently as well.

Research Objective

This research consisted mainly of a search for patterning in order to investigate the construction of logistically oriented subsistence organization, domesticity, and demography as an index of "behavioral modernity". From the literature, in many analyses specialized hunting (or impressions and opinions thereof) are treated virtually as a proxy index of Modernity. The patterning I sampled was taphonomic, faunal, and spatial in nature. I'd like to know: 1) how representative of the entire assemblage is the currently excavated sample? 2) Are there multiple, interacting, redundant household units, as at Pincevent, or does the distribution of materials appear to be limited to a single household? 3) How do faunal categories (dental age classes, teeth, bones, animal sex, left/right elements) correlate across space and what conclusions may be drawn? The main objective of this study was to undertake a rigorous, empirical analysis and description of the fauna from VBC Level II22 , combined with taphonomic, geoarchaeological and geophysical data (where possible as applicable) to understand the material content and configuration at the site. At the level of the faunal assemblage, how were carcasses treated, both economically and spatially? Is there any indication that fluvial activity has oriented (any of) the bones, since the site occurs immediately near the Oise river? Point provenience data of elongate excavated items could indicate and isolate fluvial patterning if, for example, long bones are found to share similar orientations. Spatial analyses of faunal patterning (i.e., which bones occur where, in which positions, and in what associations?) will be undertaken. What demographic and behavioral information may be preserved in the content and configuration of the assemblage? The fauna from VBC have already, as above, produced data indicative of seasonality and prey selectivity.

I endeavored to gauge the general patterning in unexcavated portions of the site. Enloe and Audouze (1991:65) indicate that VBC may represent a logistical hunting or bush camp. There is evidence at the site of ephemerally repeated fall occupations, clearly geared toward reindeer acquisition and the selective outgoing transport of prime meat-bearing elements. This apparent behavioral focus resulted in the accumulation of redundant artifacts and spatial patterning (i.e., knapping refuse dumps, butchering rings, hearths, and 'blank spots' lacking obvious artifacts). Despite the long history of excavations at VBC, there are only indirect indices of the site's lateral extent. Buried artifactual deposits continue beyond the limits of the excavation. How big *is* it? And what can the spatial configurations of unexcavated material contribute to understanding economic and social organization? Is there spatial variation between VBC 190 and 202 II.22 in terms of faunal treatment or skeletal element location? Surfer 9.0 density distribution maps were constructed of individual element classes in both areas of VBC relevant to the study in order to analyze such possible patterning.

At the level of the site, I wanted to determine whether VBC represents a modular site, with previous excavations revealing only portions of a larger entity, or if what was excavated represents more or less the continuous entirety. The horizontal extent of the site was be tested geophysically, through the use of ground penetrating radar. If GPR "sees" previously unrecorded, unexcavated material at the site, it should then be possible generally to delimit cultural accumulations, and to isolate them from the background sediment matrix. We can predict the rough characteristics of occupations at VBC from previously excavated (and redundant) material. But we don't know the total site area, nor do we know what patterning may exist in unexcavated portions of the site.

Uncertainty regarding the actual dimensions and material patterning of unexcavated portions of the site presents a considerable interpretive difficulty. Despite the long previous history of excavations at VBC, as above, we have as yet no substantive data regarding the physical size of the site itself; this means we have only rather vague metrics of the total horizontal area over which human behaviors operated. How incomplete is the sample? There may be substantial variation in faunal treatment, artifact distribution, and patterning that remains undocumented in unexcavated areas. We do not know as yet how large this site is, and there is a poor contemporary understanding of its vertical componentry. There may be structural patterning that emerges only after GPR data gathered from previously unexcavated areas can be analyzed at different scales of resolution, different time-depths, etc. How does faunal treatment vary across space, if at all? What discernible scalar differences can we "see" in terms of spatial patterning? For answering these questions, we need a quick, inexpensive method for subsurface testing that offers the capability of shifting between different analytical scales and features outstanding, manipulable three dimensional graphic capabilities. If GPR "sees" more of the same redundant data in unexcavated portions, the site can be virtually confirmed as a model logistical site. It would difficult to posit such a firm diagnosis without good data acquisition from unexcavated areas at VBC. If we find evidence of different buried material scale, configuration, orientation, distribution, or frequency, we may be able to posit GPR-visibility of some aspects of human behavior. The assumption here is that the radar survey can be combined methodologically with faunal analysis to give a better estimate of site and intrasite function than with method could alone.

The most common geophysical methods for subsurface testing in archaeology are magnetometry, resisitivity, electromagnetic conductivity, and ground-penetrating radar (Conyers 2004:3). For the majority of archaeological projects, time and budget constraints require archaeologists to use cost- and time-effective, non-destructive, and statistically representative geophysical methods with accurate three-dimensional modeling capabilities (Conyers 2004:4). At VBC, the requirements above accord very well with the capabilities GPR confers. GPR surveys using very dense grid spacing can be expected to produce high resolutions of some buried targets, as well as object orientations, certainly with accuracy adequate to estimating the horizontal "limits" of the unexcavated areas at VBC. Time-slicing (using two-way reflection times of radar waves to measure features at pre-selected depth) should portray subsurface patterning of unexcavated areas. Conyers (personal communication) suggests that VBC presents a very promising venue for such applications of GPR.

Methodology

The methodology for this study featured a detailed faunal analysis 1) to assess taphonomic agencies, 2) to test the visibility and configuration of behaviorally structured spatial patterning, and 3) to gauge faunal evidence for systematization, standardization, and consistency. In simplest terms, this program was an attempt to find answers using what's "there" in the dataset. The database for the faunal analysis consisted of both skeletal and dental materials from VBC.

As above, differential excavation methods were used for the 190 and II.22 faunal assemblages. Whereas each secteur at VBC was excavated in 1 x 1 m units, each artifact from II.22 was excavated with precise, three-dimensional coordinate provenience data. The photocopied dossiers that I have for VBC 190 do not record individual artifact provenience within 1 x 1s, instead listing the artifacts to unit only (no 3D provenience). A methodological accommodation for interassemblage spatial comparisons and contrasts of artifact distributions was performed at the least common spatial analytical unit shared between these assemblages, or the 1 x 1 m² unit. So long as the interassemblage comparisons are consistently framed within such commensurate spatial parameters, there should be no persistent epistemological concerns, since this material derives from the same site and is limited to

analysis of *Rangifer* specimens only. There is an additional methodological issue relating to the international disposition of portions of both the VBC 190 and II.22 collections. Although every effort has been made to study this material *in toto*, some isolated VBC 190 specimens were spotted and identified at a regional museum in France. These items have been included in faunal quantifications. However, two mandibular fragments were also located in this museum with articulating teeth. These teeth could have been used in constructing age profiles for VBC 190. So those data are missing. Moreover, in spite of two trips made to France to analyze this fauna in 2009, a few additional specimens from II.22 were located too late for incorporation into this dissertation. This research is therefore contingent upon slight future revision should those specimens from both secteurs be analyzed in the future. Much of the faunal material from VBC 190 is in unusually excellent conditions (Figures 4.6 and 4.7 below). Microsoft Excel and dbase were the primary data handling software for recording artifact attributes. SPSS was used for performing statistical analyses. Although faunal refits between paired elements were sought, no interassemblage pairings were found, between 190 and II.22. Since it is often possible more accurately to gain prey species demographic information from dentition, the dental sample was analyzed first, with dental identifications conducted as follows: position in the dental arcade, taxon, side, maxillary vs. mandibular dentition, sex, and age as possible, using crown height methods for aging. The teeth were quantified for estimates of NISP and MNI, used to serve as an internal check on similar estimates drawn from the skeletal sample.

Postcranial elements in the VBC sample were also treated as above. The fauna will be identified to the level of taxon, element, side, sex, and age as possible, using relevant diagnostic landmarks where present (Lam et al. 1999). The elements were quantified for estimates of NISP and MNI. Element representation can then be used to estimate site functions and taphonomic disturbance. Indices of age, sex, and seasonality were recorded so as to construct demographic profiles of the faunal assemblage and to evaluate possible spatial differentiation in the treatment of differentially aged carcasses. The program detailed above provided answers to the questions regarding human subsistence patterning that I posed. Estimating human subsistence offers the most productive way to gauge human social organization at VBC. The data results generated for VBC 190 and II.22 were then used to undertake a series of bivariate correlation comparisons between the element proportional representation and bone density, marrow cavity volume, and meat drying utility from 190 and II.22 and similar data from other archaeological sites (as well as form at least one other level at Verberie) and analyzed statistically using Microsoft Excel and SPSS. Those correlations indicated positively or negatively for any patterning due to bone density (if density mediated attrition is a key physical patterning agent), marrow cavity volume, or drying utility (if either marrow acquisition/extraction or meat-drying were behavioral agencies of patterning).

Per Kooyman (2006), the analytical frame for spatial differentiation in fauna was one of functional activity boundaries. Presumably, the material distribution at VBC represents good integrity with its primary anthropogenic deposition (Audouze and Enloe 1997). Spatial segregation between areas were therefore regarded as evincing functional boundaries; such boundaries will be more socially impermeable when associated with primary butchering, and more socially permeable when associated with secondary subsistence processing (Kooyman 2006). Methodologically, there was a problem in comparing VBC 190 with 202 II.22 in that the two assemblages were not excavated in commensurate manners. VBC 190 does not have level attribution consistent with II.22. Since this methodological discontinuity cannot be rectified now, my conclusions must remain in large measure inferential and speculative.

During the field season of 2006, a GSSI SIR-3000 ground penetrating radar unit was used at VBC. The sampling format included GPR samples taken at one meter, half-meter (50 cm), 25 cm, and 10 cm sampling intervals along both x and y axes, over excavated and unexcavated portions alike, using both 400 MHz and 900 MHz antennae. When promising subsurface targets were located, finer sampling formats (i.e., decimeter-spaced transects and tie lines) were used in order to gain higher subsurface resolution for more accurate imaging and 3D modeling. GPR "time-slicing" of any detected target surfaces was then compared/contrasted with vertical provenience data from previous excavations in order to augment our understanding of both the horizontal and vertical componentry. The sampling interval was adjusted based upon field requirements; i.e., some targets were detected at lower resolution, to be sampled later at a finer scale. One explicit aspect of this study was simply to determine the feasibility of applying high-resolution GPR subsurface sampling at an open-air Paleolithic site.

In order to "calibrate" and assess the GPR imagery, two parallel sets of experimental procedures were conducted using a 2 x 2 m above-ground sandbox and a 2 x 2 m subsurface excavation (a pseudo-site). In both experiments, similar sorts of artificial lithic, bone, and lithologic materials (flint/chert, bone, and limestones) were used to "seed" the sandbox and pseudo-site with patterned features that could reasonably be expected to occur at Upper Paleolithic open-air sites. The patterns and features themselves included false limestone hearths, false small-scale landforms (a fluvial channel and upwardly fining graded gravel/sand), and "middens" composed of bones, lithics, and limestone cobbles and combinations of the three materials. It was felt that problems in getting good subsurface imagery in any of the three parallel GPR applications might indicate a general problem with the applicability of the method to Paleolithic open-air sites, whereas success would indicate its general utility thereto.

Processing of the GPR data was accomplished primarily through the use of software suite and methodological approach that could be called the Conyers-Lucius Method

(http://mysite.du.edu/~lconyer/misc_software.htm). Basic GPR plan-view mapping was done in Golden Software's Surfer 9. Profile views of individual GPR sections were constructed using Conyers – Lucius GPR Viewer (http://mysite.du.edu/~lconyer/misc_software.htm). Alignment and slicing of the GPR sections was accomplished using Lucius – Conyers GPR Process.

Test Implications

Since the GPR methodology above was successful in determining, or at least more accurately approximating, some untested lateral extent and structural patterning of artifacts, it may be possible then to determine whether the site conforms more to a radiating or circulating, foraging or logistical collecting model based on previous (very well-documented) research at the site. This is treated below. If VBC does not represent an ephemeral, seasonal camp, we should have found some evidence of localized "different" activity areas (i.e., knapping areas, hearths, 'empty' zones, etc.) in the material distribution that do not resemble earlier patterning detected at the site. If the site does correspond to an ephemeral, seasonal camp near a kill site, the GPR methodology above should have detected more data redundancy (i.e., more of the same spatial patterning). The faunal and spatial analysis of reindeer remains from Level II22 was then used to refine our understanding of which model most closely approximates that level's material and spatial distribution. Evidence for differential treatment of older vs. younger carcasses (according to presumed nutritive value, = less valuable for old) wasvisible in this sample. It may be that the behaviors involved in conditioning the material inventory at VBC fail to conform with either Binford's (1980) or Mortensen's (1972) models for hunter-gatherers. It is possible that past human societies exhibited a wider range of behavioral variations than can be observed or abstracted today (Wobst 1978). High-resolution archaeology offers the best means to assess such theoretical considerations. Age profiles from dental crown heights should portray any potential carcass age differences between VBC 190 and II.22 illustrative of interassemblage age discrepancies.

Conclusion

In my opinion, the program detailed above yielded useful results for VBC. Being successful, this research may also elicit some answers to more general theoretical questions concerning the future research of past human subsistence. How much *can* we expect to learn from the geophysical sampling of unexcavated material remains at a Paleolithic open-air site? How much "behavioral modernity" can we actually ascribe to an archaeological site through faunal analsys, and in what ways was the Magdalenian "behaviorally modern"? Is the spatial integrity at VBC adequate for such an approach? How can cutting-edge geophysical technology, like GPR, assist the archaeologist in assessing spatial patterning of unexcavated areas? Can GPR accomplish this at an open-air site with a stratigraphically homogenous matrix? Most sites do not offer the possibility for such fine-grained archaeological research as at Verberie. How can research of such an exceptional site be extrapolated to guide our theoretical framework for formulating productive research programs at other sites? How can geophysical data augment understandings of material patterning and orientation? How consistently and systematically are behavioral indices at VBC expressed in the faunal assemblage and spatial data? These are but a few of the questions the methodology above seeks to answer.

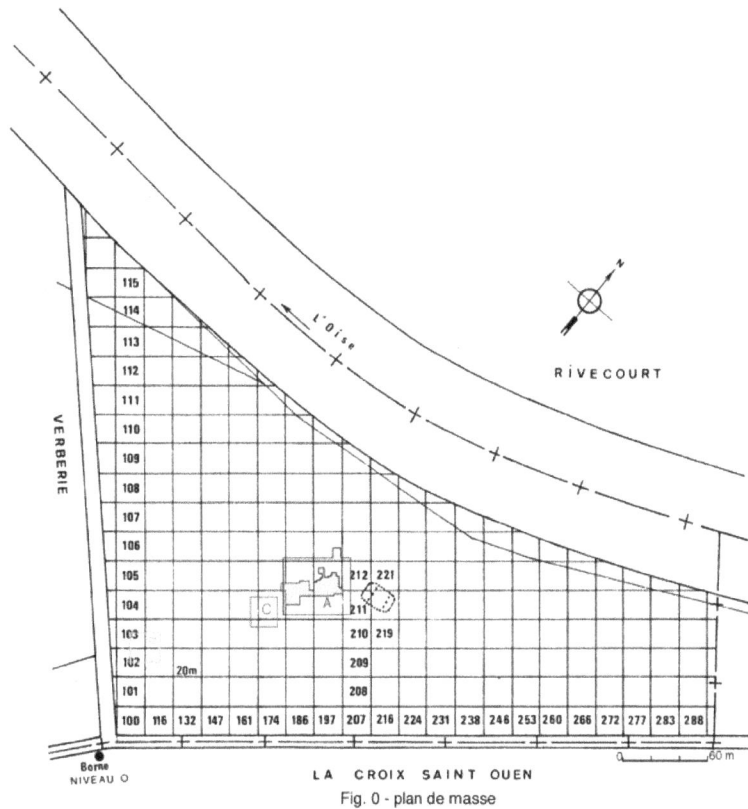

FIGURE 4.4. PLANE VIEW SCHEMATIC MAP OF VBC. RADAR GRIDS IN RECENT EXCAVATIONS RED POLYGON A; OLDER EXCAVATED AREAS YELLOW B AND GREEN C.

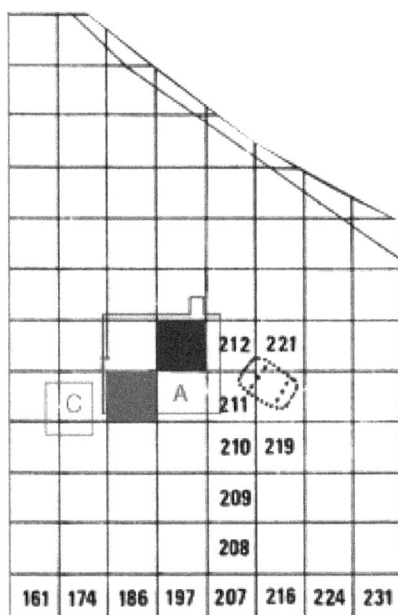

FIGURE 4.5. VBC SECTEUR 190 IN RED, SECTEUR 202 IN BLUE. NOTE RADAR GRIDS INDICATED BY RED POLYGON AND IRON AGE BARN AT RIGHT.

FIGURE 4.6. VBC 190 UNITS B-E 14-16. NOTE EXCELLENT FAUNAL CONDITION AND ARTIFACT DENSITY.

43

FIGURE 4.8. VBC LEVEL II.22 UNIT I 15. BLADES AND BONES.

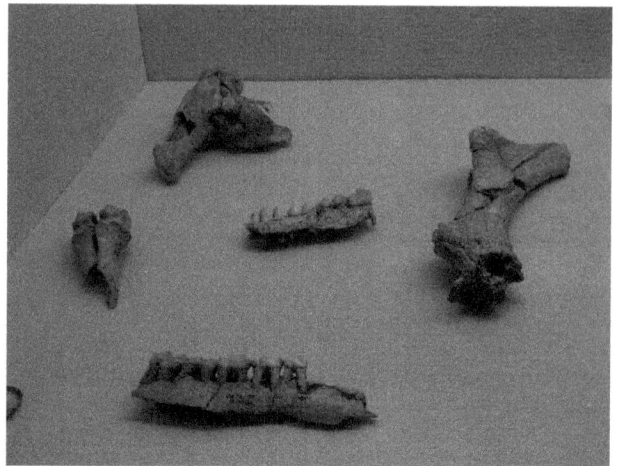

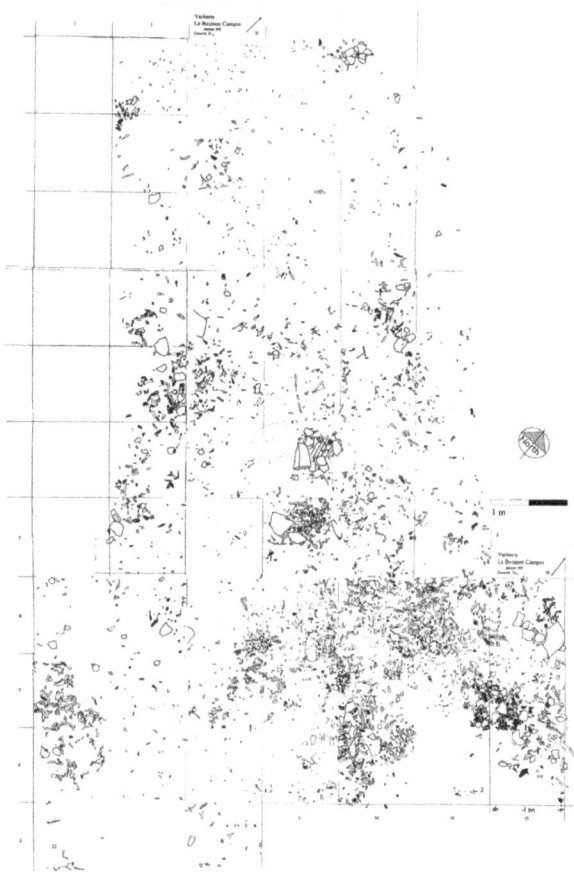

FIGURE 4.7. VBC LEVEL II.22. NOTE DISTRIBUTION, AND HEARTHS AT CENTER.

FIGURE 4.9. VBC 190 FAUNA IN COMPIÉGNE, ANTOINE VIVENEL MUSEUM. CLOCKWISE FROM UPPER LEFT: RIGHT ASTRAGALUS, DISTAL TIBIA, AND "ANKLE"; LEFT MANDIBLE WITH ARTICULATED 4P-3M; ANTLER FRAGMENT; RIGHT MANDIBLE WITH ARTICULATED P2-M2; DISTAL METATARSAL. NOTE EXCELLENT CONDITION OF THE BONE AND HEAVILY OCCLUDED CHEEK TEETH IN MANDIBLE AT LOWER LEFT.

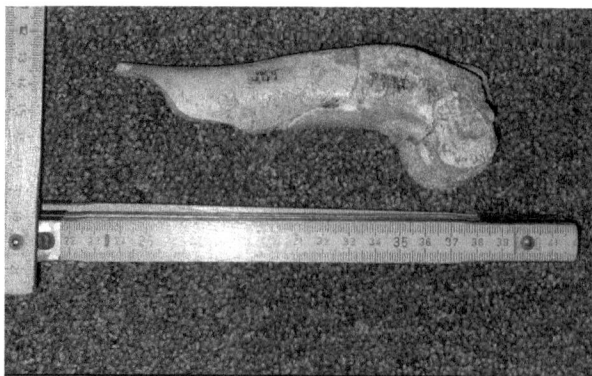

FIGURE 4.10. VBC 190 LEFT DISTAL HUMERUS. NOTE EXCELLENT CONDITION OF THE BONE AND THE GREEN SPIRAL FRACTURE WITH SHARP EDGES, AND FIELD OR LAB RECONSTRUCTION.

Chapter 5: Faunal Analysis and Taphonomy

Two separate faunal samples were analyzed from VBC for the purposes of this research. Both samples derive from an archaeological site located in a field adjacent to the Riviere Oise that's been under active cultivation for hundreds of years, beginning at least in the Iron Age. One portion is a faunal sample attributed to one level from Secteur 202, Level II.22, consists of 1,610 bones, teeth and fragments, of which 386 are identifiable. The material from Level II.22 was excavated from a lens of material occurring at (in fact partially defined on the basis of) a subsurficial depth of between 1.32 and 1.345 m (Audouze and Enloe 1997:200). This material was excavated by teams overseen by Dr. James Enloe and Dr. Francoise Audouze over VBC field seasons 1993 to 1998. The other sample is from Secteur 190, located about ten to fifteen meters to the southwest of II.22, consisting of 1,855 bones, teeth, and fragments, of which 1,566 are identifiable.

The 190 sample is rather problematic in comparison to that from Level II.22 for several reasons. This fauna was excavated, cleaned, labeled, and bagged by teams under different directorships, beginning as early as 1974 or 1975. Moreover, there is a question relating to the completeness of the 190 sample, since several diagnostic specimens (including a large reindeer antler, a complete reindeer 'ankle' joint, a complete reindeer 'knee' joint, two partial reindeer toothrows, and several intentionally marrow-cracked metacarpals and metatarsals with impact and spiral fractures) were "found" in the Paleolithic collection of the Musee d'Antoine Vivenel located in the nearby town of Compiegne. These items were located during a casual visit over the 2009 VBC field season. With respect to the specimens in the museum, perhaps the matter best serves as a caution regarding the sorts of unexpected things that can bias zooarchaeological samples. It is, at the least, a *very* curious aside.

Another interesting aspect of the 190 fauna relates to its near absence of unidentifiable bones, teeth, and fragments. Although both samples are numerically similar (1,610 to 1,855), the proportions of identifiable specimens are roughly 5:1, skewed heavily toward 190. While a very competent preliminary analysis and sorting was done on the 190 fauna, either few of the unidentifiable specimens were retained and archived, or there simply *were* few fragmentary specimens in poor states of preservation to retain at all. While the II.22 sample has many unidentifiable fragments in it, the 190 sample does not. This phenomenon (lack of many 190 unidentifiable specimens) is rather counter-intuitive, since the Level II.22 material was positioned stratigraphically lower than much of the 190 sample, and should have been less exposed to more destructive intrusion from agricultural activities.

We can assume that the shallower material should bear more taphonomic effects from cultivation than the deeper. Instead, the opposite is true: the often shallower 190 material exhibits a much better state of preservation than the deeper sample from Level II.22.

Since there were many (in fact a vast numeric majority) unidentifiable specimens from the Level II.22 sample, some questions immediately emerged: Were both samples subjected to the same sorts of physical taphonomic processes at VBC but just exhibited different effects? Why should they? Are their human behavioral or site functional agencies identifiable in analyses of the remains that might help to explain differences between the samples? What sorts of human agencies might be involved in the conditioning of this fauna that could help to account for the discrepancies between stratigraphic depth and preservation states? The analyst is left to try and explain why the shallower 190 material, collected by completely different teams with differential levels of archaeological expertise, handled much more frequently over the years and transported between at least three archiving facilities, should exhibit such a markedly *better* state of preservation than that from II.22, along with other observable patterns in the data. Given the comparative effects of virtually *all* potential post-depositional and post-recovery processes, the 190 fauna should be in rougher condition instead of better, yet it isn't.

Comparison Assemblages

I selected a group of faunal assemblages from other archaeological sites in order to provide a degree of intercomparability and explanatory power for the discussion on density-mediated representation and destruction. For even the best, most rigorous and detailed faunal analysis from any site is essentially just a point estimate of zooarchaeological variability. It seems reasonable to compare and contrast with other faunal assemblages to avoid over-interpreting the results from any one isolated site or assemblage. The following three French datasets were selected because of the presence of reindeer in the faunal assemblages and publication of requisite data, since the method requires publication of both MNI and MNE measures, and not all faunal analyses include this information: Le Flageolet and Roc De Combe were chosen for the reindeer portions in their assemblages; Prolom was chosen mainly as a carnivore assemblages, while it also features a reindeer component. All three are cave sites. The inclusion of multiple reindeer sites from both open-air and cave contexts, as well as carnivore data, is intended to offset any potential biases.

VBC Level II.1 (Enloe 2004)

The level II.1 I from Secteur 201 and 202 at VBC, probably represents a later (final Magdalenian of VBC) occupation than II.22, and perhaps some of VBC 190 as well. The radiocarbon age estimate is 12,430 +/- 120 BP (Enloe 2004:149), and is nearly 100% reindeer. This level was selected for obvious comparability with both VBC 190 and II.22, as well as to gauge potential taphonomic differences between occupations. Enloe (2004:161-162) found very weak linear correlations between bone density and survivorship in the fauna from VBC II.1 (r^2 values of 0.076, 0.054, and 0.022).

Prolom Cave (Enloe et al. 1997)

Prolom Cave (Prol), a Middle Paleolithic site on the Crimean Peninsula, dating between 135 to 60 ky, was selected for its interesting mix of anthropogenic and carnivorogenic accumulations of between 8 and 18 faunal taxa, with a highly relevant portion of reindeer for cmparative and contrastive purposes (Enloe et al. 1997).

Roc de Combe (RDC) (Grayson and Delpech 2008)

This cave site's faunal assemblage was selected because of its possible transitional interstratification of Middle and Upper Paleolithic lithic industries (Mousterian, Chatelperronian, Aurignacian), because of its cave context, and because of its multi-taxonomic assemblage with strong reindeer representation (Grayson and Delpech 2008).

Faunal Analysis of both 190 and II.22 Assemblages

I separated and segregated the bones from the teeth in both samples first, mainly as a means of identifying parallel sample biases that may have been present in the fauna. Table 5.1 below lists the itemized counts for VBC 190, Table 5.2 below lists the same for VBC II.22. The fauna was quantified and the data recorded in spreadsheet form in the Microsoft Excel program. A complication of the initial

spatial analysis relates to the absence of three-dimensional provenience data for the 190 sample. Whereas the II.22 sample was excavated with the use of a laser theodolite, and accurate x, y, and z coordinates were recorded for each item, the 190 material was not. The 190 sample basically antedates such fine spatial technology. In order to make the two samples spatially comparable, I was forced to deal with the 190 coordinates I did have and to treat the II.22 accordingly: I used provenance to 1 x 1 meter excavation units as the main spatial component of analysis. There remain issues of intercomparability between data collected as discrete levels (202 II.22) and those lacking such levels (190). Once those initial hurdles were crossed, the samples became comparable in terms of observed patterning.

For this analysis, I used the Percent Survivorship of individual skeletal elements calculated as the minimum number of elements (MNE) divided by the numbers of elements expected if there was a net survival of 100% of the material suggested by the largest calculated MNI (minimum number of individuals). This seemed the best way to deal with actual element proportions in terms of the overall identifiable assemblages for VBC 190 and II.22. This method also allowed for the generation of plotted graphic representation through analyses of the correlation and linearity of the correlation between % survivorship and bone density (after Enloe 2004; Lam et al. 1999). The resulting indices allowed me to generate statistics to use for estimating bone survivorship as a function of bone density and economic "utility" in the study (Andrews, 1995; Binford and Bertram 1977; Butler and Lyman 1996; Chase et al. 1994; Conard et al. 2008; Grayson 1984; Kent 1993; Lam et al. 1999, 2005; Marean and Assefa 1999; Metcalfe and Jones 1988; Morin 2006, 2007b; Munson and Garniwiecz 2003; Olszewski 2004; Rogers 2000; Yellen 1977). The resulting % survivorship values were then entered in SPSS to perform bivariate correlations and linear regressions. Enloe (2004) has recently performed some similar research on the fauna from VBC Level II.1, providing some data for that particular dataset.

Table 5.1 VBC 190 Elements.								
Item	No.	Left	Right	Unsided	%	MAU*	MNI	MNE
Antler	2				0.13			
Astragalus	14	5	6	3	0.89	7	6	11
Bovid Molar	2				0.13			
Bovid Prem.	2	1	1		0.13			
Caudal Vert.	8				0.51			
Calcaneum	18	9	8	1	1.15	8.5	9	17
Grand Cunei.	1				0.064			
Cervical Vert.	13				0.83			
Carpal	45				2.9			
Crania	28				1.8			
Epiphysis	15				0.96			
Flat Bone	7				0.45			
Femur	77	18	23	36	4.9	38.5	18	41
FUBTH	1				0.064			
Humerus	100	27	28	45	6.4	50	28	55
Incisor micro.	12		1	11	0.77			
Innominate	54	6	7	41	3.45	27	7	13
Long Bone	53				3.38			
Lunate	2				0.13	1		
Mandible	85	28	21	36	5.43	42.5	28	49
Metacarpal	73	30	15	28	4.66	36.5	30	45
Metapodial	43			43	2.75	21.5		
Metatarsal	74	18	24	32	4.73	36.5	23	41
Navicular	6	3	3		0.38	3	3	6
Phalanx 1	75	39	31	5	4.79			
Phalanx 2	70	18	34	18	4.47			
Phalanx 3	47	4	4	39	3			
Unid. Phalanx	1				0.064			
Unid. Premol.	1				0.064			
Rib	72				4.6			
Radioulna	130	55	54	21	7.98	65	55	109
Sacral Vert.	17				1.09			
Scapula	43	9	11	23	4.73	21.5	11	20
Sesamoid	13				0.83			
SN	4				0.26			
Tibia	49	11	22	16	3.13	24.5	22	33
Tarsal	4				0.26			
Thoracic Vert.	33				2.11			
Teeth	228				14.56			
Trapezium	10		1	9	0.64	0.5	1	
Tusk (mamm.)	1				0.064			
TW	1				0.064			
Vertebra	32				2.04			
Total	**1566**				**100**			

Table 5.2 VBC II22 Elements									
Item	No.	Left	Right	Unsided	Ant/Post	%	MAU*	MNI	MNE
Antler	1					0.2			
CB	2					0.5			
CL	3		3			0.8			
CPF	2	2				0.5			
CPI	2		2			0.5			
CPS	1		1			0.2			
CPU	1		1			0.2			
Cranium	8	5		1	2A	2.1			
Flat Bone	2					0.5			
Femur	23	5	8	10		6.2	11.5	8	13
Humerus	11	4	3	4		2.9	5.5	4	7
Innominate	7	4	1	2		1.9	3.5	4	5
Long Bone	73			73		19.7			
LTM	1	1				0.2			
MN	17	7	10			4.4			
MC	23	11	7	5		6.2	11.5	11	18
MMP	3		1	2		0.8			
MMR	1					0.2			
MP	19	3	2	14		5.1	9.5	3	5
MR	8		8			2.1			
MT	28	9	11	8		7.5	14	11	20
PHF	23	10	12	1		6.2			
PHR	14	6	6	2		3.7			
PHS	16	5	9	2		4.3			
PHT	6	3	3			1.6			
PRF	3		2	1		0.8			
Rib	10	1	2	7		2.7			
Radius	8	2	2	4		2.1	4	2	4
RDU	5	2	1	2		1.3	2.5	2	3
SED	4					1.08			
SEM	1					0.2			
SC	3		2	1		0.8	1.5	2	3
SEP	6					1.6			
Tibia	24	8	6	10		6.5	12	8	14
Ulna	11	3	4	4		2.9	5.5	4	7
UN	1					0.2			
VT				1		0.2			
VLM	5				5A	1.3			
VSA	1				1A	0.2			
VL	1				1A	0.2			
VTH	6				6A	1.6			
Total	**386**					**100.0**			

Element Representation According to Bone Density

Linear regressions and bivariate correlations in SPSS were conducted for datasets from both VBC 190 and II.22, as well as reindeer portions of the faunal assemblages from the French cave sites of le Flageolet, Prolom, and Roc de Combe. The rationale of this statistical exercise was to test the strength of correlation and relationship linearity between the percent survivorship of identified skeletal elements and bone mineral density calculated by computerized tomography (Enloe 2004; Lam et al. 1999). Weak or inverse correlations and linear relationships between skeletal percent survivorship and bone mineral density might indicate human behavioral conditioning on the fauna; strong correlations and linearity may indicate differential bone preservation due to density-mediated attrition (Enloe 2004). The assumption is that, in the absence of carnivore ravaging (for which there is no evidence at VBC) and density-mediated physicomechanical destruction, human conditioning will be left as a proximate causal mechanism.

The method was as follows. Percentage survivorship was calculated by dividing the MNE (minimum number of elements) for each skeletal element by the measure of the MNI (minimum number of individuals) of the most frequent element (Enloe 2004:154).

This method calculates the percentage survivorship as a function of the percentage of a given element that is actually present against what would be present if 100% preservation had occurred. This percentage can then be plotted against other applicable variables (such as bone density) to test strength of bivariate correlation and the linearity of (possible) relationships between them.

After the appropriate data were entered into SPSS 14.0, I selected to analyze the data by bivariate correlations. In the correlation parameters, I selected Pearson's r, Kendall's τ, and Spearman's ρ. The bivariate correlation between percentage survivorship and bone mineral density was very weak for both VBC 190 and II.22. The coefficients for VBC 190 were 0.238 (Pearson), 0.163 (Kendall's), and 0.168 (Spearman's). The coefficients for VBC II.22 were 0.220 (Pearson), 0.177 (Kendall's), and 0.241 (Spearman's). Table 5.3 below summarizes the correlation coefficients for VBC 190 and II.22 ; Table 5.4, the significance estimates.

The linear regressions likewise indicate very low correlations between bone survivorship and bone density at VBC. For the 190 sample, the r^2 score associated with the regression was 0.057 while for II.22 the r^2 score was an even weaker 0.048.

Table 5.3. Bivariate Correlation Coefficients.

VBC	Pearson's r	Kendall's t	Spearman's r
190	0.238	0.163	0.254
II.22	0.22	0.177	0.241

Table 5.4. Significance

VBC	Pearson's r	Kendall's t	Spearman's r
190	0.198	0.202	0.168
II.22	0.235	0.176	0.191

Regarding the regressions, the F scores were only 1.738 for VBC 190, and an even lower 1.474 for II.22. I also ran bivariate correlations and linear regressions for fauna from Le Flageolet, Prolom, and Roc de Combe, in order to see if and how the variables survivorship and density interplayed in those contexts. Table 5.5 below summarizes the correlation results.

Table 5.5. Sites

	Pearson's r	Kendall's t	Spearman's r
Le Flageolet	0.183	0.092	0.088
Prolom	0.661[b]	0.444[a]	0.577[a]
Roc de Combe	0.589[b]	0.485[a]	0.635[a]
[a] significant at 0.05 level			
[b] significant at 0.01 level			

In regards to the bivariate correlations, the rockshelter site Le Flageolet appears broadly similar to VBC 190 and II.22 in the weakness of the covariance between bone survivorship and bone density. At the cave sites of Prolom, and Roc de Combe, however, very strong correlations exist between the variables (Table 5.5 above). It should be reiterated that Prolom is also a carnivore accumulation. When the linear regressions were run for LF, Prol, and RDC more interesting patterning resulted. Le Flageolet exhibited statistically weak correlation, with a linear r^2 value of 0.034, similar to VBC (recall 190 value of 0.057 and 0.048 for II.22). The regressions for carnivore site Prol accorded well with the strong bivariate correlations. The r^2 value for Prol is 0.437. The regression for RDC, with an r^2 value of 0.347, also supported the indicated strong bivariate correlation for that site.

Table 5.6. Sites

	r	t	r	r^2
VBC 190	0.238	0.163	0.254	0.057
VBC II.22	0.22	0.177	0.241	0.048
le Flageolet	0.183	0.092	0.88	0.034
Prolom	0.661*	0.444*	0.577*	0.437*
Roc De Combe	0.589*	0.485*	0.635*	0.347*
* = significant relationship				

Three general subdivisions are obvious from the data in Table 5.6 above. First, the two French reindeer datasets from Verberie (190 and II.22) and le Flageolet show similarly weak associations between bone survivorship and density. The data from Roc de Combe and Prolom indicate rather strong, statistically significant correlations between bone survivorship and density. The assumption was that taphonomic agencies would operate in similar fashions upon bone in each of the site types and areas, and the data are interpreted to support this. One potential caveat to this methodology is in trying to assess the taxonomic intercomparability of faunal assemblages. All of the French material consisted of reindeer samples. Lam et al. (1999) indicate that bone density is quite consistent between quadrupedal mammals, so that reindeer skeleta from these sites should be quite intercomparable. For the data reviewed in this analysis Lam et al's (1999) findings appear to be generally confirmed.

Element Survivorship at VBC and Marrow Cavity Volume

In order to give another estimate of bone or element deletion from once whole, articulated skeletons, I again made use of Brain's (1969) percent survivorship estimate, this time attempting to correlate it with marrow cavity volume. This method involves dividing the minimum number of elements (MNE) by the MNI (minimum number of individuals) with the highest frequency (MNE / MNI = % survivorship). Adjustments must be made for MNEs generated from paired elements (i.e., mandible, femur) and for elements in series (i.e., vertebrae), either by first diving the MNE by 2 or by the number of elements in the series. Enloe (2004) used this method to evaluate reindeer assemblage integrity at VBC Secteur 202 Level II.1. Using Enloe's (2004) estimates for element percent survivorship as a baseline, I calculated percentage survivorship estimates for the major marrow-bearing reindeer elements from VBC 190 and VBC II.22 (Table 5.7 below).

Table 5.7. Context

	MN	HM	RDU	MC	FM	TA	MT
190	44.5	50	99.1	40.9	37.3	30	37.3
II.22	81.8	31.8	31.8	81.8	59.1	63.6	90.9
II.1	35	45	68.13	93.75	21.25	48.13	48.13

These data were then entered into SPSS to test bivariate correlations at VBC between % survivorship and marrow cavity (medullary cavity) volume (Binford 1978; Morin 2006). If marrow-cracking was a primary activity in VBC 190, II.22, or II.1, a negative correlation should exist between bone survivorship and marrow cavity volume, since the bones with the largest medullary cavities should be disproportionately absent. Table 5.8 below summarizes the results.

Table 5.8. Sites

	r	t	r	r²
VBC 190	-0.405	-0.69	-0.812	0.164
VBC II.22	0.94	0.138	0.116	0.009
VBC II.1	-0.753	-0.552	-0.667	0.567

It appears from the inverse correlation between bone survivorship and medullary cavity volume for marrow-bearing bones in VBC 190 and Level II.1 that marrow-cracking was indeed a primary on-site activity (Table 5.8 above), while a positive correlation between survivorship and medullary cavity volume exists for VBC II.22, contraindicating the results from 190 and II.1. Thus it seems marrow-cracking was not as primary an activity in the II.22 material as in 190 and II.1. The linear regressions of the survivorship/marrow cavity volume relationship for VBC 190 is $r^2 = 0.164$ and for VBC II.22 is $r^2 = 0.009$.

Element Survivorship at VBC and Meat Drying

Since the results above seemed to indicate that VBC 190 and VBC II.1 assemblages were perhaps subjected to more intensive marrow-cracking than that from II.22, I wanted also to determine if there was any correlation between element survivorship and Binford's (1978) meat-drying index, mainly to test if the fauna were being prepped for storage. Whereas Table 5.8 above lists the % survivorship at VBC 190, II.22, and II.1 for major appendicular (except the mandible) marrow-bearing bones, table 5.9 below lists the % survivorship for major reindeer axial elements that are often subjected to meat-drying (Binford 1978; Friesen 2001). My rationale was that an inverse correlation between bone survivorship and meat drying utility could indicate the transport of dried, axial elements from the site.

Table 5.9. Context

	CERV	SCAP	TH	LUM	SAC	PELV	RIB
190	23.64	20	60	0	30.91	12.73	65.45
II.22	0	18.18	54.55	45.45	9.09	36.36	18.18
II.1	18	37.5	16.07	8.2	30	45	7.41

I entered the data into SPSS and ran bivariate correlations and linear regressions on them. Table 5.10 below summarizes the results.

For the VBC 190 assemblage, there is moderate positive correlation between bone survivorship and the meat drying index, which suggests some of the axial elements were perhaps transported away from the site according to their drying qualities but not many or most of them. Fauna from VBC Level II.22 show a patently weak positive correlation for Pearson's, while the linear r² value was > 1.09 E, which is an obvious error in that the linear value cannot exceed 1. This suggests that there is neither positive nor negative

50

Table 5.10. Site				
	r	t	r	r
VBC 190	0.750	0.390	0.487	0.562
VBC II.22	0.100	0.450	0.527	> 1.09 E
VBC II.1	-0.584	-0.586	-0.757	0.341

correlation between axial element survivorship and the meat drying index for VBC II.22. The inverse correlation ($p < 0.05$) between axial element survivorship and the meat drying index for the VBC II.1 fauna indicates that axial elements from this assemblage were quite likely transported from the site according to their drying values.

Spatial Distributions of Burned and Butchered Items

In order to give some spatial dimension to the faunal patterning in this study, I plotted two 20 m x 20 m 'secteurs' to represent both VBC 190 and VBC 202 Level II.22. As above, although excellent 3D x, y, and z coordinate provenience exists for the II.22 material, 190 completely lacks such detail. To make these samples inter-comparable, I was obliged to deal in spatial units, or excavation squares, of 1 m². I then plotted the unit positions of burned/butchered items for both 190 and II.22 (Figure 5.1. below). Even at the relatively arbitrary analytical level of the 1m x 1 m squares, the spatial distribution of these items portrays sensible patterning. Figure 5.1 below highlights those units in each of the two secteurs that produced fauna, and also shows the positioning of one hearth (Unit L8) from Level II.22 vis a vis two other hearths that conform to the overlying Level II.1 for some idea of the spatial distribution of hearths.

Burned/butchered items in 190 occur in a large undifferentiated "mass" of bones, concentrated mainly in Units B14 and 15, C13, 14, 15, 16, D 14, 15, 16, and E 13, 14, 15, and 16, as well as another accumulation located mainly in Units E, F, 6, 7, and 8 (Figure 5.2 below). The burned and butchered items from II.22 appear much more structured, interestingly, being situated *around* the hearth located in Unit L8 (Figure 5.2 below). Bones, when plotted by 1 m² units, largely conform to the generally *different* spatial patterns in 190 and II.22. Audouze (personal communication) has informed that *no* hearths were found in Secteur 190. The spatial distributions of the humerus, radioulna, femur, tibia, and phalanges in 190 tend to collocate within large bone masses, or middens, located roughly in the northwest and southwest quarters of the 20 m² area. The distributions of these same elements in II.22 appear much more diffuse and yet also arranged relatively symmetrically around a more or less circular area centered around the L8 hearth.

It is also interesting to consider the scenario of VBC 190 containing burned bone, but containing no hearths. In Secteur 202, as above and in Figure 5.2 below, the burned material is clearly oriented to and around the

hearth in Unit L8. It's quite clear the burned material was most likely burned *in situ* or nearby. The implication is however that the burned material in 190 came from one of the hearths elsewhere on the site, whether currently known or unknown. It does tend to suggest quite strongly, given the absence of hearths in 190, that already burned and butchered material was moved into that secteur at least sometimes. In both VBC 202 and 190, appendicular elements constitute the vast majority of burned bone; VBC 202 burned bones consist of two distal metacarpals; VBC 190 burned bones include six phalanges, five long bones, one distal metacarpal, and an unidentified flat bone. This would indicate that at least some appendicular elements were probably cooked and consumed on-site, at least distal extremities. In the case of the burned material in VBC 190, it may be that they were dumped in that secteur as well.

Individual skeletal element density distribution maps were constructed using Golden Software's Surfer 9.0 GIS mapping program. In this analysis, areas with higher element frequencies appear in brighter colors, while lower element frequencies are shown in more neutral, lighter colors. Surfer density maps were constructed for crania, femur, humerus, metacarpal, metatarsal, phalanges, radioulna, rib, tibia, verbtebrae, and unidentified long bone shafts (Figures 5.3-5.13 below). The element density maps for skeletal material appear to portray a similar distribution of material to that for burned and butchered items in Figure 5.2; i.e., material in Secteur 190 appear to show a consistent distribution in two main areas with no apparent selectivity for individual elements while material in 202 II.22 appear to show some selectivity in distribution according to element.

Dental Analysis

Based upon the dental analysis of reindeer teeth and tooth fragments, it is possible to say the following regarding the archaeofauna from Sector 190 at VBC: There are 8 right M_3 and 7 left M_3 present in this sample. Thus, as based upon the MNI for this particular tooth, at least 8 adults are present. Several of these are paired with other teeth from 190. Two left and right M_3 (Units C15 and D16) are paired from the same individual adult, and may indicate some degree of past anthropogenic interaction between these excavation units. A portion of right mandibular toothrow (P_4 through M_2) is paired with left M_1 and M_2, although these lack provenance data. Also present are paired left and right adult M_2 and M_3 (one each) that lack provenance data.

There are two 2nd year juveniles present in the sample. Two partial mandibular toothrows attest to this. This juvenile dental material consists of right teeth 12-5 with $P_2 - P_4$ buds underneath (Unit D15). A left mandibular toothrow with teeth 12-5 missing $P_2 - P_4$ with buds underneath. At least two fawns are present in the sample. Right $D_3 - D_4$ and an isolated right D_4 are present (separate individuals). This archaeofauna also contains: 7 right P_2, 13 premolars (third or fourth), 14 right molars (first or second) 3 left P_3, 7 left P_4, and 6 left molars (first or second). The VBC 190 Dental MNI = 12 (eight adult right third molars, two juvenile mandibular toothrows, two fawns) It is possible to conclude from the VBC 190 dentition that at least 12 individual animals are represented in the faunal assemblage.

VBC 202 Level II.22

Two paired mandibles from different 1 x 1 units were present from II.22, both adults; the refit mandibles were from L7/M7 and O5/K9. Another refit mandible derived from unit K9. Isolated right mandibles occurred in K13 (2nd year juvenile), J9, N10, and O6. The dental MNI was calculated to be at least 7 from specimens of M^2. A total of seventeen deciduous teeth, including two milk teeth (nursing fawns) were noted. At least seven individual animals are present in the II.22 faunal assemblage.

Dental Mortality Profiles for VBC 190 and II.22

The VBC 190 and II.22 dental samples were subjected to a crown height analysis in order to estimate the mortality profile of the animals comprising the assemblage (Gifford-Gonzalez 1991; Klein and Cruz-Uribe 1984). Due to uneven dental occlusion within individual dental series (i.e., cheek teeth wear faster than other teeth), many or most reindeer mortality curves overestimate the actual ages of the animal peer cohorts in any given sample (Enloe and Turner 2005). However, as a means of gauging the general age cohorts present within a skeletal population, the method is adequate. Evaluation of absent or rare age classes does roughly indicate seasonality of an assemblage at death (Enloe and Turner 2005). The age classes are based on a series of class categories from 1-10 and 10+, premised upon measured dental wear. For this method, less dental wear indicates a generally younger age class profile, more dental wear indicates generally an older measure.

In order to formulate a cohesive mortality profile estimate from this sample, the teeth were initially sorted into maxillary and mandibular categories. I then compiled a final dental dataset consisting of all VBC 190 and II.22 reindeer teeth with verified provenience (unprovenienced teeth were not included in the mortality profile). The tooth crowns were then measured with digital calipers in the UI Zooarchaeology Lab. The resulting crown height measures were then entered by hand into Verberie's revised crown height equations (Enloe and Turner 2005:132, Fig. 6), which when resolved provide dental "age estimates" in months, which are then easily converted into years (see Figure 5.14 below for Enloe and Turners 2005 equations). These were entered into Microsoft Excel for recording and tabulating, and SPSS for data manipulation and to run a check on my hand calculations. In order to check my statistical hand calculations, I used SPSS to perform a bivariate scatterplot of measured crown heights against the equations' age estimates by month. The scatterplot (Figure

5.15 below) indicates a consistent, trimodal distribution of reverse age estimate curves (higher crown height = younger age, lower crown height = older age) with no apparent calculation errors (which would be visible as outliers). If the crown height calculations were in error, then they were perfectly consistently in error, according to the scatter plots. This is true when either months (as the equations provide) are used, likewise when the months are converted into years (Figure 5.16 below). When a bivariate correlation was run on crown height vs. age in years, the inverse correlation was found to be highly significant, validating the accuracy of the crown height method (Figures 5.17 and 5.18 below).

The mortality curve indicated by the crown height distribution for VBC 190 is trimodal, and heavily biased towards older animals. Nearly 40% of the variation in this dental sample of wear distribution is attributable to wear class 10+. The next most abundant wear class, Class #8, represented 12.61% of the variation. Wear Class #4 contained 9.1% of the variation in the dental sample. Figure 5.19. below portrays the averaged results of the separate VBC 190 age classes, not corrected for specific eruption age. At least for VBC 190, the results suggest a very different age composition than noted for VBC II.1 (Figure 5.14 below, from Enloe and turner 2005). For VBC 190, there is a distinct bias toward older animals, whereas several other levels from VBC seem to indicate

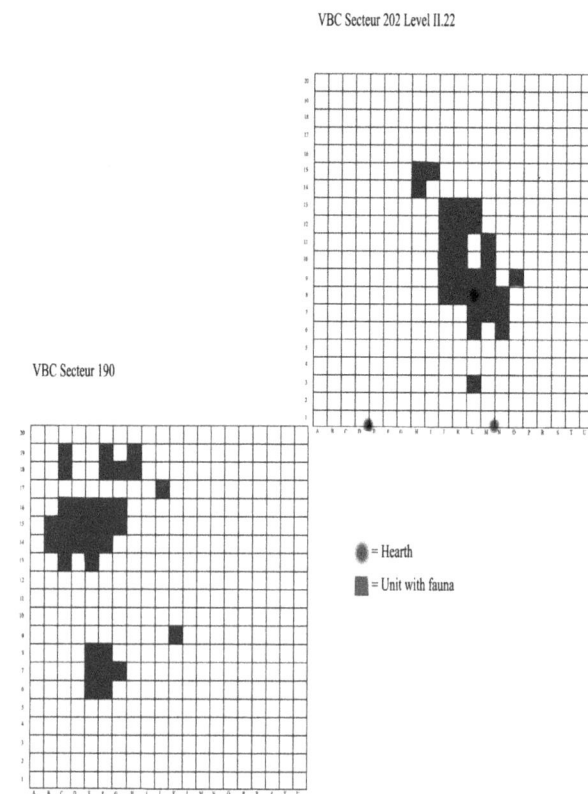

FIGURE 5.1. VBC 190 AND 202 II.22 FAUNA AND HEARTHS.

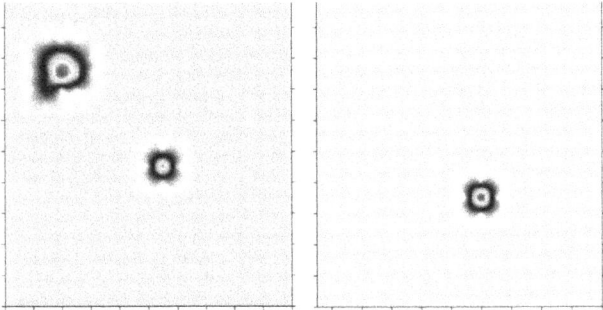

FIGURE 5.2. SURFER 9.0 DENSITY DISTRIBUTION MAP OF 20 X 20 M SECTEURS VBC 190 (LEFT) AND 202 II.22 (RIGHT) BURNED AND BUTCHERED FAUNA. MARKS AT TWO METERS.

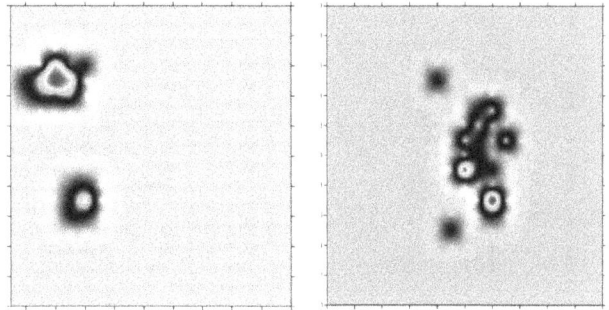

FIGURE 5.6. SURFER 9 DENSITY-DISTRIBUTION MAP OF 20 X 20 M SECTEURS VBC 190 (LEFT) AND 202 II.22 (RIGHT) METACARPAL. MARKS AT TWO METERS.

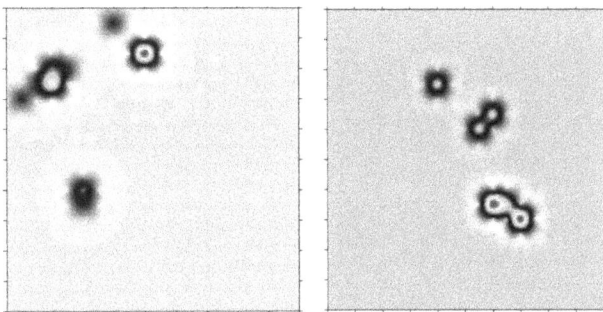

FIGURE 5.3. SURFER 9 DENSITY-DISTRIBUTION MAP OF 20 X 20 M SECTEURS VBC 190 (LEFT) AND 202 II.22 (RIGHT) CRANIA. MARKS AT TWO METERS.

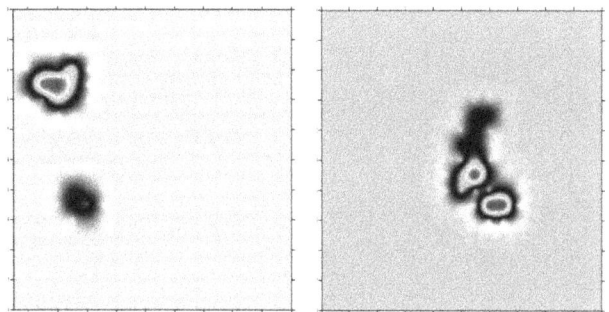

FIGURE 5.7. SURFER 9 DENSITY-DISTRIBUTION MAP OF 20 X 20 M SECTEURS VBC 190 (LEFT) AND 202 II.22 (RIGHT) METATARSAL. MARKS AT TWO METERS.

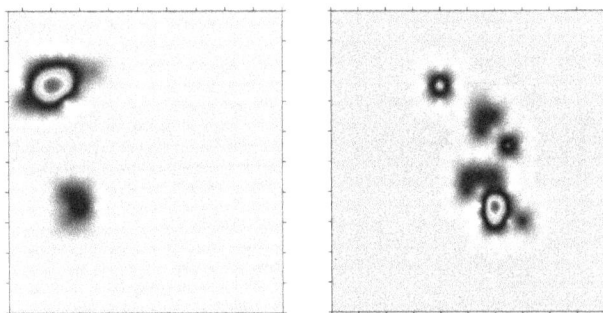

FIGURE 5.4. SURFER 9 DENSITY-DISTRIBUTION MAP OF 20 X 20 M SECTEURS VBC 190 (LEFT) AND 202 II.22 (RIGHT) FEMUR. MARKS AT TWO METERS.

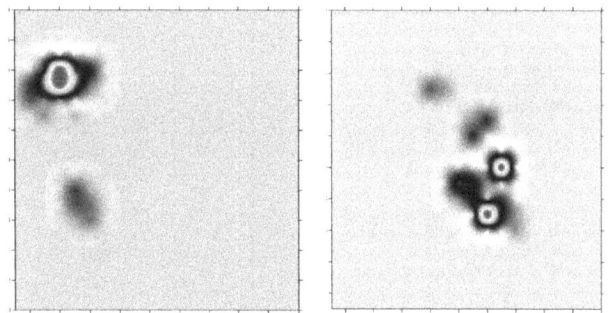

FIGURE 5.8. SURFER 9 DENSITY-DISTRIBUTION MAP OF 20 X 20 M SECTEURS VBC 190 (LEFT) AND 202 II.22 (RIGHT) PHALANGES. MARKS AT TWO METERS.

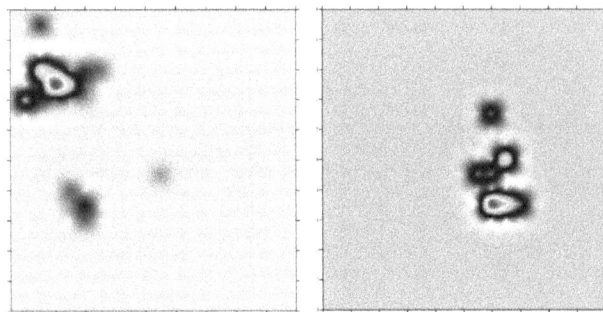

FIGURE 5.5 SURFER 9 DENSITY-DISTRIBUTION MAP OF 20 X 20 M SECTEURS VBC 190 (LEFT) AND 202 II.22 (RIGHT) HUMERUS. MARKS AT TWO METERS.

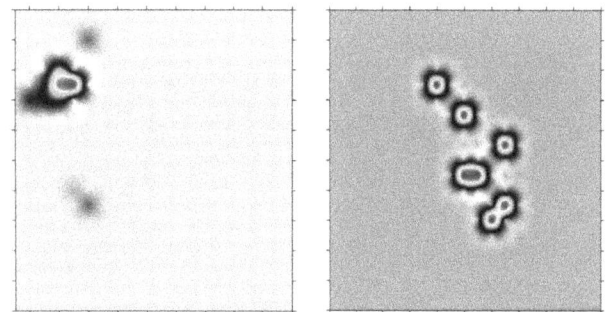

FIGURE 5.9. SURFER 9 DENSITY-DISTRIBUTION MAP OF 20 X 20 M SECTEURS VBC 190 (LEFT) AND 202 II.22 (RIGHT) RADIOULNA. MARKS AT TWO METERS.

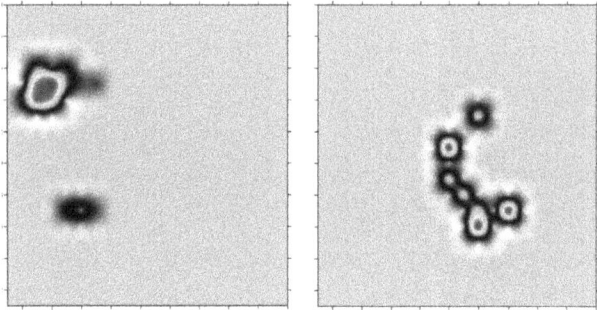

FIGURE 5.10. SURFER 9 DENSITY-DISTRIBUTION MAP OF 20 X 20 M SECTEURS VBC 190 (LEFT) AND 202 II.22 (RIGHT) RIB. MARKS AT TWO METERS.

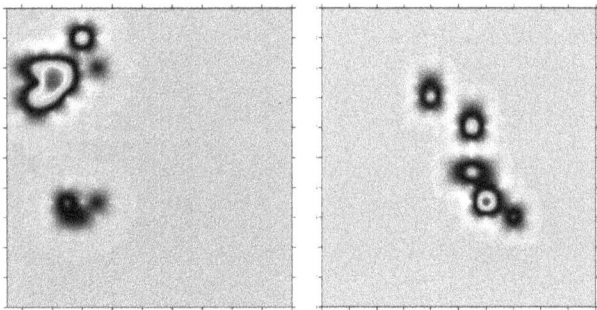

FIGURE 5.11. SURFER 9 DENSITY-DISTRIBUTION MAP OF 20 X 20 M SECTEURS VBC 190 (LEFT) AND 202 II.22 (RIGHT) TIBIA. MARKS AT TWO METERS.

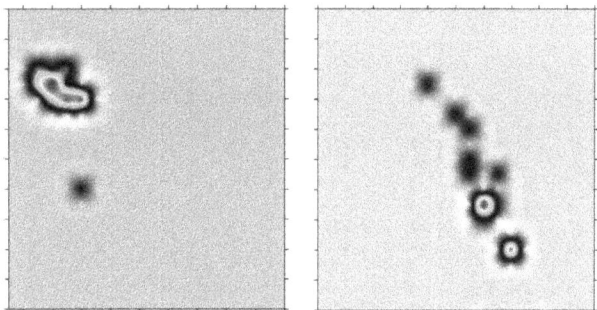

FIGURE 5.12. SURFER 9 DENSITY-DISTRIBUTION MAP OF 20 X 20 M SECTEURS VBC 190 (LEFT) AND 202 II.22 (RIGHT)

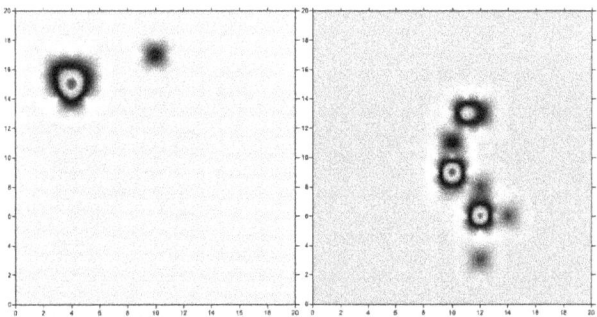

FIGURE 5.13. SURFER 9 DENSITY-DISTRIBUTION MAP OF 20 X 20 M SECTEURS VBC 190 (LEFT) AND 202 II.22 (RIGHT) UNIDENTIFIED LONG BONE SHAFTS. MARKS AT TWO METERS.

$$P_3 \, Age = 200 - (2(200-24)(CH/19.49)) + ((200-24)(CH^{1.5})/(19.49^{1.5})) + (((19.49-CH)^2)/1.25$$
$$P_4 \, Age = 200 - (2(200-24)(CH/20.67)) + ((200-24)(CH^{1.5})/(20.67^{1.5})) + (((20.67-CH)^2)/1.25$$
$$M_1 \, Age = 200 - (2(200-5)(CH/18.76)) + ((200-5)(CH^{1.6})/(18.76^{1.6})) + (((18.76-CH)^2)/3)$$
$$M_2 \, Age = 200 - (2(200-12.5)(CH/18.89)) + ((200-12.5)(CH^{1.6})/(18.89^{1.6})) + (((18.89-CH)^2)/3)$$
$$M_3 \, Age = 200 - (2(200-24)(CH/18.11)) + ((200-24)(CH^{1.6})/(18.11^{1.6})) + (((18.11-CH)^2)/3)$$

FIGURE 5.14. MODIFIED VERBERIE CROWN HEIGHT EQUATIONS (FROM ENLOE AND TURNER 2005:132, FIG. 6).

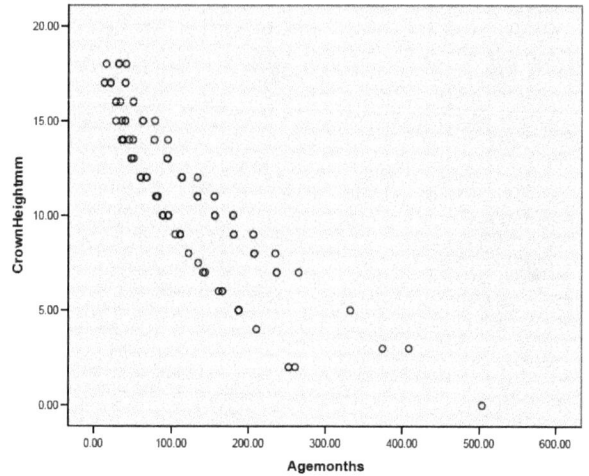

FIGURE 5.15. SPSS SCATTERPLOT OF VBC 190 CROWN HEIGHT VS. ESTIMATED AGE IN MONTHS.

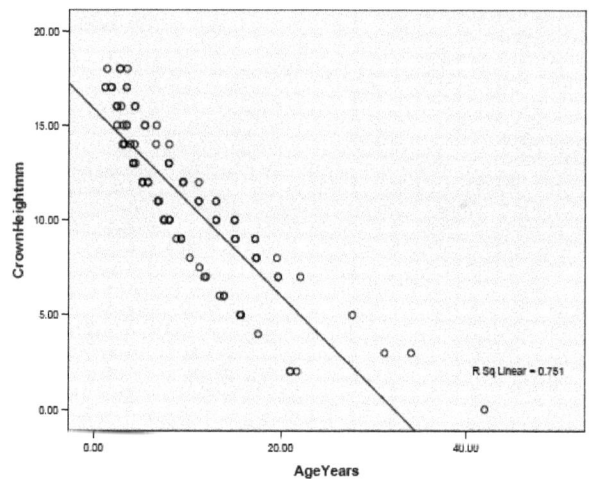

FIGURE 5.16. SPSS VBC 190 R^2 LINEAR SCATTER PLOT.

Correlations

		Crown Heightmm	AgeYears
CrownHeightmm	Pearson Correlation	1	-.867**
	Sig. (2-tailed)		.000
	N	111	111
AgeYears	Pearson Correlation	-.867**	1
	Sig. (2-tailed)	.000	
	N	111	111

**. Correlation is significant at the 0.01 level (2-tailed).

FIGURE 5.17. VBC 190 PEARSON CORRELATION BETWEEN CROWN HEIGHT AND AGE IN YEARS.

Correlations

			Crown Heightmm	AgeYears
Kendall's tau_b	CrownHeightmm	Correlation Coefficient	1.000	-.771**
		Sig. (2-tailed)	.	.000
		N	111	111
	AgeYears	Correlation Coefficient	-.771**	1.000
		Sig. (2-tailed)	.000	.
		N	111	111
Spearman's rho	CrownHeightmm	Correlation Coefficient	1.000	-.911**
		Sig. (2-tailed)	.	.000
		N	111	111
	AgeYears	Correlation Coefficient	-.911**	1.000
		Sig. (2-tailed)	.000	.
		N	111	111

**. Correlation is significant at the 0.01 level (2-tailed).

FIGURE 5.18. KENDALL'S AND SPEARMAN'S CORRELATIONS BETWEEN CROWN HEIGHT AND AGE IN YEARS.

a selectivity for younger, prime animals (Enloe 1997:99, Figure 5). Several possible explanations for this apparent difference in prey populations might involve either time-successive, diachronic shifts in focus over time, diachronic differences or changes in site functions, or sampling bias. Another potential explanation, one with particular possible promise, might be differential treatment of differentially aged animals. Younger, prime age carcasses and older individual may have been subject to different butchering and treatment activities as based upon differential nutritional quality. If younger animals, or specific elements therefrom, were transported from the site more frequently than geriatric specimens, a skewing toward older age classes would result irrespective of how the older carcasses were processed. Or were different animal age

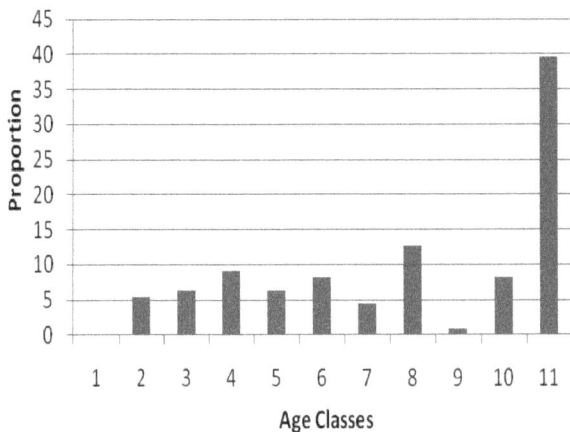

VBC 190 Mortality Profile

FIGURE 5.19. VBC 190 MORTALITY PROFILE, NOT CORRECTED FOR ERUPTION AGE.

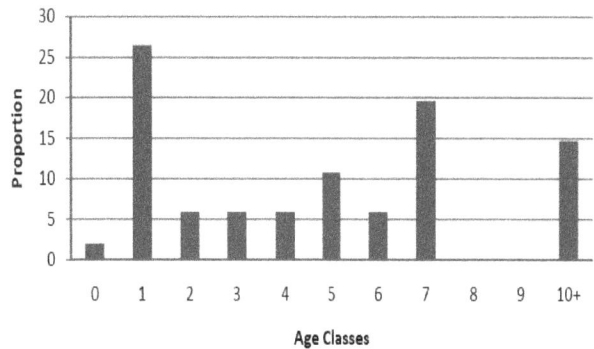

VBC II.22 Mortality Profile

FIGURE 5.21. VBC II.22 MORTALITY PROFILE.

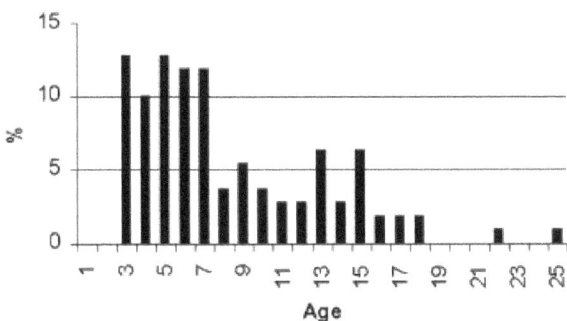

FIGURE 5.20. AGE CLASS PROFILES FROM VBC (FROM ENLOE AND TURNER 2005:135, FIGURE 18).

Correlations

		CrwnHgt	AgeMo
CrwnHgt	Pearson Correlation	1	-.785**
	Sig. (2-tailed)		.000
	N	74	74
AgeMo	Pearson Correlation	-.785**	1
	Sig. (2-tailed)	.000	
	N	74	74

**. Correlation is significant at the 0.01 level (2-tailed).

Correlations

			CrwnHgt	AgeMo
Kendall's tau_b	CrwnHgt	Correlation Coefficient	1.000	-.675**
		Sig. (2-tailed)	.	.000
		N	74	74
	AgeMo	Correlation Coefficient	-.675**	1.000
		Sig. (2-tailed)	.000	.
		N	74	74
Spearman's rho	CrwnHgt	Correlation Coefficient	1.000	-.807**
		Sig. (2-tailed)	.	.000
		N	74	74
	AgeMo	Correlation Coefficient	-.807**	1.000
		Sig. (2-tailed)	.000	.
		N	74	74

**. Correlation is significant at the 0.01 level (2-tailed).

FIGURE 5.22. VBC II.22 SPSS CORRELATION COEFFICIENTS FOR VARIABLES CROWN HEIGHT/AGE IN MONTHS.

VBC II.22 produced a much younger mortality profile. Figure 5.11 above indicates that VBC II.22 contains many fewer geriatric animals as a proportion of its fauna, and also a higher proportion of very young.

Figure 5.23 above shows the strong inverse correlations between dental crown height and age in months for VBC II.22.

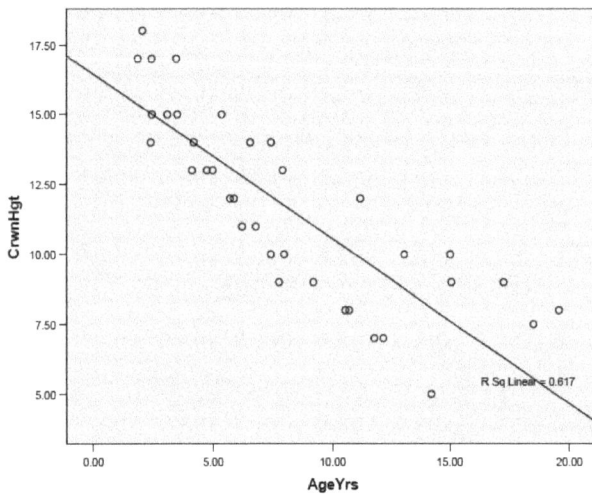

FIGURE 5.23. SPSS VBC II.22 R^2 LINEAR SCATTER PLOT.

In Figure 5.9 above, it will be noted that Enloe's results (1997:99) indicated slightly differing mortality profiles for each of the VBC levels (compare with Figure 5.21 above for VBC II.22). As above, these levels (II.1, II.2, II.21, II.22, II.3, etc.) have been interpreted as different occupations, separated by an as yet unknown interval. The differing mortality profiles might therefore indicate fluctuating proportions of age peer cohorts in herd populations over time, suggestive of dynamic herd demographics. This indicates that at VBC there may also be an age-mediated spatial component to faunal locations.

In order to help answer questions regarding age-mediated conditioning of space, I also calculated the mean crown height "age" estimate per excavation unit. This allowed quick comparison and data analysis to determine if any spatial patterning appeared to relate to age class (in either X or Y axes). For example, for the E series of units, for those units that produced reindeer teeth the mean crown height age classes were as follows: E7 5.73 years; E14 8.33 years; E15 12.89 years; E16 13.55 years (Figure 5.24 below). Similar patterning was also noted for the B and C series of units.

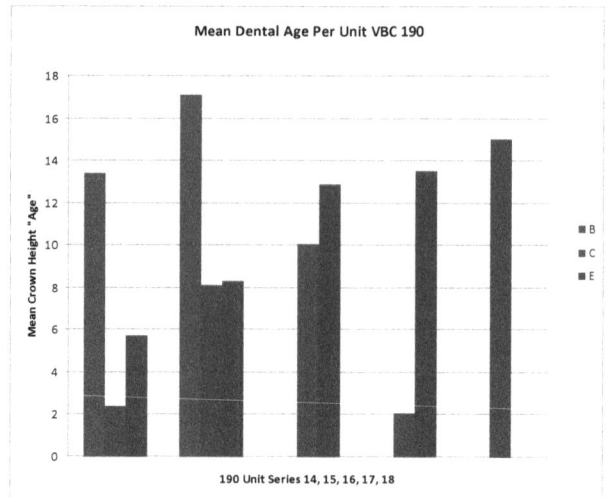

FIGURE 5.24. VBC 190 MEAN DENTAL AGE PER UNIT.

For the B series of units, for those units that produced reindeer teeth, the mean crown height ages in years were: B14 13.39; B15 17.11 (Figure 5.24 above). For the C series of units, the mean crown height age in years were: C13 2.41; C14 8.13; C15 10.05; C18 15.06 (Figure 5.24 above).

At VBC, the 20 m² secteurs increase in numeric value from south to north, and in letter value from west to east. In other words, the mean crown height ages of the age classes *tend* to increase from south to north. I then analyzed the mean crown height age estimates across the numeric series, from west to east (across B14, C14, D14, etc.). For the 14-series the mean age classes were: B14 13.39 years; C14 8.13 years; D14 5.85 years; E14 8.33 years. For the 15-series, mean age classes in years were: B15 17.11; C15 10.05; D15 9.05. In other words, the mean carcass age estimates *tend* to increase from west to east. The farther south and east the fauna at VBC 190, the younger it generally is in terms of crown height age class. This is an interesting phenomenon in that most of the hearth areas are to the south and east of the VBC 190 fauna. These are, however, subtle phenomena, and I am only summarizing the trends.

The age-mediated directional pattern of spatial location in 190 is, however, not apparently similarly present in VBC II.22. Instead, for II.22 it appears there is neither directionality nor actual patterning in the distribution of animal age classes. In VBC II.22, the age classes are simply dispersed around the hearth in L8. There seems to be no general trend at all in the distribution of age classes in II.22 outside a general dispersion around this hearth. This is visible even in a rudimentary plotting of the mean age classes per tooth-bearing unit (Figures 5.25 and 5.26 below). VBC 190 seems to lack any handy similar "landmark"; instead the fauna (teeth, bones, burned, and butchered) share a monotonous "piled" or stacked arrangement (see also Figures 5.1, 5.2).

Faunal Taphonomy

The fauna from both VBC Secteur 190 and VBC Secteur 202 II.22 were subjected to a detailed taphonomic analysis. A brief explanation of the taphonomic methodology is in order. Taphonomic data categories (individual fields) in spreadsheet form include Weathering, Burning, Butchering, Breakage, gnawing, and Root Etching (vermiculation due to plant root acidification and etching of bones). Beneath each of these primary taphonomic data categories, I recorded the estimated extent of the attribute concerned.

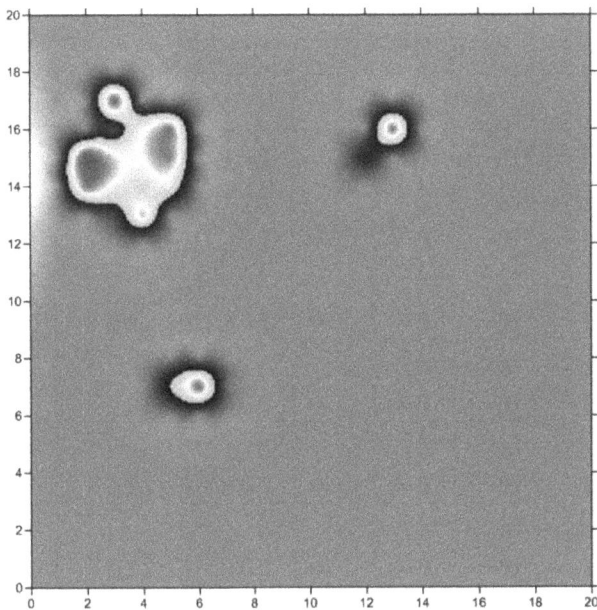

FIGURE 5.25. MEAN AGE CLASS DISTRIBUTION PER TOOTH-BEARING UNIT VBC 190. BRIGHTNESS = INTENSITY.

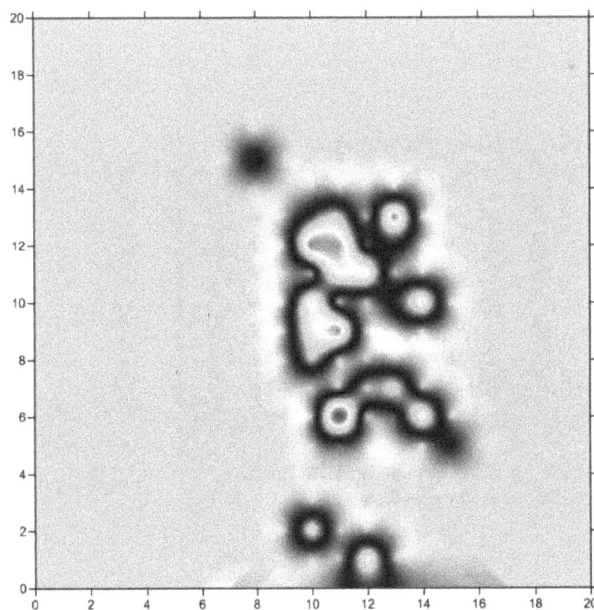

FIGURE 5.26. MEAN AGE CLASS DISTRIBUTION PER TOOTH-BEARING UNIT VBC II.22. BRIGHTNESS = INTENSITY.

For example, for Weathering, I would record a measure of the degree of bone weathering falling between a 0 to 7 interval from unweathered to completely fragmentary. For burning, the data ranges from none to completely carbonized; butchering from 0 no evidence thereof to 8 cuts and impacts. For the breakage category, two data fields are collected, the first category being morphology (breakage 'type', such as none or spiral, crushed, etc.) and the second category being freshness (freshness *at the time of breakage*, for instance green in the case of immediately post-mortem fracture).

When the two samples are compared for taphonomic attributes, the more fragmentary nature of the II.22 fauna had some serious effects on this portion of the study. Whereas the individual analyst may entertain particular preferences for highlighting various taphonomic indices, it has been my customary approach to deal first with evidence for burning and butchery of the fauna. Especially concerning sites at which evidence exists for the use of fire, any evidence of burning can be interpreted as an index of human behavioral conditioning on the material. Butchery marks offer an obvious index of human behavior. For the 190 sample, thirteen burned items were observed, many of which also bore evidence of butchering. Five of these burned items were long bone fragments. One is a flat bone with cutmarks. Four burned phalanges were also observed in the 190 sample, all of which bore cutmarks. One burned proximal metacarpal was noted in 190, as were two humeri (one right humeral head and a right distal humerus, both with chopmarks). From the II.22 sample, *no* burned material was observed in the sample. Four items featured butchery marks, all of which were on metatarsals, with chopmarks, scrapes, and impact scars. We will turn to a spatial analysis of the burned/butchered material below.

With respect to the other taphonomic attributes in the fauna, II.22 is remarkable for its abject *lack* of taphonomic patterning whatsoever. 99% of the fauna from II.22 is basically unweathered (Figure 5.28 below), and not significantly etched by root vermiculation. Diagnostic breakage and fracturing was identifiable on only four items from II.22 (less than 0.5%). About 85% of the 190 fauna is moderately root-etched. In terms of bone breakage patterning for the 190 sample (Figure 5.29 below), roughly comparable percentages are noted for unbroken bones (17.4%), spiral green fractures (11.9%), transverse (14.5%), longitudinal (16.5%), crushed items (18.9%), and items with indeterminate breakage characteristics (16.4%). In terms of weathering, the 190 material (Figure 5.27 below) also appears to feature a more diverse range of weathering indices. Thus, the material from II.22 bears fewer taphonomic indices and is much more fragmentary, while the 190 sample bears many more taphonomic indices and is much less fragmentary.

In a recent analysis of fauna from a later occupation at VBC, Enloe (2004) documented that density-mediated physical degradation of the material could not explain the survivorship of the bones from Level II.1. Although many studies have suggested that bone density should be regarded as a primary conditioning agent at archaeological sites (Binford and Bertram 1977; Ioannidou 2003; Lam et al. 1998, 1999; Lyman 1994), if bone density can be eliminated as a serious causal agent for faunal assemblages then we need to account for other, perhaps behavioral, causes for observable faunal patterning (Enloe 2004). As above, for typically non meat-utilitarian elements at VBC (vertebrae, carpals, tarsals, ribs, and phalanges) the presence and comparative proportions seem in accordance between 190 and II.22. The appendicular elements portray the most variance between the two assemblages. A consideration of the spatial distributions of these elements may help to evince possible causes.

In terms of basic probabilities and taphonomy, the burned and butchered fauna is essentially numerically insignificant. What is present is tantalizing, but extremely sparse and highly diffuse. The probability of encountering any given faunal item from VBC 190 would be: 1,855 items / 34 units = 1:55. The probability of encountering any given faunal item from II.22 would be: 1,610 items / 31 units = 1:52. It is, however, interesting to consider the basic probabilistic dispersion of the identifiable fauna across VBC 190 and 202 II.22. For VBC 190, 1,566 NISP were excavated from 34 1 x 1 m units, which equates to approximately a 1:50 probability that any individual identifiable faunal item comes from any one of the 34 fauna-bearing units. Also for II.22, 31 units produced at least 386 faunal NISP, which is about a 1:12.5 probability that any individual identifiable faunal item comes from any one of the 31 fauna-bearing units. This is an indirect measure of both the numerosity and dispersion of the fauna in the respective Secteurs 190 and 202 II.22, as well as the degree to which the samples were degraded by on-site processes. In other words, although the identifiable fauna are distributed over a commensurate amount of space (31 m^2 in 202.II.22 compared to 34 m^2 in 190), and despite the association of the II.22 fauna with a basically central hearth, there is a higher basic per item probability (1:12.5) that the identifiable II.22 material will occur or be encountered in within any of the units in that secteur that bear fauna in contrast to those from VBC 190 (1:50). This higher rate of encounter is completely due to the very low number of identifiable fauna in II.22 in proportion to the total sample size. II.22 portrays a highly deteriorated sample. Recall also that both secteurs produced similarly sized total faunal assemblages (1,855 total for VBC 190, 1,610 total for II.22). This is a rough index of just how "patterned" (or 'systematized') the relative few identifiable fauna appear to be around the 202 II.22 hearth area, despite the degree of overall faunal degradation. VBC 190 appears to invert this pattern; in 190, many more identifiable fauna (bones in better condition) appear to have much less "structured" patterning.

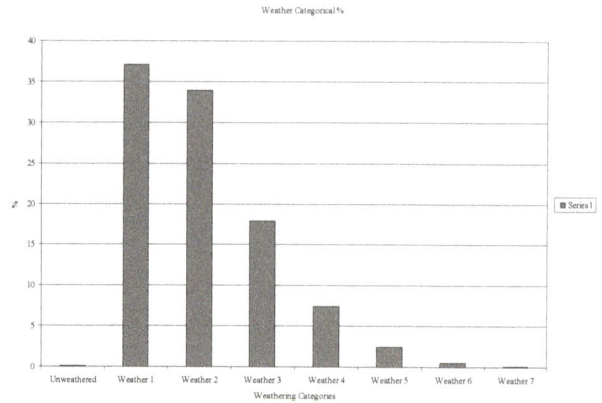

FIGURE 5.27. VBC 190 BONE WEATHERING.

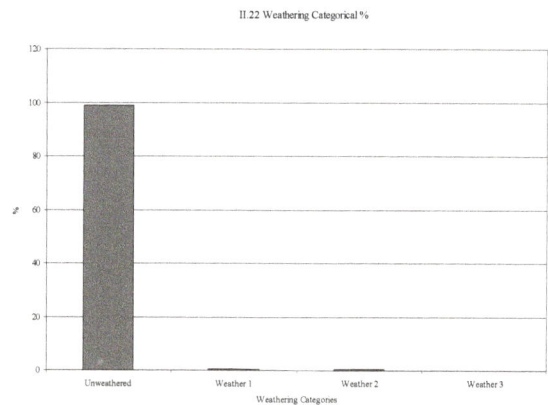

FIGURE 5.28. VBC II.22 BONE WEATHERING.

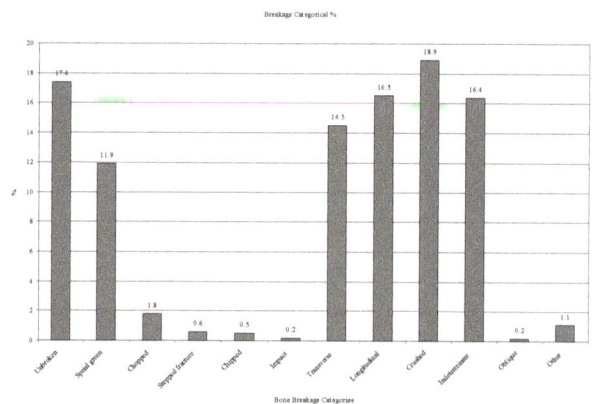

FIGURE 5.29. VBC 190 BONE BREAKAGE.

As above, the samples also differ with respect to bone breakage. Although both samples featured evidence of crushing and otherwise indeterminate breakages, II.22 exhibits these breakage categories to such a degree that it was impossible adequately to portray graphically. It was simply unproductive to attempt construction of a bone breakage histogram similar to Figure 5.29 for VBC 190, above. Whereas the 190 sample exhibits much evidence of traditionally diagnostic "green fracturing", such as spiral and stepped, longitudinal fractures, perhaps indicative of marrow-cracking, the II.22 material is simply pulverized. To reiterate, definitive bone breakage categories could only be attributed to a small minority of the II.22 assemblage.

The majority of burned/butchered items in both samples are lower limb elements bearing impact scars and spiral fracturing. The proportional representation of forelimbs and hindlimbs seems to differ between 190 and II.22; 190 lacks the forelimbs while II.22 lacks the hindlimbs, while similar proportions of all other elements seem generally to accord quite well (Figures 5.30, and 5.31 below). The axial elements appear nearly identical in spite of differences in sample sizes. Unfortunately, no other matching was found between paired bones linking 202 II.22 and 190 beyond the two proximal phalanges. Three distal metacarpal pairings were found between VBC 190 and Secteur 202 Level II.1. There were isolated examples of tooth pairings located inside both 190 and 202 II.22, but no dental matches between. For although the taphonomic analysis is somewhat sketchy owing to the lack of diagnostic taphonomic indices in the II.22 sample, I interpret the spatial distribution of the 190 sample to represent essentially jumbled bone dumps or refuse middens (one in the NW, one in the SW of Secteur 190), composed somewhat haphazardly of disarticulated items from many different individual reindeer. Although there is no hearth in 190, there are burned/butchered items located in this sample. Likewise, although there are many different elements distributed around the L8 hearth in II.22, the distributions do not evince the same jumbled, piled pattern visible in 190.

It would appear that, discounting differential bone preservation owing to bone density, we're left with human behavioral conditioning as the primary accumulative and distributional agent in both samples. The discrepancy between 190 and II.22 in bone condition and preservation states, and in terms of the proportion of identifiable specimens, may relate to an entirely different style of processing intensity and goal direction. The more fragmentary faunal material from II.22 occurs around a hearth, in the presence of tools (Audouze, personal communication), and was apparently subjected to much more intensive processing by humans. The more integral material from 190 was perhaps simply processed less. Moreover, while II.22 can be reasonably interpreted as conforming to a single occupation at VBC, there is no similar indication for 190. The presence of burning and butchery marks on low meat-utility lower limb elements and phalanges suggests that marrow extraction was a principal activity among humans at VBC. The burning and very similar transverse fractures on phalanges suggests that these items were perhaps first cooked or at least heated in or near a fire and then snapped or smashed open relatively systematically, for marrow procurement, as were other lower limbs.

With respect to the general spatial distribution of fauna in 190 and II.22, it may also be instructive to consider briefly the evidence for multiple occupations as defined remnant stratigraphy. Enloe and Audouze (1997) have suggested that at least five separate occupations occurred in Secteur 202, conforming to a succession of levels as delineated above. The difference in limb proportions between 190 and II.22 could thereby indicate some degree of functional differentiation between them. Since the upper limbs are generally the highest meat-utility items, a sample of faunal material from one seasonal occupation could easily show different general limb proportions when compared with a dumping midden composed of the subsistence remains gathered and centrally accumulated over multiple seasonal rounds.

These two samples appear not to indicate any sort of cultural difference in terms of faunal treatment over time, nor is there evidence in this dataset of a "multi-family" encampment with different, interacting site functions.

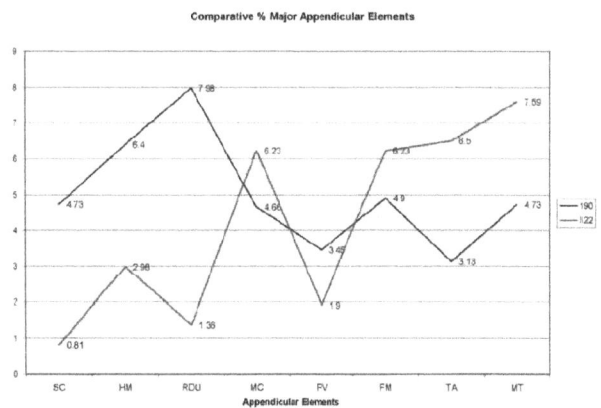

FIGURE 5.30. PROPORTIONAL REPRESENTATION OF AXIAL ELEMENTS 190 AND II.22.

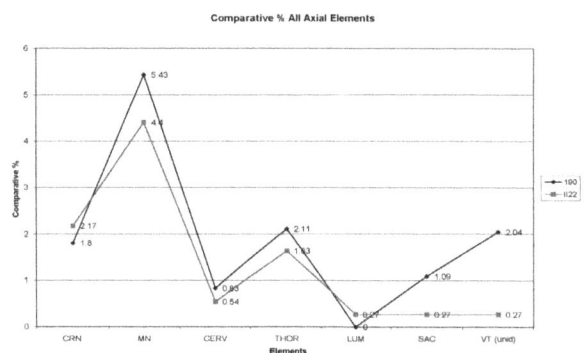

FIGURE 5.31. PROPORTIONAL REPRESENTATION OF APPENDICULAR ELEMENTS 190 AND II.22.

Moreover, the more "complete" articulations as noted in photographs of the 190 material (complete vertebral columns and limb joints, etc. Figure 5.32) might indicate that the 190 loci were selected for refuse dumping because of simple proximity to the primary kill or butchering locus. 190 might in fact BE the primary butchering/disarticulation locus. VBC 202 II.22 may represent an occupation to which things were generally moved for further processing, while 190 may represent a locus from which things were moved.

Whereas VBC 190 seems generally to consist of the after effects of repeated activities, it, serving as some form of residential loci, have produced similar representation patterns due to generally similar repetitious accumulations of fauna. Regardless of whether these three sites were truly "residences", it appears that multiple sequences of faunal acquisition, processing, and discard have contributed to the formations of these assemblages and to their general similarities in appendicular patterning. In this study, VBC II.22 patterns may be indicative of ephemeral occupation for faunal acquisition and processing. For VBC II.22, in fact, there exists the possibility that we are in effect seeing one seasonal occupation's more dispersed, differentiated instance of faunal distribution and processing in contrast to the more "jumbled" nature of VBC 190. There seems no question that the spatial distribution of fauna in VBC II.22 is clearly oriented in relation to the hearth found in unit L8 of that level, while 190 lacks any similar locus of intra-site centrality or apparent focus.

Binford (1983:137, Figure 75) proposed that reindeer processing stations among the Nunamiut consisted of multiple discard loci that in the abstract seem, at least at the level of one such locus, to resemble VBC 190 especially in term of bone aggregation and frequency patterns. At such processing sites, kinship or other social divisions were, he claimed, visible in multiple occurrences of hearths and "activity areas" that were separated by space (Binford 1983). These socio-spatial divisions were perhaps relatively impermeable, in that each particular kinship group or lineage was responsible for undertaking its own provisioning and processing activities on the acquired reindeer carcasses. Irrespective of the length of occupation or regardless indeed whether a given processing station served as a residence, the pattern was clear: where possible, people choose to re-use such stations, especially if there were hearths and associated raw materials already at a site (lithics, bones from previous occupations) (Binford 1983:120-128). Despite the numeric abundance of bones in VBC 190, it produced no hearths.

Refits

There were ultimately no secure metric or mechanical refits found between VBC 190 and VBC 202 that could be used to assess some degree of contemporaneity between the secteurs. Some potential false-positives occurred, such as several pairs of phalanges and metapodials, but such pairings were very weak in relation to the pervasive

structural differences between these assemblages. The best potential refit was of two juvenile distal metacarpals with two unfused distal epiphyses (four total bones). Claiming refits for those four specimens required a certain measure of confidence that 1) unfused distal epiphyses can be rearticulated with their matching diaphyses/metaphyses, and 2) that the diaphyses themselves were formerly associated in life. There were several examples of unfused metapodial distal epiphyses, all similarly sized, that could be plausibly reassociated with several distal metapodial diaphyses. The potential matches included both metacarpals and metatarsals, indicating that any claimed refit of such items would be purely speculative. Another analyst might easily refit them differently. Its jumbled and spatially tight pattern of element representation (virtually all elements represented, in just a few units) suggest that VBC 190 conforms to a "midden", or perhaps, given the frequency and often excellent physical condition of the material, the primary butchering area of Verberie le Buisson Campin. It was noted above that 190 material was often found at shallower depths than the II.22 material. This could be explained by Secteur 190's reuse over at least several occupations as a primary butchering locale, while the hearth areas of Secteur 202 may represent successive consumption/task/habitation areas located at some distance from the butchery refuse.

With respect to the dental crown height age profiles, and the apparently large age discrepancy between VBC 190 and VBC II.22, there are a number of factors that must be considered. It is unquestionable that the age profile for VBC 190 indicates a much older animal population than that of II.22. If there were an occupational cause for this discrepancy, it could be a result of accumulation during different seasons, focus on differentially aged animals at different times for whatever reason, or even simply that older animals were easier to hunt and were acquired in greater numbers for VBC 190. Furthermore, it could simply be that older animals were processed more frequently in 190, while younger ones were processed

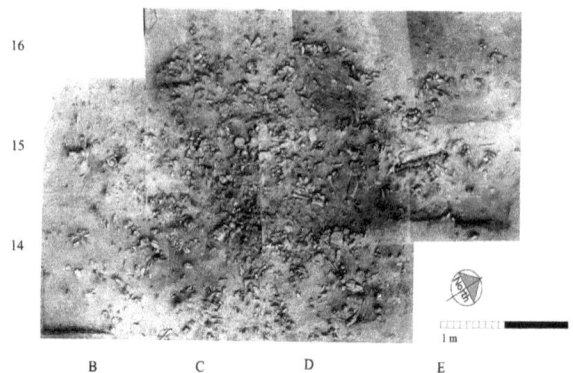

FIGURE 5.32 NORTH BONE MIDDEN IN VBC 190. NOTE ARTICULATED VERTEBRAE ABOVE E.

more frequently in II.22. Perhaps older animals were less nutritious and more fat-depleted and were more heavily processed on-site, while more nutritious younger and prime age carcasses and carcass segments were preferentially transported out, with higher nutrition better able to underwrite the transport costs.

There is, however, a simpler possibility. VBC 190 (Tables 4.1 and 4.2 above) contains a larger number of identifiable fauna, and of those fauna a larger number of crania and teeth. This seems reasonable, assuming that heads were removed generally nearer the kill or butchering site as opposed to residential areas. VBC 190 also contained a higher number of vertebrae and ribs, perhaps indicative of systematized, anatomical differences between the two areas based upon selective transport of limb elements into Secteurs 201 and 202, leaving axial elements behind in Secteur 190. The apparently larger number and proportion of older animals in VBC 190 may simply be skewed because of a preponderance of heads and teeth and other axial elements, and may not be age-mediated at all.

This interpretation would seem to support the identification of VBC 190 as the, or at least a, possible butchering/dismemberment area of the site in relation to the residence/hearth/activity areas. Yet, this too is problematic upon consideration of the simple proportion of crania and mandibles per each of the two secteurs. VBC 190 contained 28 crania and 85 mandible (sum = 113), which for a total NISP of 1,566 is 7.2%. Secteur 202 Level II.22 contained 8 crania and 17 mandibles (sum = 25), out of a total NISP of 386, or 6.48%. The head and mandible proportions are thus quite comparable in relation to NISP in both 190 and II.22.

If the head and mandible proportions are similar, then it is difficult to invoke supernumerosity of heads and mandibles in 190 as a skewing agent for the divergent crown height age profiles. Similar proportions of heads should result in similar age profiles for the two secteurs as long as the populations were similar. This in itself suggests strongly that very dissimilar age cohorts composed the fauna in VBC 190 and 202 II.22. Whereas it could be noted that VBC II.22 may represent a single occupation while 190 might represent several, one needs to reconsider Figures 5.8 and 5.9 above. Even if 190 represents a succession of occupations, the general age profile would not be greatly affected. For VBC 202, crown height age profiles from levels II.1, II.2, II.21, and II.3 are highly concordant. VBC 190 is highly skewed towards animals estimated to be of age 10 + years. It is a very different sample.

Based upon the currently available evidence, it appears that different carcass age classes are present in VBC 190 and 202 II.22. These differing age class cohorts have resulted in a very different age structure in the two secteurs, based upon the very different carcass ages. This structural difference can be interpreted several ways; 1) as a superfluity of geriatric carcasses in 190; 2) as a general but magnified absence of younger to prime-age carcasses in 190; 3) some combination of both 1 and 2. This structural difference between 190 and 202 II.22 is not relative to a functional difference between the two so much as it is based upon an apparent spatial segregation of geriatric from younger carcasses. In other words, it might represent a faint glimpse of a subsistence strategy premised upon the age-mediated differential evaluation and treatment of carcasses.

Chapter 6 GPR Results

Herein are discussed the various results of the three GPR applications relevant to the study: the sandbox, the saddle club pseudo-site, and Verberie, France. In each of the three applications, highly encouraging results were obtained for use on buried Paleolithic materials. Furthermore, the results detailed herein should serve as examples for further methodological/experimental research in the application of GPR to solve archaeological problems. The studies are presented sequentially, beginning with the experimental applications and ending with Verberie.

GPR Results from the Sandbox

GPR surveys were taken of the sandbox in October 2007 and May 2008. The 2.5 m² sandbox of one meter depth was surveyed using the University of Iowa's GPR panoply of a Geophysical Survey Systems, Inc. (GSSI) SIR-3000 radar unit, with 400 MHz and 900 MHz antennae. Sample (profile) intervals were 25 cm for the 400 and 10 cm for the 900. Standard radar settings were used for passes: 512 samples per scan, 64 scans per second, 40 scans per meter, hi-pass filtering at 800 MHz and low-pass filtering at 200 MHz. Due to the restricted size of the sandbox, a survey wheel for automatically entering distance metric data was unusable. Metric distance data was entered by hand for the sandbox, with ticks at 25 cm intervals. The data analysis included the use of Dr. Larry Conyer's software (GPR_Process, GPR_Viewer, available at http://mysite.du.edu/~lconyer/), as well as the commercial software Surfer, LView, and Slicer-Dicer. The best of all the sandbox results are summarized here.

Of the targets listed above in Table 5.2, five produced reflections of detail sufficient for quality imaging by the GPR. The visible targets were the Pincevent flint core, the pseudo fluvial channel and point bar in the base-level gravel, the simulated limestone hearth, and two "bone scatters", numbers 3 and 5. The fluvial channel (and its false point bar) and hearth were expected to be visible, being the two largest and materially densest of the targets. Both produced reflections of good detail. Figure 6.1 below details the channel, Figure 6.2 the hearth. The next most visible target was the Pincevent core, figure 6.3 below. Of the bone and lithic scatters from Table 5.2 above, only numbers 3 and 5 were visible in substantial detail (Figures 6.4 and 6.5 below). The sheep skeleton was entirely absent. In both sandbox surveys conditions were dry.

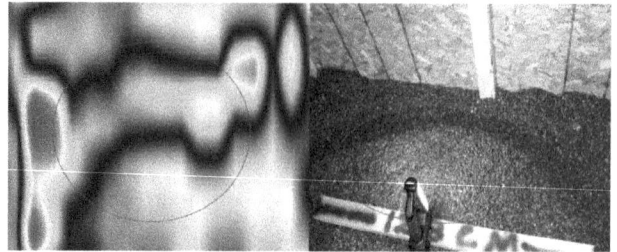

FIGURE 6.1. PSEUDO CHANNEL AND POINT BAR, RED OVALS, NOTE ROUNDED SHAPE OF TARGET AT LEFT.

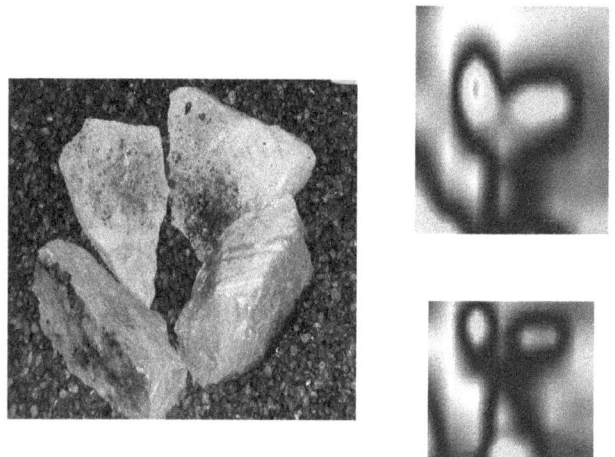

FIGURE 6.2. HEARTH AT LEFT, GPR IMAGES 10.5 NS (UPPER RIGHT) AND 11 NS (LOWER RIGHT). NOTE GPR IMAGING DETAIL OF INDIVIDUAL STONES.

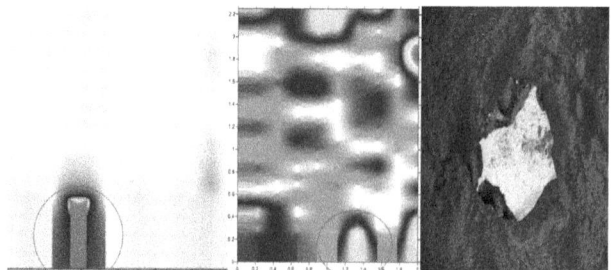

FIGURE 6.3. PINCEVENT FLINT CORE: LEFT, 900 MHz IMAGE AT 3.5 NS, (MIDDLE) 400 MHz ANTENNA AT 5 NS, PHOTO AT RIGHT.

62

Figure 6.4. Scatter #3 above red oval, 900 MHz image at 6.5 ns below.

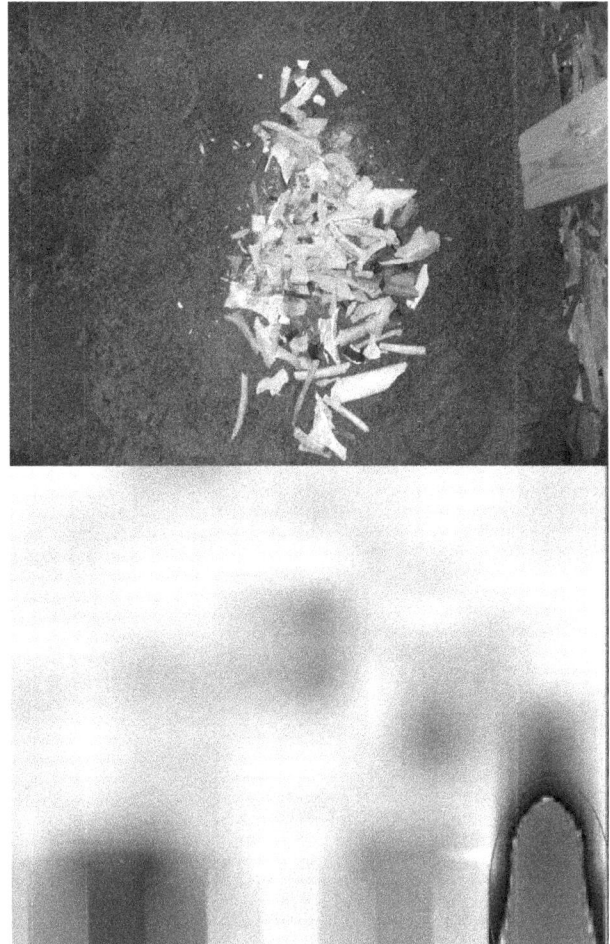

Figure 6.5. Scatter #5 above, 900 MHz image at 1.5 ns, note shapes and edge of sandbox wall at right in photo.

Gilman Saddle Club Results

GPR surveys were taken at the main show arena of the Gilman Saddle Club in March 2009 under fully saturated moisture conditions and July 2010 during a rare dry Iowa summer interval. The exposed area was surveyed using the University of Iowa's GPR panoply of a Geophysical Survey Systems, Inc. (GSSI) SIR-3000 radar unit, with 400 MHz and 900 MHz antennae. Sample (profile) intervals were 25 cm for both antennae. Standard radar settings were used for passes: 512 samples per scan, 64 scans per second, 40 scans per meter, hi-pass filtering at 800 MHz and low-pass filtering at 200 MHz. Since the pseudo site was situated outside it was not restrictive as the sandbox, so a survey wheel for automatically entering distance metric data was usable. Metric distance data was entered automatically by a survey wheel for the saddle club test, with ticks at 1m intervals. The data analysis included the use of Dr. Larry Conyer's software (GPR_Process, GPR_Viewer, available at http://mysite.du.edu/~lconyer/), as well as the commercial software Surfer, LView, and Slicer-Dicer. The best of all the saddle club results are summarized here.

In general, the saddle club results were "better" than those from the sandbox test. As above, the saddle club experiment was constructed with only four targets, each of which was situated at a generally consistent elevation of about 50 cm below surface. The sandbox experiment has consisted of eleven targets, at different elevations, some situated atop others. Lacking superimposed targets, the saddle club imagery is of a much higher 3D quality. The sheep skeleton at the saddle club, as in the sandbox (in fact, the very same skeleton to the bone), indicated generally poor GPR visibility. The skeleton was, however, at least partially visible under both saturated and dry sampling conditions, which indicates a very fertile area for future research. The remaining three targets (false hearth, false lithic scatter, and a composite lithic/bone/stone scatter) proved highly visible (Figures 6.6, 6.7, 6.8, 6.9, 6.10, and 6.11 below).

FIGURE 6.6. GILMAN SADDLE CLUB PSEUDO SITE, LOOKING NORTH.

FIGURE 6.6. GILMAN SADDLE CLUB PSEUDO SITE, LOOKING NORTH.

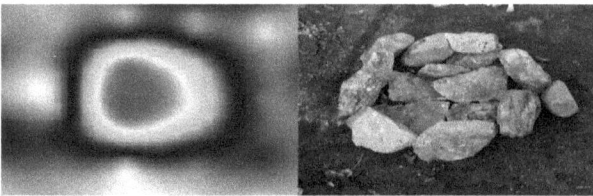

FIGURE 6.7. 2009 GPR IMAGE 400 MHz AT 7 NS LEFT, HEARTH PHOTO AT RIGHT.

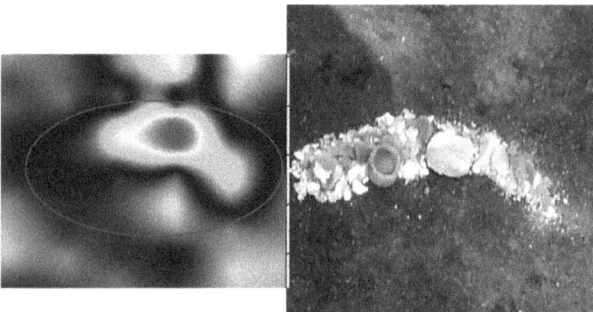

FIGURE 6.8. 2009 GPR IMAGE 400 MHz AT 8 NS LEFT, LITHIC ARC PHOTO AT RIGHT.

FIGURE 6.9. 2009 COMPOSITE SCATTER, GPR 400 MHz IMAGE AT 4 NS, PHOTO AT RIGHT.

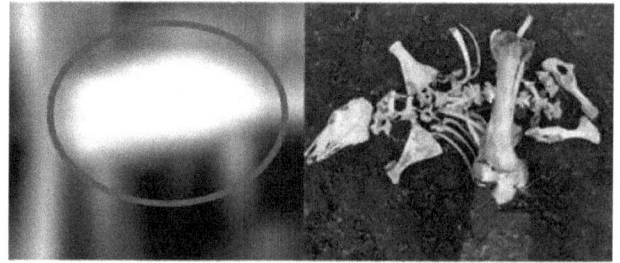

FIGURE 6.10. 2009 SHEEP SKELETON, 400 MHz IMAGE AT ~5 NS LEFT, PHOTO AT RIGHT. NOTE ANGLE ORIENTATION SW TO NE (FROM THOMPSON AND STOREY 2010, FIGURES 8 AND 14).

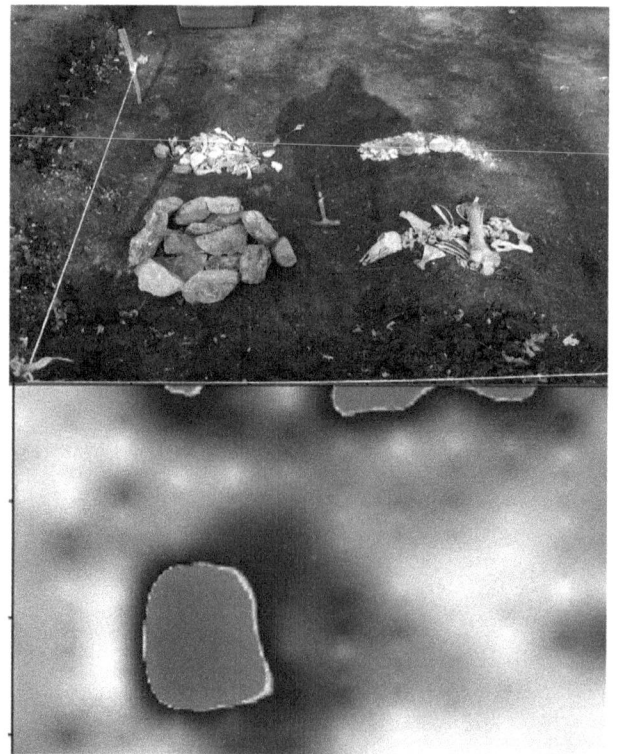

FIGURE 6.11. 2010 SADDLE CLUB PHOTO ABOVE, GPR IMAGE 900 MHz AT 28 NS BELOW. NOTE COMPLETE ABSENCE OF SHEEP SKELETON.

As can be seen, the two GPR experiments were quite successful in producing plan-view, two-dimensional images of the target items in both the sandbox and at the saddle club. With the exceptions of some superimposed, palimpsest target orientations in the sandbox, the targets were revealed, in generally good detail. Superimposition of targets in the sandbox, however, seems to have had the effect of removing much of the 3D information from the GPR sections, even from the largest, densest targets. The sheep skeleton, both in the sandbox and at the saddle club, was very difficult to image. Under the wet conditions of the March 2009 saddle club survey, the skeleton was more visible than under the dry 2010 conditions. This might relate to the pooling of water or ice around and/or beneath the skeleton under saturated conditions. Under dry conditions, the sheep skeleton was basically absent, even using the higher-resolution 900 MHz antenna (Figure 6.11 above). Surface slope gradient (essentially variable at the saddle club in 2009 due to high saturation), target surface slope gradient, and soil moisture content (differential soil electrical conductivity) clearly impacted the differential 2D results from the two separate surveys of the saddle club (Thompson and Storey 2010). Simultaneous imaging of multiple targets was best under dry conditions, despite the apparent difficulty in imaging the sheep skeleton.

3D GPR Images at Gilman Saddle Club

GPR's ability to produce three-dimensional images represents one of the technology's most attractive benefits for application in archaeology, including Paleolithic archaeology. In both the 2009 and 2010 surveys at the Gilman saddle club, high-quality three-dimensional imagery of the targets was produced. As above, the 2009 survey produced better images of the sheep skeleton—or, perhaps more accurately, images of the sheep skeleton plus water or ice pooled beneath and around it—than was the case in the 2010 survey. The simulated hearth, lithic arc scatter, and composite bone/lithic/stone targets produced particularly outstanding 3D images during the 2010 900 MHz survey (Figure 6.12 below). Note the "depth" of this 3D imagery, especially of the false hearth.

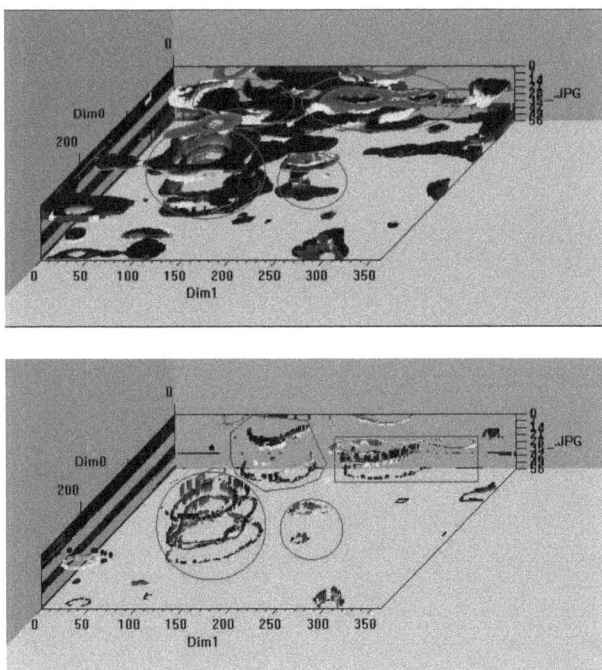

FIGURE 6.12. TOP: 3D SLICER-DICER IMAGE WITH ALL TARGETS "OVALED". BOTTOM: 3D SLICER-DICER IMAGE SHOWING BASAL LEVEL OF ALL TARGETS: LARGE OVAL = HEARTH, SMALL OVAL = SKELETON, POLYGON = COMPOSITE TARGET, AND RECTANGLE = LITHIC ARC (FROM THOMPSON AND STOREY 2010, FIGURE 6).

Yet, excellent 3D results of the composite target and the hearth were also produced during the saturated 2009 survey (Figures 6.13 and 6.14 below).

Figure 6.15 below clearly shows a compacted clay layer on which the fake hearth is sitting. This clay layer was visible to the radar under wet conditions in 2009 but not when dry in 2010. Another part of the same clay layer is also visible in Figure 6.13 above, showing the composite multimaterial target. GPR's ability to image target shape, depth, and the 3D aspects of and associations between material entities is unquestionably and starkly visible.

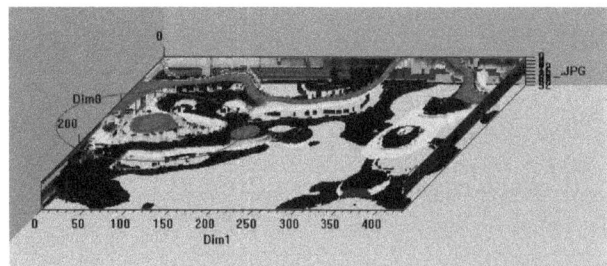

FIGURE 6.13. 2009 3D 400 MHz IMAGE OF COMPOSITE TARGET, NW QUAD SADDLE CLUB, OVALED.

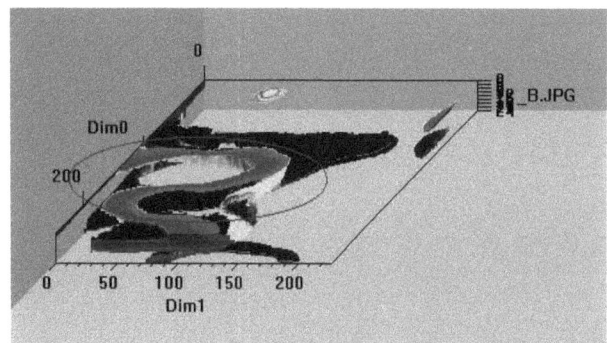

FIGURE 6.14. 2009 3D 400 MHz IMAGE OF HEARTH, SW QUAD SADDLE CLUB, OVALED. NOTE CIRCULARITY AND DEPTH OF THE FEATURE. COMPARE TO FIGURE 6.15 BELOW.

GPR at Verberie

During the field season of 2006, a detailed series of GPR surveys were conducted at the site of Verberie. A multi-tiered format was used to attempt to develop the highest resolution subsurface imaging of unexcavated portions of the site: signature reflections of archaeological deposits were established in the field through the use of 1 m, 50 cm, and 25 cm profile grid spacings, mainly using the 400 MHz antenna. Once signature reflections of intact archaeological deposits were established, tighter profile intervals of 12.5 and 10 cm increments were employed using the 900 MHz antenna. As a general rule, GPR antennae with lower MHz resolution offer deeper subsurface penetration but sacrifice target resolution. Higher MHz antennae offer much higher target resolutions, but sacrifice subsurface penetration.

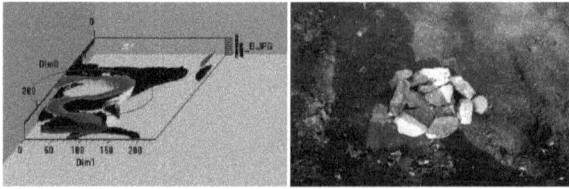

Figure 32. 3D Slicer-Dicer Image of Hearth SW Unit (oval). Hearth Clearly Sitting On Darker Basal Surface. Compare Shapes.*

*Scale relates to pixel numbers not actual spatial scale.

FIGURE 6.15. SIDE-BY-SIDE 3D 400 MHz GPR IMAGE OF HEARTH AT LEFT, PHOTO AT RIGHT. NOTE DARK SURFACE IN GPR IMAGE AND COMPACTED CLAY SURFACE IN PHOTO.

The complementary use of both a 400 MHz and 900 MHz antenna offer a very wide range of subsurface sampling and imaging capabilities.

The primary focus of the 2006 surveys were the areas to the northwest, north, and directly east of the known, excavated portion of the site located in Secteur 202. The cessation of major excavations in 2002 left at least one north profile exposure of significant middens (Figure 5.1 above). Figure 6.16 below is an oblique aerial photo of VBC looking basically west. Figure 6.17 below indicates the locations of the known archaeological deposits in 202. GPR grids (see also Table 5.3 above). Of the 23 grids total,

FIGURE 6.16. OBLIQUE AERIAL PHOTO OF VBC. SITE IS ON BROWN PLEISTOCENE POINT BAR AT CENTER.

only three are actually featured herein: Grids 3, 7, and 23, all of which partially overlap the primary archaeological deposits in Secteur 202. Unfortunately, while nearly all of the Verberie GPR grids revealed some useful information, time and space limitations force a focus on only those grids most directly relevant to this research. For example, the total number of GPR profiles (hence individual radar files) taken during VBC 2006 was 1,899. The profiles consist of both x profiles (taken west to east) and y profiles (taken south to north).

An overview of materials GPR was expected to image at VBC may serve to explain the necessity of variable survey parameters. Figure 6.19 below shows an actual archaeological exposure from VBC detailing the sorts of material and spatial configurations GPR would need to

image; Figure 6.20 shows actual GPR images of grids 3, 7, and 23 superimposed on the main basemap of plotted, excavated artifacts. Recalling Figure 5.1, above, the unexcavated materials at VBC can be expected to consist of both thin discontinuous layers as well as much denser, more continuous accumulations, quite similar to excavated material in most respects. Thus, the GPR sampling format needed to be able to image relatively dense features as well as sparse or even absences of artifactual material (or 'voids'). In terms of individual material size, the sampling format needed to detect or "see" objects from small submeter size (10-20 cm diameter at depths ranging between 50 to100 cm) to much larger and denser potential hearths, even middens and scatters spread across multiple units.

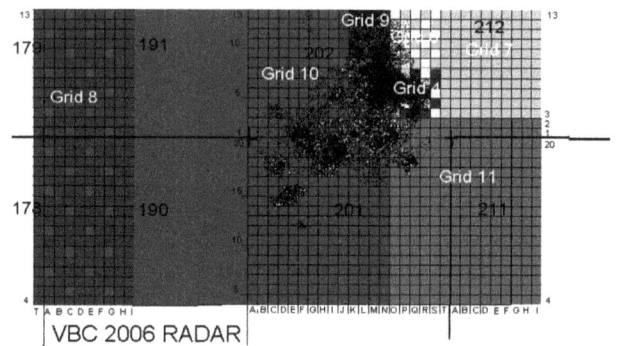

FIGURE 6.17. 2006 GPR GRIDS AT VBC (NOTE BLACK ARCHAEOLOGICAL MATERIAL) PLAN VIEW.

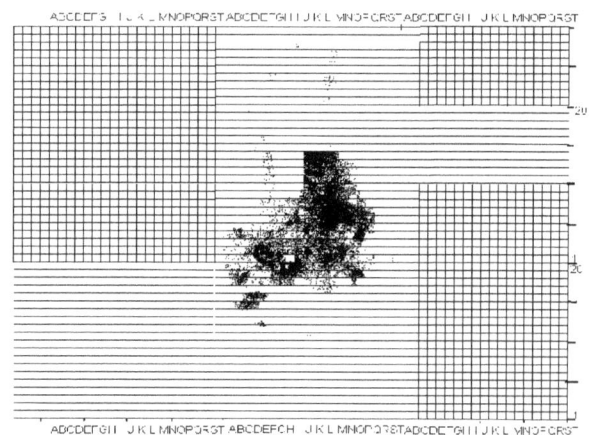

FIGURE 6.18. SECTEUR 202 KNOWN ARCHAEOLOGICAL DEPOSITS PLAN VIEW.

FIGURE 6.19. VBC EXCAVATION, SHOWING HEARTH AT CENTER RIGHT, LITHIC, BONE, AND FCR SCATTERS.

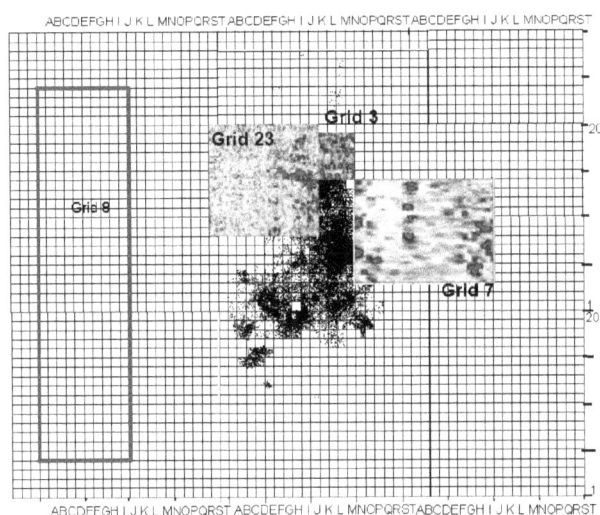

FIGURE 6.20. GPR IMAGES OF GRIDS 3, 7, 23 SITUATED ON PLOTTED EXCAVATION BASEMAP.

Verberie

GPR Results: Grids

Grid 3

VBC Grid 3 (5 m²) was emplaced immediately north of the exposed north wall of Secteur 202, Units J-N (Figure 5.1 above). The survey was performed with the 900 MHz antenna and survey wheel apparatus, at 25 cm profile intervals, at a time-depth interval of 30 nanoseconds. Since there were actual photos of the unexcavated material along the southern margin of Grid 3, direct side-by-side comparisons were possible between photos and GPR images. Figure 6.21 and 6.22, below, show such comparisons. In them it is possible to see both larger, dense archaeological "midden" deposits, consisting of lithics, bones, and various limestones, and even very fine, detailed items such as individual rocks, breaks, and disconformities in the stratigraphy. In some cases the disconformity

between the Pleistocene sand matrix of the site and the humic silt overburden was visible. Such minute details were unexpected. They suggest that the radar sampling design performed very well at this site. Had the survey not produced correspondences between the photos and the GPR images the GPR research design would likely have been seriously flawed.

The plan views of the Grid 3 GPR survey also produced excellent imagery, which was again conducive to a more or less direct, side by side (or 'edge-on') comparison with an actual exposure photograph, in Figure 6.23 below. In this instance, the same photo from Figures 6.21 and 6.22 above was used, to generally good and informative effect. It shows the excellent correspondence between the materials exposed and the GPR time-slice (10-12 ns). Figure 6.23 also clearly shows the straight, truncated southern edges of the archaeological deposits that resulted from partial excavation and leaving the material in the wall. Since both profiles and time-slices were successful in imaging subsurface material, it was then possible to look for similar kinds of material targets in other areas of the sites, at similar depths, perhaps (but not necessarily) in similar scales, distributions, and configurations. A sense may be gained of the three dimensional configuration of the unexcavated material in Grid 3 in Figure 6.24 below. In all the GPR images, from the profiles, to the plan-view time-slices, to the 3D constructions, a set of three primary accumulations is visible, tapering off towards the north away from the hearth area of Secteur 202.

Grid 7

VBC Grid 7 (165 m²) was emplaced immediately east of the hearth area of Secteur 202, in the previously excavated Units O-T, 3 to 13, and Secteur 212 Units A-I, 3 to 13 (Figure 6.20 above). This survey was performed with the 400 MHz antenna and survey wheel apparatus, at 50 cm profile intervals, at a time-depth interval of 15 nanoseconds. The wider spacing and shallower depth calibration relate to the prior excavations; the finding of little new material was expected. In accordance with that expectation, if there was any Paleolithic occupation in Grid it appears most of this rather large area was previously excavated, with the possible exception of the southeast corner (Figure 6.25 below). Archaeologically empty or retired/excavated space shows primarily as white or light blue. A large linear feature was noted in Grid 7, measuring approximately seven meters in length, one meter width. Notwithstanding its unusually symmetrical dimensions, this feature is also oriented quite obviously according to the site grid parameters, tracking directly map North and map South. Figure 6.26 below portrays a 3D image of this feature, which seems pretty clearly to be a trench. Whether this feature is a test trench or a drainage feature for removing runoff is difficult to determine.

At the western (left) extremity of Grid 7, there is a very symmetrical, cylindrical target, perhaps one meter or less in diameter. This feature appears to continue below the depth sampling threshold (15 ns) for Grid 7, so there is no way from these data to gauge this item's depth. This target first becomes visible at 12 ns, which in this matrix sediment probably equates to approximately 72 cm in depth. The item is visible as a red circle in Figure 6.25 below, and the 3D images in Figures 6.29 and 6.30 below show its cylindrical shape and symmetry. Given the strength of this target signal and its symmetry, it does appear it could be the poured concrete site datum used during excavations to calibrate the theodolite.

Along the eastern edge of Grid 7, are several areas that appear potentially to be intact archaeological deposits, although based on the signal strength of the targets they are more likely to be some type of post-backfilling disturbance. In most of the VBC GPR images, strong subsurface signatures show as red and orange. The material in the eastern margin of Grid 7 are also red and orange, indicating a strong GPR reflection amplitude difference between the sediment matrix and the materials (Figure 6.31, below). These materials are, however, quite strongly oriented linearly in relation to the grid, both between and on gridlines. It is unlikely that *in situ* archaeological material would show such strong linearity in conjunction with an arbitrary grid. In Figure 6.32 below, this "linearity" can also be seen to have a distinct three dimensional quality. It would appear that the material in the eastern portion of Grid 7 is related to previous excavation disturbance and backfilling, according to the site grid schematic. None of the other archaeological deposits at VBC feature such strong tendencies towards grid linearity. For example, one might expect this feature to have a linear eastern margin, since that would represent the eastern edge of the Grid 7 itself. Yet, Figure 6.32 below shows that the feature also has a visible *western* linear edge to it, which one would not expect from archaeological deposits. It would be very unlikely indeed for the archaeology to be oriented according to our grids.

Grid 23

VBC Grid 23 (144 m²) was emplaced immediately northwest of the hearth area of Secteur 202. The grid occupies Secteur 191 Units S-T 8-19, and Secteur 202 Units A-J 8-19 (Figure 5.1 above). The survey was performed with the 900 MHz antenna and survey wheel apparatus, at 10 cm profile intervals, at a time-depth interval of 15 nanoseconds. Grid 23 revealed excellent imagery of what are very likely to be *in situ* archaeological deposits, oriented and located clearly in relation to the hearth area of Secteur 202 (Figures 5.1, above and 6.33, below). The main feature, located in Secteur 202, Units E-J 10-14, is approximately 7 meters in length and perhaps 1.5 meters in width. The feature is clearly oriented from the hearth area to the northwest of the VBC grid (Figure 6.33, below). Strong amplitude differences between this target and the surrounding sediment suggest the feature is materially

very dense. The Grid 23 feature is present in time-slices between 11 ns and 14 ns, making it approximately 20 cm in depth, average depth about 70 cm.

Three-dimensional imaging of the feature in Grid 23 proved very successful, as evinced by Figures 6.34 to 6.39 below. Unlike the material in the east edge of Grid 7, the Grid 23 feature is apparently neither linearly oriented in relation to the site grid nor does it indicate any linear affinity to a superimposed grid (Figures 6.33, below, see also Figures 6.37, 6.38, 6.39). When a 3D image of the feature was rotated along a pitch axis to the north, no apparently linearity is observed from above or below it (Figures 6.35 and 6.36). No indication of linear orientation appears when a 3D image of the feature was rotated counterclockwise along its vertical axis (Figures 6.37, 6.38, and 6.39 below). Given the feature's high amplitude reflections, its thickness, its scale and configuration, and its evident association with previously excavated material, it appeared quite likely that it was composed of *in situ* archaeological deposits.

In the field season of 2009, ten 1 x 1 units were excavated in and around Grid 23. Those units were Secteur 202, Units D-C 19-20, D 9, F 19, H 9, I 9, H-I 14-15. These ten units are shown in Figure 6.40, below, four of which (H-I 14-15) intersected with the large Grid 23 feature and produced artifacts. Multiple occupation surfaces were encountered arranged in a palimpsest manner, corresponding to previous Levels II.1, II.2, II.22 and II.3. Figure 6.41, below, portrays a photograph of Units H-I 14-15, Level II.22 from Secteur 202, showing the artifacts from that level in relation to the GPR imagery. Level II.4 in Unit I 14 and I 15 is visible in Figure 6.42 and 6.43 below. In this case, GPR successfully located a pattern that appeared to be anthropogenic. When the area containing the observed pattern was sampled, archaeological material was indeed located *in situ*. Lithics, bone, and fire-cracked rock were each present in the 2009 excavations, indicating that the GPR was able to detect multiple materials at variable depths, just as it had done in the sandbox and saddle club experiments. By any measure this was a successful application of very detailed GPR tomography at a Paleolithic archaeological site.

Summary

Above was summarized a tripartite research agenda to use ground-penetrating radar to assist in pattern recognition at a Paleolithic open-air site. An extensive battery of experimental tests was used to calibrate and refine the methods by which anthropogenic patterning visible in unexcavated Paleolithic archaeological deposits could be identified. The two parallel and complementary experimental applications indicated that GPR would be usefully applicable in estimating buried material scale, orientation, and configuration at a Paleolithic site. The field application of GPR is augmented by such complimentary experimentation and methodological refinement. Having established the successful application of GPR at Verberie, the topic now at hand is interpreting the patterning observed along and the material excavated, both in relation to previously established material patterning, configuration, and content.

Software used for the analysis of this gpr data also allowed for the development of a technique for correlating gpr imagery "time-slices" or depth slices to produce images at predetermined depths. What follows is a very tedious description of an exceedingly tedious procedure. For example, Storey calculated the radar wave velocity at VBC 2006 to be 0.1058 m/ns. If that is an accurate velocity, what this means is that the radar wave travels through VBC sediment at a rate of about 10.6 centimeters per nanosecond, or just over one decimeter. A one-nanosecond depth slice at VBC is therefore 10.58 cm in thickness; a two-nanosecond depth slice is 21.16 cm thick, a three-nanosecond slice is 31.74 cm, etc. These thickness measures also indicate the maximal sampling depth of depth slices; i.e., "snapshot" views of reflections at -10.58 cm for a 1 ns slice, -21.16 cm for a 2 ns slice, etc. Let's assume the gpr was set to collect data from 0 to 40 ns (in some grids at VBC it was, in some it wasn't). Since we know that the radar wave at VBC penetrated 0.1058 m/ns, the total depth sampled at VBC would be a function of $0.1058 \times 40 = 4.232$ meters in total depth. If the gpr was set for 0 to 15 ns, the total depth would be $0.1058 \times 15 = 1.587$ meter total depth. Previous methods for creating and using time- or depth-slices with gpr have been to accept slices produced by software at the familiar whole number nanosecond intervals (i.e., 1, 2, 3, etc.) where actual imaging depth can by calculated by multiplying the time-depth in nanseconds by the radar wave velocity through the substrate to get an estimate of actual depth. Moreover, much attention has also been paid to appropriateness of radar transect spacing. Data for time-slices should be derived from closely-spaced, parallel profiles spaced less than one half the wavelength of reflections returned from the smallest target to be mapped (Conyers and Goodman 1997).

The gpr software used in this research allowed for the analysis of radar reflections at much finer time-depths, such as fractions of one nanosecond. Using the radar wave velocity of 0.1058 m/ns it is possible to set the software to produce images at fractional intervals, such as 1/10 of one nanosecond. For example, if a one-nanosecond depth slice at VBC penetrated to -10.58 cm depth, a 0.10 ns slice would penetrate -1.058 cm. Likewise, a 0.0945 ns slice would penetrate 1.0 cm, which is attainable by solving the equation $0.10/.01058 = x/.01$ where $x = 0.0945$.

What this means is that the processing software can be set to sample radar reflections from depths that correlated at VBC with known occupation surfaces, accurate to the centimeter. Audouze and Enloe (1997) suggested that discrete occupation surfaces at VBC in Secteurs 201 and 202 were found at the following elevations: Level II.1 = -1.15m; Level II.2 = -1.225 m; Level II.21 = -1.27 m; Level II.22 = -1.315 m; Level II.3 = -1.345 m; and Level II.4

= -1.39 m. If unexcavated archaeological materials were also deposited in discrete occupation surfaces, it is now possible to make depth slices accurate to the centimeter, and so we can image even unexcavated material distributions at the level of the occupation surfaces to which they may belong, which was accomplished for Grid 23 (Figures 6.44 through 6.49 below). This methodology has allowed for very precise imagery of Grid 23, correlated to the occupation surfaces listed in Audouze and Enloe (1997).

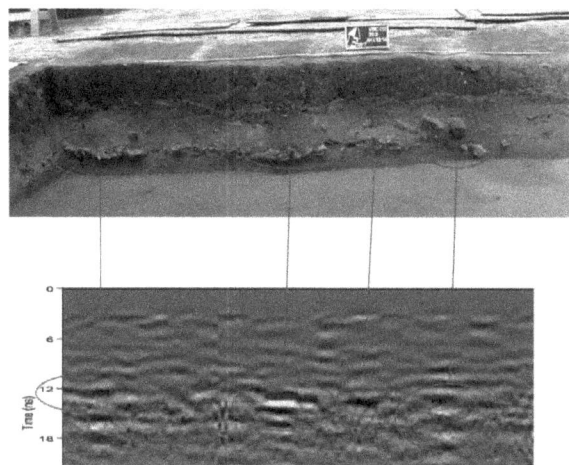

FIGURE 6.21. COMPARISON BETWEEN PHOTO AND GPR PROFILE GRID 3. NOTE CORRESPONDENCES BETWEEN ARCHAEOLOGICAL DEPOSITS.

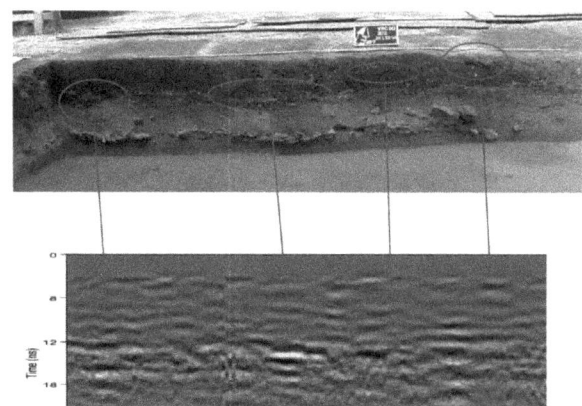

FIGURE 6.22. COMPARISON BETWEEN PHOTO AND GPR PROFILE GRID 3. NOTE CORRESPONDENCES BETWEEN STATIGRAPHY AND SMALL ITEMS.

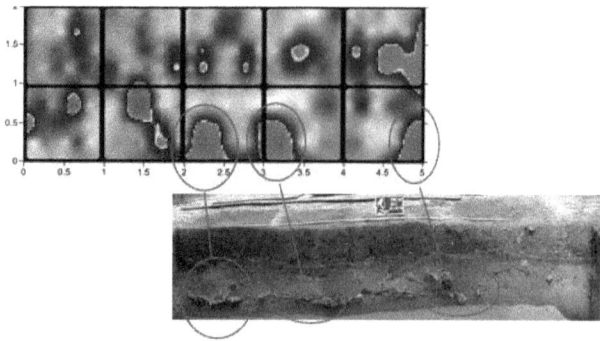

FIGURE 6.23. COMPARISON BETWEEN GPR PLAN VIEW TIME-SLICE (AT 10-12 NS) IN GRID 3. NOTE CORRESPONDENCES BETWEEN MATERIAL IN PLAN AND PROFILE, AND DIMENSIONS, DISTANCES.

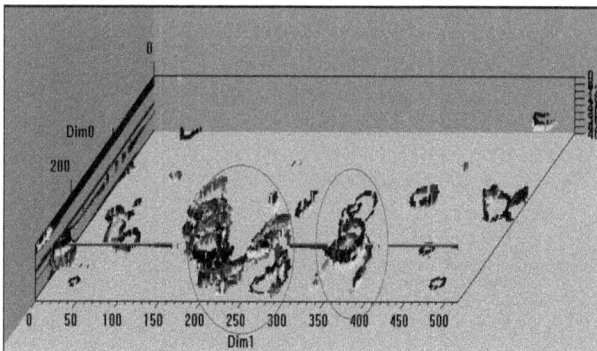

FIGURE 6.26. GRID 7 3D IMAGE. NOTE LINEAR TRENCH FEATURE, RED POLYGON.

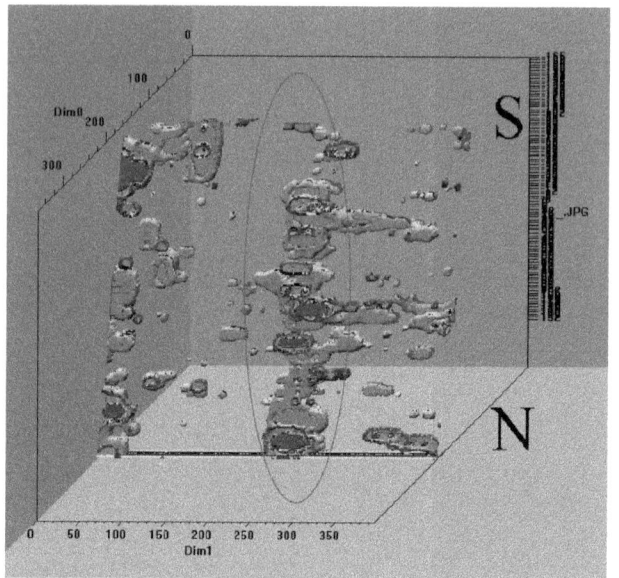

FIGURE 6.24. GRID 3 3D IMAGE SHOWING ASPECTS OF TARGET DEPTH CONFIGURATIONS.

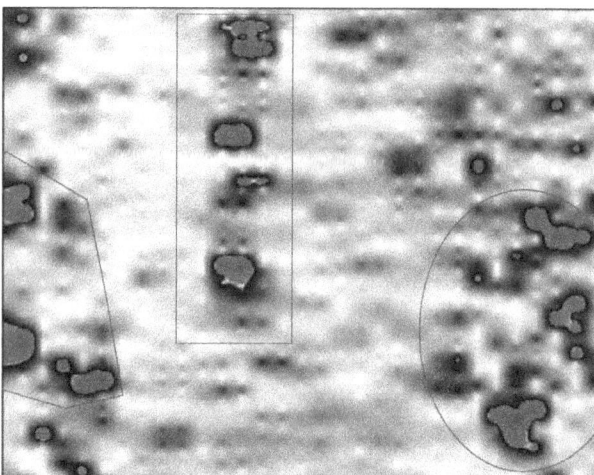

FIGURE 6.27. 3D GRID 7 IMAGE, INFERIOR VIEW OF LINEAR FEATURE RED OVAL.

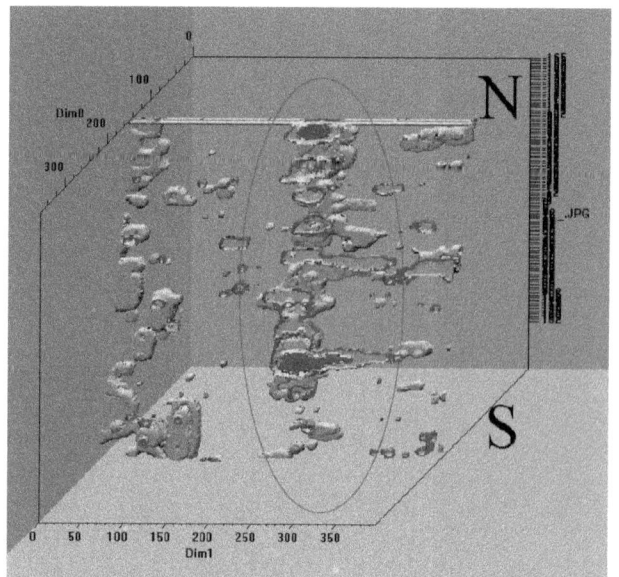

FIGURE 6.25. GRID 7 GPR TIME-SLICE (13 NS). NOTE POSSIBLE ARCHAEOLOGICAL MATERIAL AT LOWER RIGHT RED OVAL. NOTE LINEAR FEATURE CENTER RED RECTANGLE. NOTE POSSIBLE CONCRETE SITE DATUM AND ASSOCIATED BACKFILLING DISTURBANCES IN LEFT POLYGON.

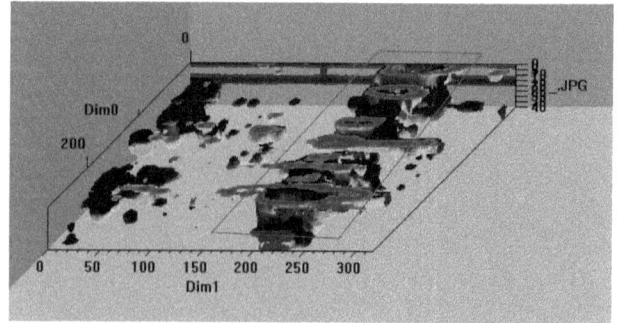

FIGURE 6.28. 3D GRID 7 IMAGE, SUPERIOR VIEW LINEAR FEATURE RED OVAL. NOTE ELONGATED PLOW FURROWS IN SUBSURFACE (ORANGE).

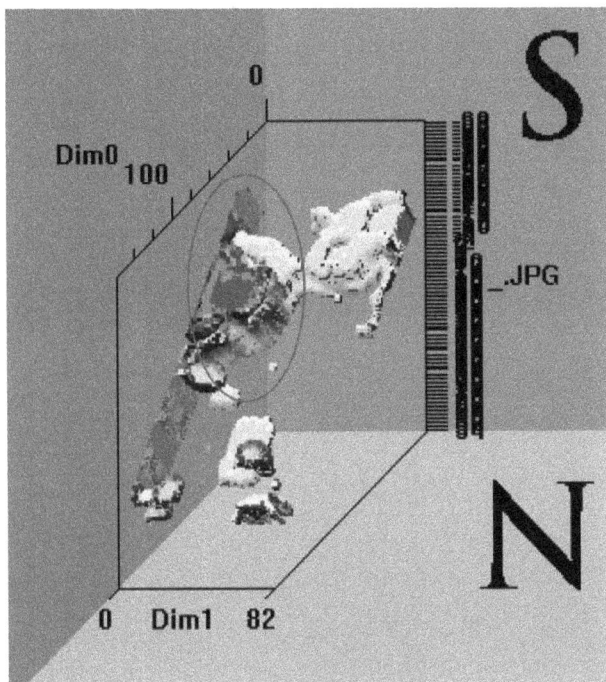

FIGURE 6.29. 3D IMAGE GRID 7, INFERIOR VIEW OF CEMENT SITE DATUM IN RED OVAL.

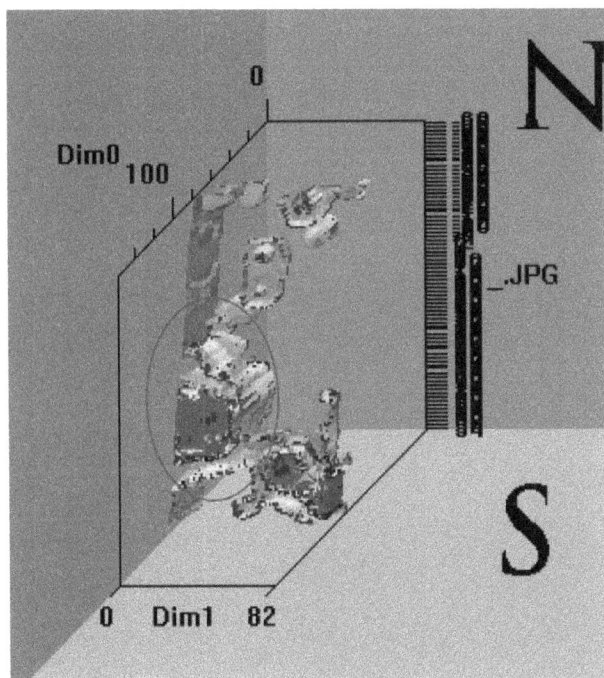

FIGURE 6.30. 3D IMAGE GRID 7, SUPERIOR VIEW OF CEMENT SITE DATUM IN RED OVAL. NOTE HIGHLY SYMMETRICAL, CYLINDRICAL SHAPE.

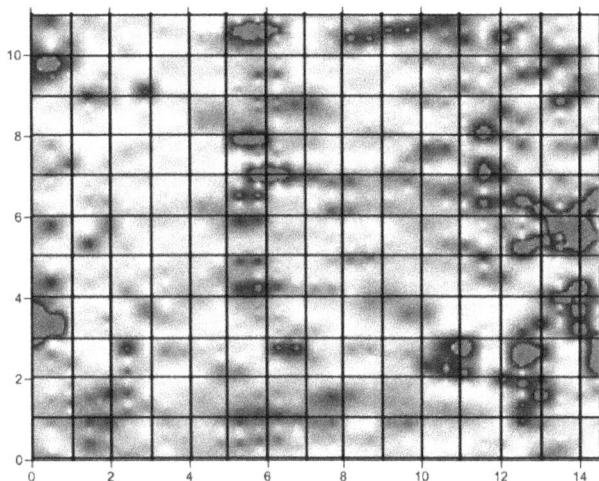

FIGURE 6.31. VBC 400 MHz 14 NS GRID 7 TIME-SLICE WITH SUPERIMPOSED GRID. NOTE MATERIALS FROM ~11 M TO EDGE OF SECTION AT FRIGHT AND LINEAR ARRANGEMENT WITH GRIDLINES. SITE DATUM AT EXTREME LEFT.

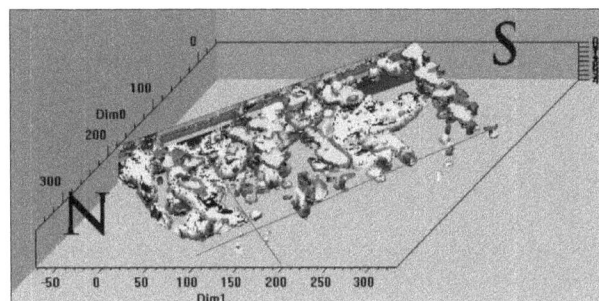

FIGURE 6.32. VBC 3D IMAGE GRID 7, LOOKING OBLIQUELY EAST. NOTE THE STRONG LINEARITY AND SYMMETRY OF FEATURES IN THE FAR EASTERN PORTION OF THE GRID. SURFICIAL PLOW FURROWS IN PURPLE.

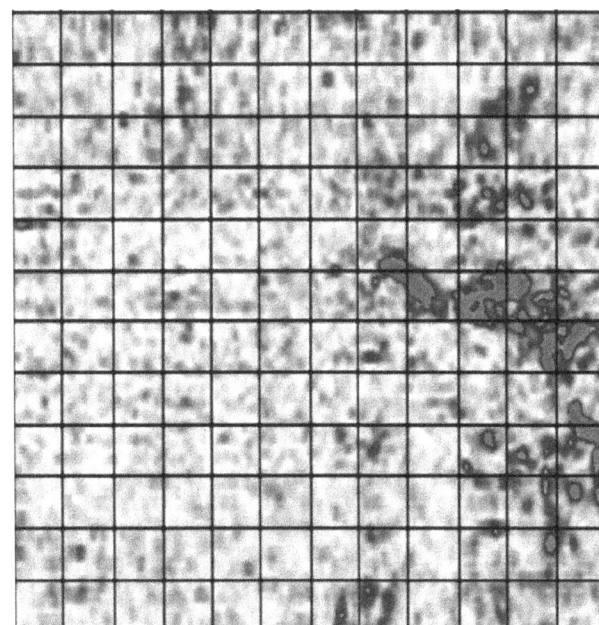

FIGURE 6.33. VBC 900 MHz 12 NS IMAGE OF GRID 23, NOTE FAR RIGHT CENTER.

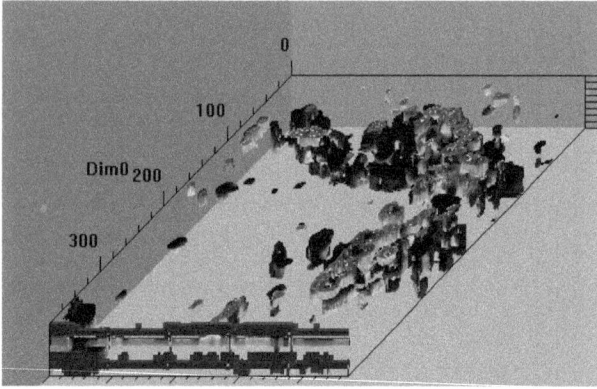

FIGURE 6.34. VBC GRID 23 900 MHz 3D IMAGE.

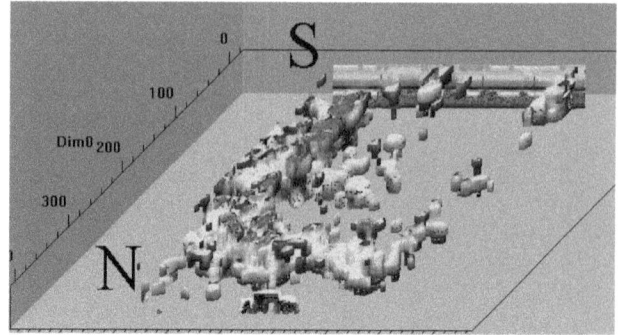

FIGURE 6.37. VBC GRID 23 3D IMAGE, OBLIQUE SUPERIOR VIEW FROM NORTHWEST.

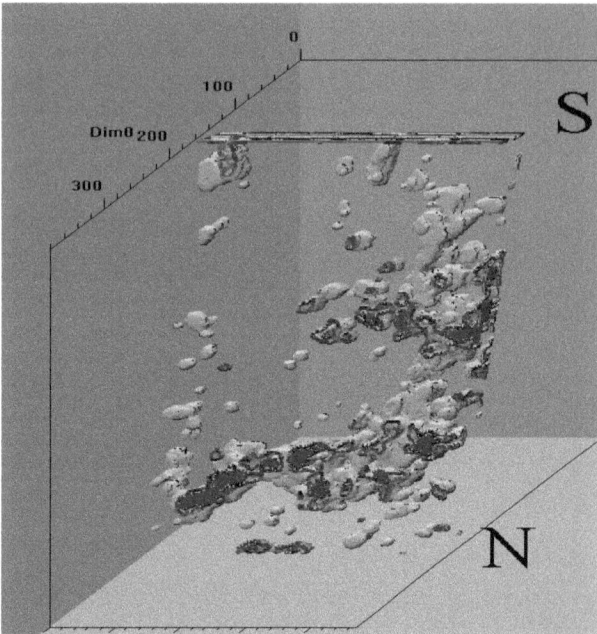

FIGURE 6.35. VBC GRID 23 3D IMAGE, INFERIOR VIEW.

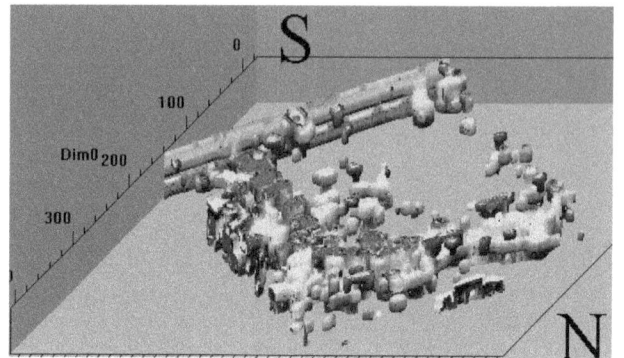

FIGURE 6.38. VBC GRID 23 3D IMAGE, OBLIQUE SUPERIOR VIEW FROM NORTH.

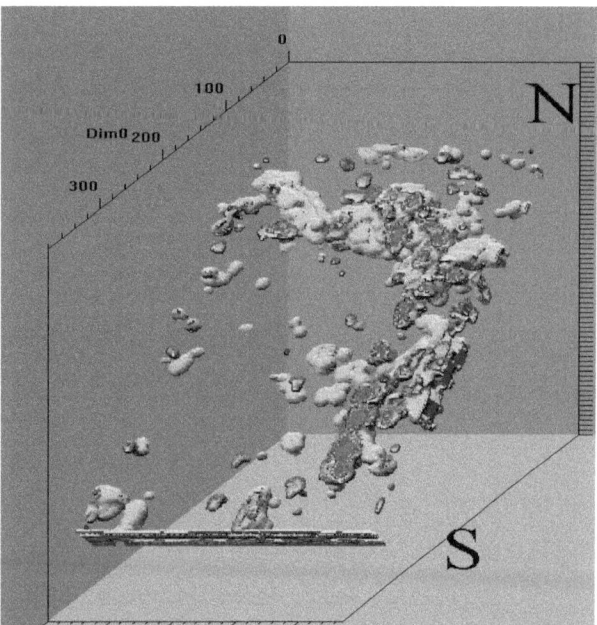

FIGURE 6.36. VBC GRID 23 3D IMAGE, SUPERIOR VIEW.

FIGURE 6.39. VBC GRID 23 3D IMAGE, OBLIQUE SUPERIOR VIEW FROM EAST.

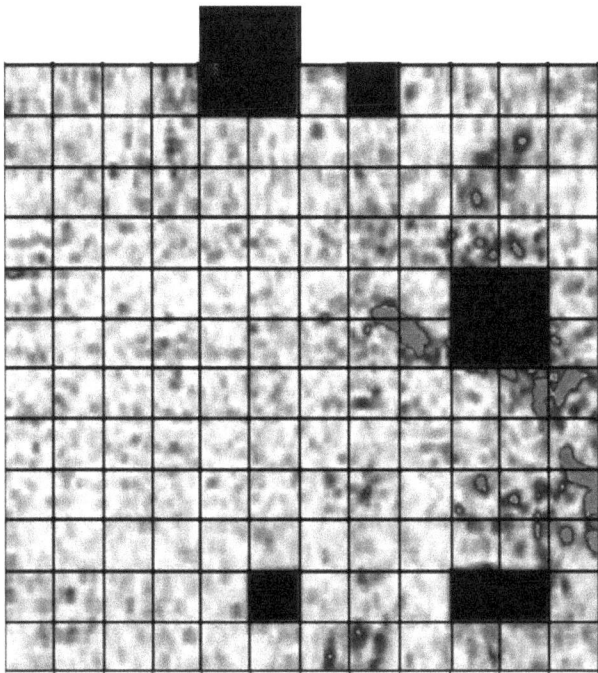

FIGURE 6.40. VBC GRID 23 900 MHz TIME-SLICE WITH GRID, 12 NS. 2009 TEST UNITS IN BLACK.

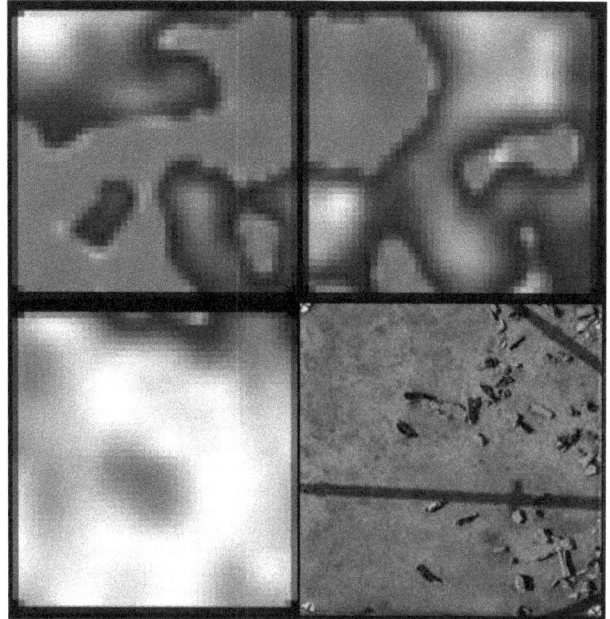

FIGURE 6.42. VBC SECTEUR 202 UNITS H-I 14-15 LEVEL II.4 (I 14 IN PHOTO).

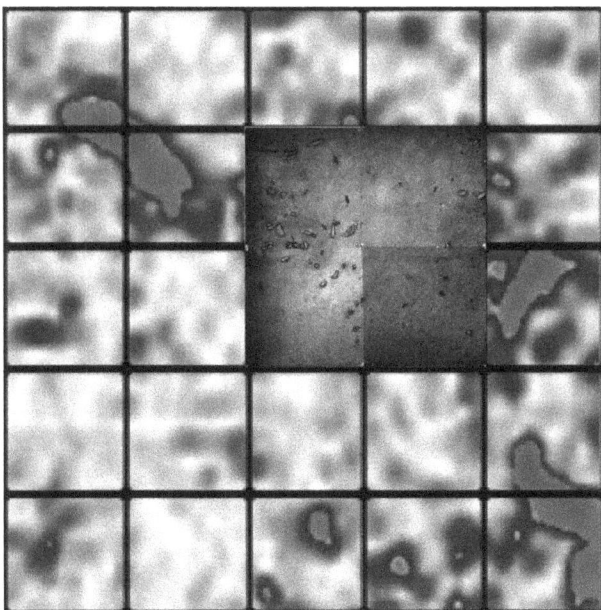

FIGURE 6.41. VBC GRID 23 900 MHz TIME-SLICE AT 12 NS. PHOTOPAN OF 202 LEVEL II.22 MATERIAL SUPERIMPOSED. 5 x 5 SECTION UNITS F-J 12-16, EXCAVATED UNITS H-I 14-15 SHOWN IN PHOTO.

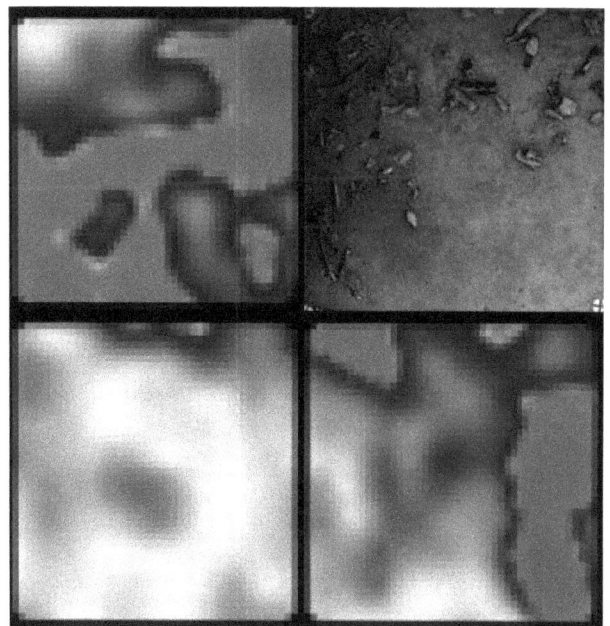

FIGURE 6.43. VBC SECTEUR 202 UNITS H-I 14-15 LEVEL II.4 (I 15 IN PHOTO).

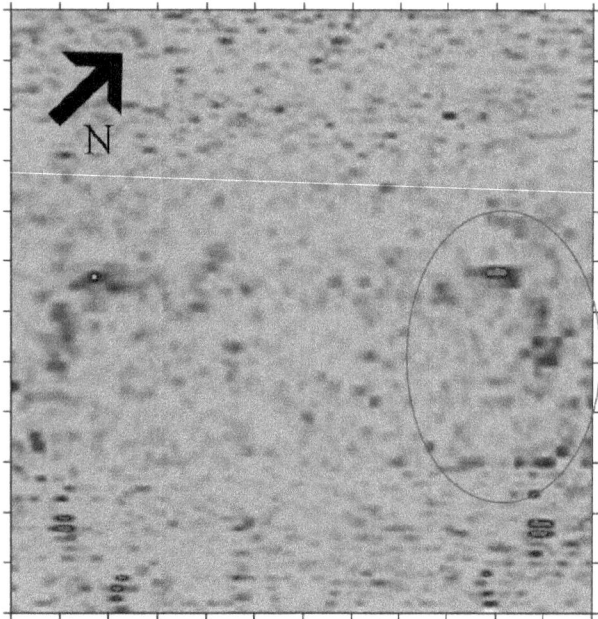

FIGURE 6.44. VBC 2006 GRID 23 "MICROSLICE" IMAGE
CORRELATED TO LEVEL II.1, -1.15 M.

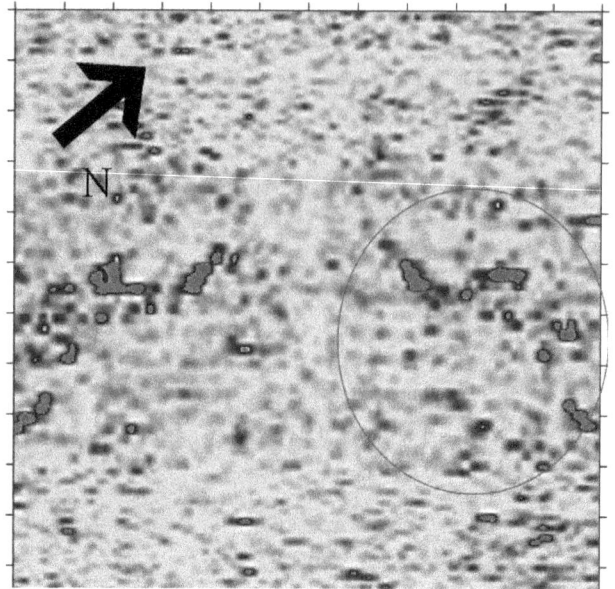

FIGURE 6.46. VBC 2006 GRID 23 "MICROSLICE" IMAGE
CORRELATED TO LEVEL II.21, -1.27 M.

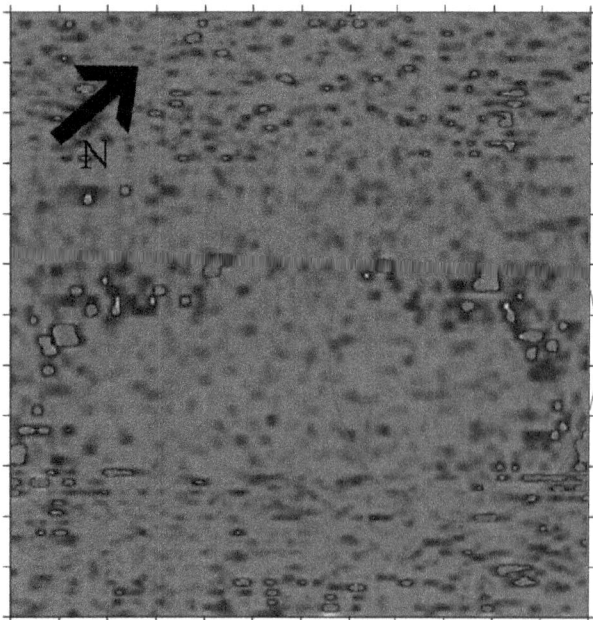

FIGURE 6.45. VBC 2006 GRID 23 "MICROSLICE" IMAGE
CORRELATED TO LEVEL II.2, -1.225 M.

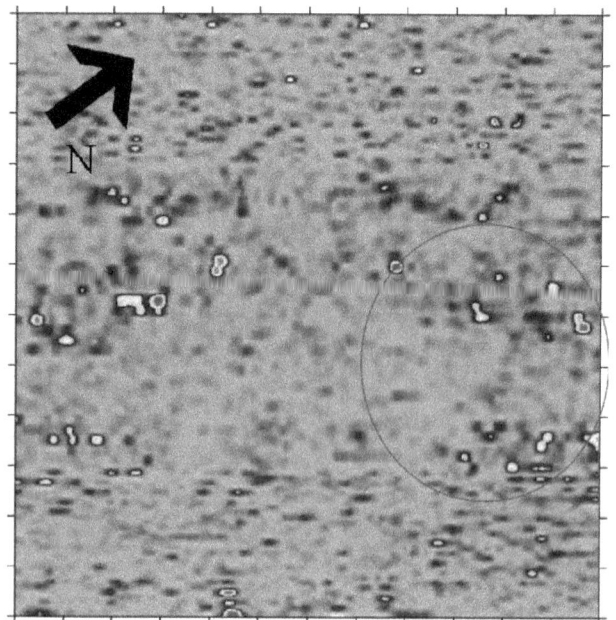

FIGURE 6.47. VBC 2006 GRID 23 "MICROSLICE" IMAGE
CORRELATED TO LEVEL II.22, -1.315 M.

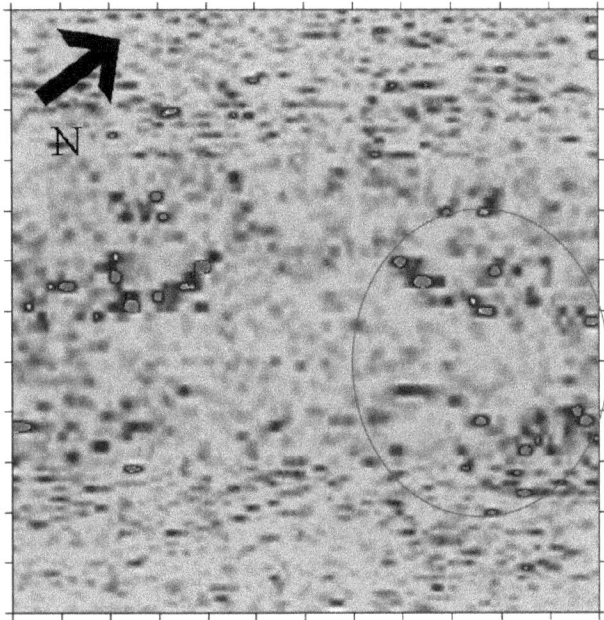

Figure 6.48. VBC 2006 Grid 23 "Microslice" image correlated to Level II.3, -1.345 m.

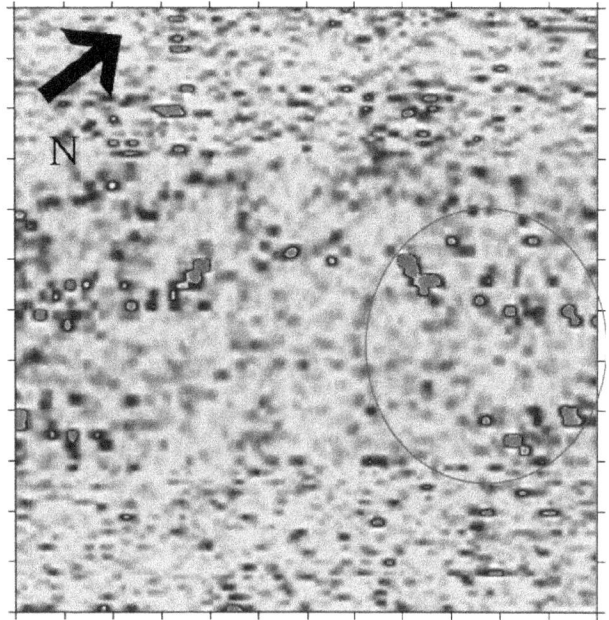

Figure 6.49. VBC 2006 Grid 23 "Microslice" image correlated to Level II.4, -1.4 m.

Chapter 7 GPR Summary

For this thesis, the exploratory and experimental use of Ground-penetrating radar was framed as a means to test material scale, configuration, and orientation in unexcavated portions at a Paleolithic open-air site. It was possible given decades of previous excavation at Verberie that, if unexcavated portions of the site were actually present then GPR should be able to "see" them, given the nature of the materials themselves and the sedimentary matrix of homogenous sand. The primary issue would be in identifying anthropogenic materials from the location, scale, configuration, and shape of target material and features at depth and through association with known materials. Resolution of this issue was proposed through pattern recognition for answering two main methodological questions: 1) How representative of the entire site assemblage is the currently excavated sample?; and 2) Are there data visible that are indicative of multiple, interacting "households" as at Pincevent, or does the material scale, configuration, and distribution appear limited to a single household?

Answering the questions above would really only be possible through experimental tomographic remote-sensing, barring expensive large-scale excavations. GPR was proposed as the most feasible remote-sensing geophysical method to employ at VBC given the method's combination of good target resolution and 3D imaging abilities. The three-part experimental and feasibility-testing program was devised to establish how *in situ* anthropogenic materials would appear to GPR, in terms of material presence/absence, shape, depth (depth to target and depth of target), scale, configuration, and orientation so that such things might be located in radar surveys at Verberie.

The sandbox experiment was constructed to evaluate lab applications and to determine how well GPR could work in imaging various predetermined arrangements of simulated archaeological material in a controlled sedimentary and moisture environment. The saddle club experiment had the same basic rationale as that involving the sandbox, but additionally to determine how well GPR could perform in the imaging of known materials in a much more "natural" sedimentary setting, under actual but differing real weather conditions. The materials consisted of simulated lithics and limestone cobbles, along with real animal bone These materials were seeded in the sandbox and artificial site according to scale of basic sizes down to submeter size (20-50 cm). In terms of configuration, shapes of features and associations between them were constructed as nearly as possible to mimic those found in excavations at Verberie. Locational association of any actual unexcavated GPR targets located in relation to previously excavated VBC materials would be quite obvious. The imaging in all three applications was both instructive and productive.

For the sandbox experiment, five of eleven targets were imaged quite well in terms of accurate scale, configuration, and shapes. Identifiable sandbox features consisted of a fluvial pseudo-channel in the gravel substrate (Figure 6.1); the hearth of limestone cobbles (Figure 6.2); a core of Pincevent flint used for fashioning replicated lithics unrelated to this research (Figure 6.3); and two lithic/bone scatters (Figures 6.4 and 6.5). In the saddle club experiment, all four out a sample population of four targets were successfully imaged with accurate scale, configuration and in three dimensions. These saddle club items were the hearth (Figures 6.7, 6.11, and 6.12); the lithic arc, including an excellent image of one Burlington chert core in the center of the target (Figures 6.8, 6.11, and 6.12); the composite lithic/bone/limestone target 9figures 6.9, 6.11, 6.12, and 6.13); and at least some portions of the sheep skeleton (Figures 6.10, 6.11, and 6.12). In both of the experiments, high-quality image suitable for the identification of specific known targets was produced, many that proved to be even more definitive when imaged in 3D.

In field applications at Verberie, surveys from three grids produced imagery that was suggestive of potential unexcavated anthropogenic materials. Images from Grid 3 showed material clearly consisting of wallbound middens known from an actual northern wall exposure photograph from VBC Secteur 202, Units J-N during the last phase of large-scale excavations in 2002 (Figures 6.21, 6.22. 6.23, and 6.24). Imagery from VBC 2006 GPR Grid 7 appeared to reveal examples of features and disturbances associated with previous excavations (Figures 6.25, 6.26, 6.27, 6.28, 6.29, 6.30, 6.31, and 6.32). Grid 7 images appear to show the permanent concrete site theodolite datum, a test or drainage trench, and a larger, rectangular backfilled excavation exposure. A suite of images from VBC 2006 GPR Grid 23 appeared to show materials of highly suggestive scale, configuration, location and association with previously excavated materials (Figures 6.33, 6.34, 6.35, 6.36, 6.37, 6.38, and 6.39). Photographs of actual 1 x 1 m unit excavations from 2009 were combined with the GPR images showing visible targets (Figures 6.40, 6.41, 6.42, and 6.43). The 2009 excavation from units in the areas indicating intact and eanthropogenic subsurface targets produced lithics, bone, and stones from at least 3 to 4 occupation levels known from previous excavations (II.1, II.2, II.22, and II.3).

In situ archaeological materials in Secteur 202 at VBC do not appear to be suggestive of any previously unknown domestic or household areas in terms of scale, configuration or location. Although a completely definitive identification of all the imaged targets would require additional excavations, there is nothing in the GPR imagery to suggest that any unknown residential areas are present in the areas GPR surveyed in 2006. The imaged, unexcavated material is clearly associated with the activity area and hearth already known from VBC 202, including material assigned to 202 Level II.22. The materials excavated in 2009 likewise conform to previously excavated material. The 2006 GPR images indicating unexcavated targets suggest that the current excavated sample is probably very representative of the site. In fact hearth features at such sites may be diagnostic, similar to kiva sites in the American southwest. The hearths in the sandbox and saddle club tests were both highly visible and recognizable, given the known materials. Since they were constructed to be as much like actual VBC hearths as possible, the quality of other VBC 2006 GPR data suggests that any unknown hearths should be at least as visible and recognizable as both the two experimental hearths and the midden area located by GPR and excavated in Grid 23. Even the saturated soil saddle club images showed excellent 3D representation of that hearth. That no other similar "hearths" are visible or even faintly indicated in VBC 202 probably indicates their absence, at least in surveyed portions of the site.

Caveats and Suggestions for Future Research

It would appear that much further work remains to be completed with both experimental and actualized GPR research, especially in terms of increasing target resolution and identification. This would include greater appreciation for factors that affect general GPR visibility. For example, it seems that the target number and density in the sandbox was simply too high and caused a kind of radar wave reverberation inside the confines of the box. Fewer targets with more "empty space" between, in both horizontal and vertical dimensions, may have produced better 3D results. It would also appear that much work remains regarding bone visibility, although this probably relates to physicochemical factors and not field or lab methodology. The sheep skeleton was, for example, more visible in the saddle club experiment than it was in the sandbox, and this might relate to the lower target density and frequency in the former. Although it appears that most targets at VBC lie on generally flat surfaces, the target surface slope has proven to be a major source of imaging difficulty in high-resolution GPR (Thompson and Storey 2010). Continuing experimental work toward accurate identification of archaeological targets oriented at variable subsurface slopes will obviously be necessary to improve both the method and theory (such as it is) of anthropological geophysics. Unquestionably future radar surveys at VBC are warranted, given that the vast majority of the site has been unsampled. VBC's outstanding spatial preservation and associational integrity make the sites ideal for refining high-resolution ground-penetrating radar methods.

Chapter 8 Faunal Summary

What would a given phenomenon look like if it was zooarchaeologically visible in the archaeological record? If we cannot conceive or predict of how or what something might even appear or appear to be in the material residues of the past, what can we learn? What would the residue or archaeologically visible after effects of a subsistence risk-mitigation strategy premised upon age-mediated carcass treatment look like? To return to the beginning, to summarize the present faunal analysis, we are presented with two rather different faunal assemblages from two Secteurs at VBC, 190 and II.22. The differences between these two samples are numerous. VBC 190 is located about 20 m southwest of VBC II.22. 190 was excavated as an entire secteur, apparently all as one level, and has been archived as such. II.22 was excavated as an individual occupation surface among several, and has likewise been archived in such fashion. Yet, aside from recovery and recording differences (which, it must be noted, do have affects upon subsequent analyses), there are also pervasive structural differences between them.

In terms of assemblage structure, despite general similarity in terms of absolute numerosity (VBC 190 consists of a total sample size of N=1,855, VBC II.22 N=1,610; II.22/190 = 86.8%, thus II.22 is nearly 90% the size of 190), the differences outweigh. From similar total sample sizes, 190 presents an NISP of 1,566, while II.22 produced a much lower NISP of only 386. In terms of NISP, II.22 is only 24.6% the size of 190's. This is a significant structural difference for assemblages consisting of the same species (reindeer) excavated from the same site. Furthermore, the dental MNI estimate for VBC 190 is for twelve individuals and seven for II.22. Kilberger and Enloe (2005:2) note the following dental MNIs for various levels. II.1 = 27; II.2 = 45; II.3 = 15; II,4 = 18; II.5 = 6; and II.6 = 2. Dividing seven (II.22 MNI) by twelve (190 MNI) provides a quotient of 58.33%. So to summarize the sample-structural differences, despite being about 87% the same sample size, consisting of nearly an estimated 60% similar number of animal individuals, VBC II.22 produced 25% as many bones attributable to NISP, in many ways the most basic of faunal quantitative units. By any measure of bone integrity, the sample from 190 is much less fragmentary and in generally much better condition than that from II.22.

Taphonomically, although the two assemblages were presumably exposed to a suite of generally similar physiochemical agencies of bone destruction, they portray different physical effects. For example, VBC 190 fauna were weathered more, and to more diverse degrees. The II.22 sample was much less weathered despite its much more fragmentary condition. In terms of breakage

patterning, the 190 assemblage did feature many indices of green breakage, perhaps for marrow-cracking. The II.22 sample is simply pulverized and reduced. The lack of identifiable bone breakage categories on most II.22 bones, as well as the small size of most fragments, does suggest a much more intensive suite of processing and treatments.

There are several differences between these two assemblages in terms of spatial distributions. Several different aspects of spatial distribution must be discussed. First, in specific terms, there appears to be an individually age-mediated component to the location of carcasses or carcass parts between 190 and II.22, at least when those areas of VBC are contrasted. According to *mean* (emphasis mine) dental crown height age, the animal individuals in 190 are estimated to be about twice as old as those from II.22. The actual sample variance is much wider than that, with averaging tending somewhat to reduce the actual crown height age variance between 190 and II.22, hiding the variability. These crown height calculations were each correlation tested to verify their accuracy and consistency, which were all verified at a 0.01 confidence level. There is also the matter of the apparently pervasive and differential spatial distribution of skeletal elements between 190 and II.22. In VBC 190, the fauna are located in what are essentially two large piles, lacking direct association with any hearths or obvious domestic/residential features. VBC 202 II.22 fauna are clearly distributed around and according to the hearth in L8. These two patterns repeat for all the fauna from the respective areas; stacked or piled in 190, while spread to the north and south around the L8 hearth in II.22.

One serious advantage at Verberie is that Enloe (2004, 2006) has convincingly demonstrated that fluvial patterning and densly-mediated bone attrition are not likely primary agents in the conditioning of fauna at the site. Physicomechanical bone degradation and hydraulic conditioning have probably impacted the site, but not in such extents as to be primary conditioning agencies. Anthropogenic activity is the likeliest remaining causal agent for the condition and distribution of fauna at VBC (Enloe 2004, 2006). Because of this anthropogenic conditioning, we can be quite certain that the differences between 190 and II.22 didn't simply result from slope processes, cryogenic effects, or other mass wasting events.

Attempting to impute a cause to this conditioning would involve reiterating the question posed above: What would the residue or archaeologically visible after effects of a subsistence risk-mitigation strategy premised upon differential age-mediated reindeer carcass treatment look like at Verberie? It seems reasonable to suggest that such a strategy would serve to distinguish between and separate geriatric reindeer carcasses from younger, healthier ones, if based merely upon the potential differences in nutritional value between old and young. Given the disparate condition of the fauna from 190 and II.22, it also seems reasonable to suggest that whatever the actual purpose for the spatial segregation of generally older carcasses in 190 from the younger animals in Secteur 202, it was probably not accidental or taphonomic in nature. We might then ask why older material would be segregated from the younger. Based on the framing of subsistence risk mitigation as partially based upon comparative valuation of prey items, the differential nutritional value of young/prime vs. geriatric reindeer in terms of differential processing is a possibility.

One criticism could be that 190 isn't actually a behavioral locus but simply a drop point or disposal midden indirectly indicative of residual anthropogenic agency, that this observed intrassemblage patterning is just a sampling artifact imposed by collection in a standardized grid coordinate system. This would also suggest site-functional distinctions between 190 and II.22. One way of investigating this would be to see if the areas of maximal faunal item frequency (i.e., those units with the highest counts of bones and teeth) produced the highest mean dental age estimates. In VBC 190, the units with the highest faunal counts, D15 (234 bones, 14 teeth) and D16 (139 bones 20 teeth), had mean crown height age estimates of 9.05 yr and 8.48 yr respectively. For comparison, the unit in 190 with the highest mean age estimate was B15, with 17.11 years; this unit only produced thirteen bones and four teeth, only two of which were sufficiently intact to measure crown heights. It does not appear to be the case either that II.22's lower mean crown height ages are a sampling artifact (i.e., a relic of small numbers of bones or teeth), for the lowest mean age in II.22 came from a unit (O5) that produced twice as many individual teeth as the unit with the highest mean age from VBC 190 (B15). If this age discrepancy does not relate to density- or chemically-mediated bone destruction, agricultural taphonomy, or sampling bias, then human agency looms large as a proximate cause.

Assuming, for the moment, that a site-functional difference exists between these assemblages (i.e., 190 was a dump, 202 II.22 was an occupational surface in a residential/domestic area), this is still not explanatory. This does not explain the structural and age differences between the faunal assemblages. Argument could commence regarding the type of human behavior that caused the animal age discrepancy between 190 and II.22. Does the geriatric bias in 190 reflect relatively poorer hunting ability by the Magdalenian hunters than in II.22? This is an interesting question, and assumes that there were possibly different human agents involved in forming the two deposits. The age profile for 190 does not *lack* young/prime animals, it simply features an unusually large proportion of old ones. It's not that young/prime animals are absent from 190, but rather that so many individuals were so old. This "spike"

in elder reindeer is not accompanied in 190 by a similar spike in infants/yearlings, so 190's profile does not appear to portray a catastrophic, or U-shaped, mortality curve. Moreover, in 190 there were also more prime age animals present than young. Presumably, calves would not be deliberately targeted for exploitation, but would accompany targeted nursing does as "riders" (i.e., acquisition of a nursing mother would be accompanied by the calf as opposed to merely letting the orphaned calf starve or fend for itself, but this is admittedly speculative based upon the writer's sensibilities and nothing deductive). It is, however, a virtual impossibility to "prove" any particular archaeological interpretation, so complete avoidance of speculation is unattainable, even within this dataset

We can question also whether 190 resulted from immediate butchery of an entire quarry, or whether it is a secondarily redeposited assemblage reflecting selective disposal of primarily older carcass parts. This is a difficult case to make, and it involves circumstantial evidence as opposed to testimony. Yet, the totality of evidence seems to suggest that 190 resulted from selective treatment. There were no hearths located in 190, and all elements and teeth, along with the burned and butchered fauna, share essentially the same "piled" or jumbled distribution within the same restricted but open space, indicative of a midden or dump. Articulated vertebra, joints, and the excellent bone condition in contrast with II.22, argue for less intensive processing. Less intensive processing is at least indirectly indicative of a more rapid disposition of the 190 fauna in comparison to the apparently more extensive treatment and processing given II.22 fauna (if it wasn't processed much more extensively, near the L8 hearth, its condition becomes difficult to explain given the condition of 190's). Given the apparent availability of numbers of young/prime animals in multiple levels of 202 (including II.22), why were so many more, older ones deposited in 190? Why weren't there more older ones in 202? In other words, even if 190 is a midden/dump, why should its faunal inventory differ so substantially from a nearby series of occupations in its age profile that, at least presumably, may have contributed somewhat to its formation (i.e., behaviors in II.22 possible correlated with some accumulation in 190)? One might expect the fauna in a dump to resemble the fauna from nearby activity areas, especially given the shared prey species unity and occupation by the same or very similar peoples.

Regarding the apparently differential treatment of fauna in VBC 190 and 202 II.22, is it possible we're seeing seasonal variation in faunal processing and treatment? Perhaps occupations during different seasons produce differing faunal assemblages through the action of rather different human behaviors. Could it be that the less intensive processing in 190 is indicative of more immediate consumption? The age profile skew towards older animals in 190 might then simply be a function of seasonal prey acquisition prior to calving season. If 190 material was consumed with more immediacy while II.22 material was prepped for extensive transport and storage/caching and delayed consumption, such differences in faunal treatment should be expected. In other words, the suite of behavioral agencies to which 190 was exposed would be fewer, perhaps consisting of butchering and filleting, as opposed to butchering, filleting, extensive marrow-cracking, and possible grease-boiling. In this construction, the higher and better quality fat content of the younger animals in II.22 might indicate their higher food and transport value, thus the more intensive treatment. So while additional effort was possibly expended wringing every last calorie from the younger carcasses, perhaps the older animals were simply butchered and filleted, and only the highest marrow-utility elements were processed from among the geriatrics. If that is the case, then this is perhaps indicative of some degree of risk-management, taking steps based on available resources to face potential future shortfalls and contingencies that may not even arise, with knowledge that past failures to do so imposed steep costs

Kilberger and Enloe's (2005) interesting MNI counts for the various levels at VBC offers another circumstantial datum. Figure 8.1, below, shows this information in graphic form. If the interpretation of these levels as occupation surfaces

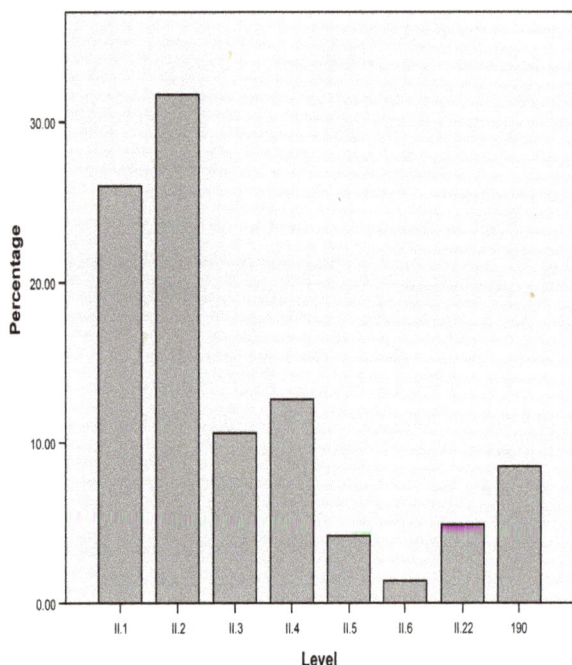

FIGURE 8.1. VBC FAUNAL PERCENTAGES BY LEVELS PLUS 190. NOTE THAT THIS IS COMPARING INDIVIDUAL LEVELS OF SECTEUR 201 AND 202 WITH 190.

is correct, then there was a wide variance in the number of prey items taken per occupation. Level II.2 contained the largest portion of the fauna (31.7%), while Level II.6 contained the smallest (1.4%, range 30.3). The mean proportion would be 12.5, while the sample of levels has a standard deviation of 10.83. This is a very wide variation of animal individuals between levels. This variance may be suggestive of fluctuating herd population characteristics and

changing herd demographics. Unfortunately, it is difficult to impossible to determine if these herd changes occurred over seasonal, annual, or multi-year intervals. Changes in herd demographics could certainly affect the age profiles of the site simply by conditioning available prey. Over some intervals more young/prime animals would be available, and over others older animals would be more numerous. After hunts during which more young/prime were taken, the herd population would be skewed toward older animals. Although imprecise, some lag time would be required before the population recovered to feature "natural" proportions of young, prime, and old individuals. A hunt that occurred during this lag, before younger age cohorts had been replenished, would be skewed towards older animals not as a function of choice but due simply to prey availability. Squabbles could then again arise over *why* the fauna was apparently segregated by age into different groups in 202 and 190. Moreover, could the diachronic variation in animals taken perhaps be reflective of variation in the sizes of human labor pools? Whether hunting primarily young/prime or geriatric reindeer, we might assume the end materials procurement goals were the same: acquisition of meat, marrow, skins, antler, and bone.

Yet, the interpretation of the VBC levels as remnant discrete occupations perhaps presents some explanation. If that interpretation is correct, then the VBC age profiles indicate that over some intervals either different prey age cohorts were available or different hunting selectivities were enacted. Why are the age profiles from 202 so much younger, per each occupation level, than 190? For that matter, why do the age profiles differ per level? We might expect differing numbers of individuals taken per occupation, based upon herd size, variable hunting success/return rates, and other factors.

Yet, why should the age profiles between two adjacent areas at VBC be so variant if 190 does not represent an intentional or intentional-functional segregation of primarily older individual animals? For example, even if the VBC levels do not indicate discrete occupations, and even if all fauna in both secteurs 190 and 202 are simply two parts of a larger aggregate assemblage, then why was such a proportion of older animals concentrated in the bone piles of VBC 190? Multiple individual levels of Secteur 202 indicate young-skewing age profiles, while the aggregate profile generated from those multiple levels indicates a very young-dominated profile. 190, however, represent a much higher proportion of old animals accompanied essentially by proportions of younger classes with profile curves generally similar to the individual levels from II.22. 190, in other words, is similar to 202 except for the much higher proportion of geriatric animals, as if the older cohorts were simply added to the younger. This could indicate a hunting episode premised upon acquiring supplemental numbers of geriatric caribou, but this is of course not the only interpretation possible, nor is it necessarily that only one may apply. Multicausality and shared causality could also seriously complicate any interpretations through equifinality.

It is interesting to note also, according to the MNIs calculated by Kilberger and Enloe (2005), a general trend of increasing numbers of caribou taken at VBC until the cessation of Pleistocene occupations. The uppermost, most recent occupations feature the largest sample sizes. Any number of questions regarding this phenomenon are possible. Does this indicate diachronically increasing sizes of reindeer herds due to general climatic amelioration in northern France? Increased herd sizes due to changes in the seasonal distribution of browse vegetation and different migration patterns? Or should we see the increased numbers of animal individuals per occupation as indicative of diachronic improvements to hunting techniques and the acquisition of superior skills? Are the differences between VBC 190 and 202 II.22 the result of behavioral variation between different social groups, possibly segregated by kinship or clan affiliations? Were perhaps the 190 hunters just bad, and could only acquire predominantly geriatric reindeer?

Compared to other levels, (II.1 and II.2, for instance) 190 only produced an MNI of 12 individuals. Perhaps under certain conditions, such as during a hunt enacted over an interval when young/prime caribou were relatively rarer, a logistical risk-avoidance or risk-management strategy would be to hunt an augmented number of older caribou to make up roughly the nutritional equivalent of the absent young/prime. Older, less nutritious animals might be needed in greater numbers to avoid a food shortfall. The possible contingencies are unlimited, and there is no way to address all the possibilities in one thesis. What would such an occurrence *look like* in the archaeological record? In what appearance and formal integrity would we expect to find the ancient, smeared fingerprint of human activity? For example, the faunal discrepancy might portray an apparently anomalous proportion of aged prey animals in accompaniment with lower proportions of more youthful animals. The collocation thereof might be the only signature. Probably no one interpretation is completely "correct". Moreover, all of the analytical frames for potential explications presented above are probably each worthy individually as entire studies of this material in their own right.

Applying Occam's Razor to the Confusion

Given that there are virtually innumerable potential explanations for the faunal differences between VBC 190 and VBC 202 II.22, it seems prudent to employ the potential explanation that presents the fewest number of variables. The process is similar to constructing an equation; in this case, we want the equation with the fewest possible variables for which we need to account. The simplest hypothesis involving the fewest possible variables is preferable for reasons of parsimony. As above, there are virtually limitless numbers of potential explanations that can be credibly mobilized in order to explicate the particular conditioning observed in the VBC 190 and II.22 fauna. So for reasons of parsimony, it is prudent to eliminate from the present consideration those potential explications that present the most complexity and the most numerous variables.

Variability in Diachronic Hunting Ability?

For example, invoking poor hunting ability for the 190 hunters (i.e., they could only bag oldsters!), or even net diachronic improvement in Magdalenian hunting techniques visible across five or six occupations (evinced by increasing MNIs in younger occupations) are not the most parsimonious explanations. If 190 hunters were just "bad" at hunting or inefficient, suboptimal subsisters, how did they or their progenitors survive the Late Glacial Maximum and the surely dynamic transition to Holocene climates? Luck? How many additional variables are needed to explain their survival if they were poor hunters? If being unskilled at hunting is bad, it is probably much worse to be unskilled at hunting during periods of wide climatic variability and change. Moreover, if hunting improved diachronically at VBC, what additional variables are necessary to explain those successive improvements? Furthermore, if hunting continually improved over time, precisely what was driving that improvement? We would be able to detect profound technological changes in the Magdalenian repertoire, and we might expect drastically improved hunting capabilities to be dependent upon technological refinement and improvement. These are not present

Mechanisms of Temporal Variability in Occupancy?

Invoking mechanisms of temporal variability in occupancy between 190 and II.22, for example, whether by seasons, years, decades, or millennia, also present additional analytical variables into consideration, as well as further complexities. Such an interpretation would, for instance, tend to contradict previous research suggestive of patterned fall occupations timed to coincide with fall herd migrations. Instead of being only seasonally available, this would also tend to suggest that caribou were available at or near VBC for longer periods, perhaps year-round. It would also indicate how little we actually know regarding the herd movements of Pleistocene European caribou, and how little we know about the actual modes of Magdalenian caribou hunting. If caribou were widely available at VBC over long periods of an annual cycle, why is there repeated evidence suggestive of fall occupations, perhaps premised upon the animals having attained a state of good nutrition after summer browsing? Evidence for seasonally repetitive occupations may be indicative of differential valuation of caribou based upon their nutritional states. If reindeer were in prime nutritional status for the fall migrations, timing VBC occupations to coincide with those fall migrations is a logical choice. Timing VBC occupations for early seasonal occupancy, prior to calving season, seems more opaque. It seems clear that future research into VBC paleoclimate and seasonality are warranted, and this indicates how crucial seasonal indices are to interpretations of this site.

Despite potential variation in occupation seasonality between VBC 190 and 202 II.22, it still remains that the respective caribou assemblages from the two areas were treated very differently by the human occupants. There were, however, small percentages of other species present at Verberie. Enloe (personal communication) has informed that a small number of horse bones, including a pelvis, have been recovered from VBC. I was also present at excavations in the 2009 field season, during which several more horse elements (appendicular extremities) were recovered in Secteur 202, from the H-I, 14-15 quartet of units. I also noted rabbit upper appendicular elements, a mandible, and teeth in the 190 assemblage; this material is not relevant to the methodological and theoretical issues of comparing/contrasting 190 and II.22, and is not treated in depth. The rabbit bones produced no cutmarks or burning, so whether they represent human provisioning is purely speculative. The horse was probably less likely to occur at the site without anthropogenic causality, and was perhaps brought to the site (Enloe personal communication). But due to the presence within a large preponderance of caribou remains of isolated small percentages of other species it is perhaps possible that active provisioning prior to the onset of the caribou hunt occurred. Such isolated non-caribou fauna may indicate such provisioning.

Temporal variation in human group size might also factor into our equation. As previously, if modeling the behavior of individuals is complicated then how much more complex is modeling interpersonal, group behaviors? If Magdalenian human groups partitioned and aggregated according to fluctuating seasonal resource availabilities, then how certain can we be that the necessary labor pools to enact a (presumably) intensive, short-term caribou hunt and transport the acquired products was uniformly available? Lacking a Paleolithic census as well as abundant seasonality indices, we are constrained merely to speculate on human group size and available labor pools. If 190 had produced any hearths, it may have been easier. Spatial and age-mediated differences in fauna, conditioning, and treatment could be linked with multiple domestic/residential features. Differences in faunal assemblage structure could then be explained, at least partially, as a function of variable intergroup behaviors, as social variation in the treatment of fauna. This could be based upon different kinship lineages, clan-based moieties, or other social mechanisms of human group partition. Yet, 190 produced no hearths, and it is impossible to prove contemporaneity of occupations between 190 and 202 II.22 in the absence of faunal refits.

VBC Secteur 190 as Bounded Social Space

There are two primary attributes common to the faunal assemblage from VBC 190 that suggest it might represent an example of an impermeable, or bounded, social space, defined by relative large differences between human roles and spatially-segregated activities over smaller spatial areas (Ashforth et al. 2000:476; Kooyman 2006): the strongly variant, outlying 190 age cohort profile calculated from dental crown heights, and the pervasive structural difference in its very well-preserved, apparently minimally processed skeleta (disproportionately higher NISPs per

II.22 in relation to MNIs). Another datum suggestive of bounded social differentiation between these two VBC secteurs is the lack of hearths or obvious domestic spaces within 190 and their presence in 202. Given the rather stark contrasts between 190 and II.22 according to those three criteria, it becomes just possible to infer social, or behavioral, conditioning on a putative role boundary between the two secteurs that is not merely a function of temporal variation in occupancy.

As above, VBC secteurs 190 and 202 are diagonally adjacent, and there is no obvious physical, topological, or relief boundary between the two visible surficially. The GPR surveys of the site thoroughly sampled the space between 190 and II.22, and there were likewise no evident subsurficial physical, topological, or relief boundaries between the two. Since in Secteur 202 there are multiple occupations indicative of repetitive fall acquisition, butchering, and processing of caribou over some as yet undefined span of time, whether seasons, years, or decades, we might expect generally similar indices in the faunal assemblage recovered from nearby areas if they shared unbounded and permeable, functionally similar human behavioral foci. For example, despite the passage of as yet unknown spans of time between human occupations in Secteur 202 (including Level II.22), the age profiles of the faunal assemblages were generally consistent, and skewed towards more youthful age cohorts. The fact that repeated occupations resulted in the accumulation of essentially similar material in 202 (not merely one instance of difference with 190, but multiple, repetitive instances) is itself strong evidence of some form of social boundary between the behaviors that conditioned the fauna in II.22 and those that conditioned VBC 190. This cumulative multiplicity of similar occurrences in II.22 is also indicative of subsistence systematization, consistency, and coherence, fully commensurate with what me might expect for humans partaking in behavioral-cognitive modernity. It is unlikely that equifinality would result in the imprinting of the same behavioral fingerprint in the same space over numerous successive intervals.

Yet, if II.22 indicates systematization, consistency, and coherence, can we say that 190 does as well? VBC 190 certainly produced a consistently and coherently well-preserved faunal assemblage. It also evinces that a consistently much older set of *Rangifer* individuals comprises its faunal assemblage. Furthermore, it appears that human activity systematically conditioned those preceding attributes. But if the activities in II.22 resulted in a palimpsest of obviously functionally and structurally related archaeological material, then *why do they all seem so different from 190 in every way*? The similarities between 190 and II.22 are very few: they contain many of the same Magdalenian tool types and they contain a vast majority of reindeer bones. Contemporaneity between VBC 190 and 202 II.22 seems almost beside the point when the behavioral fingerprints the people who made the site left behind seem so vastly different. For example, regardless of mutual occupational synchronicity, it appears that the people who accumulated the 190 fauna saw some value in geriatric reindeer that multiple, successive groups using II.22 did not see. Binford (1978:354) notes that different people performing different tasks of necessity occupy different spaces.

It appears, therefore, that multiple levels of boundaries exist between VBC 190 and 202 II.22. There may be a chronological boundary between human occupancies, or at least there is no strong evidence of occupational synchronicity. There appear to be stark, impermeable functional boundaries between the suites of human behavioral conditioning to which these respective fauna were subjected. Simply repeating that VBC 190 is a midden or refuse dump and that 202 II.22 was a domestic or activity area explains nothing. For instance, the arrangement and spatial distribution of material *around* the L8 hearth in VBC 202 II.22, given their more or less semicircular shapes and placement, might correspond to Binford's (1978:339-340) drop and toss zones. To take an extremely pessimistic slant, however, if we discount anthropogenic conditioning for the disjunctive faunal structures, spatial arrangements, and age profiles at VBC 190 and 202 II.22, having already discarded extensive hydraulic effects and density-mediated bone attrition, there are few remaining plausible alternatives for explanation. To continue in that pessimistic vein, we have no unambiguous evidence that the *Rangifer* death assemblage (skeletal remains and dental material) at VBC actually corresponded to living individuals. Perhaps the teeth derive from one herd and the skeletal elements from another. Furthermore, for all we *know* (sarcasm intended) each animal individual at VBC originated from different herds. We have no conclusive mitochondrial DNA data suggestive of lineal descent amongst the caribou. But which line of argument presents the fewest variables with which to contend?

Differential Seasonality of Site Occupations in VBC 190 and VBC 202 II.22.

An additional potential explanation for the differences between VBC 190 and VBC 202 II.22 may relate to different seasons of occupation and variable nutritional states between the two faunal datasets. The younger mortality curve for fauna from VBC 202 II.22, which was subjected to a higher degree of post-butchering processing and fragmentation could relate to a greater human investment in it to extract fats from marrow-cracking and grease-boiling. An inference can therefore be made that VBC 202 II.22 could indicate younger, healthier prime-age animals. The chronologically much older mortality curve for the VBC 190 fauna, which was subjected to less intensive post-butchering fragmentation might thereby indicate an assemblage of much older animals in a fat-depleted state. VBC 202 II.22 might therefore correspond to a fall occupation after animals had summered and fattened. VBC 190 fauna might indicate a contrasting spring occupation, during which older animals were taken in fat-depleted states after stressful wintering. In any event, seasonality looms very large as a potential explanation for

the very different conditions of these two faunal datasets, one the author currently favors based upon the toality of evidence. A very interesting aspect of this explanation is that the different spatial patterns and configurations of the above faunal assemblages would in the author's opinion be radar-visible, which indicates that at Verberie such intensive ground-penetrating radar surveys of the entire site area could estimate seasonality based upon our knowledge the areas VBC 190 and 202 II.22.

Summary and Preliminary Conclusions

Based upon the above research, it appears that the faunal assemblage in VBC 190 most closely corresponds to what would be expected of a disposal midden or bone dump. Virtually every skeletal element present in VBC 190 shares a highly uniform spatial distribution, with little to no compartmentalization specific to any of the bones. The presence in 190 of articulating joints, often with distal portions of long bones in articulation with carpals and tarsals, and articulated vertebrae indicates that the primary butchering locus might be nearby assuming VBC 190 itself is not it. The excellent condition and preservation of the bones and teeth suggests that they were not subjected to intensive postmortem processing. The age profile, skewing heavily towards geriatric animal individuals, perhaps gives some justification for *why* 190 fauna was apparently minimally processed: comparative prey valuation.

The assumption here is that older carcasses would be valued less due to lower fat content in meat and marrow, and the presence of various degenerative conditions that lowered their caloric value. The older animals were perhaps simply not "worth" the investment of labor, time, and effort for extensive processing in terms of systematic marrow cracking (more like marrow-smashing in 202 II.22) and grease-boiling. I proposed the analytical frame of subsistence risk-mitigation or risk-management (i.e., subsistence 'insurance') as a potential heuristic device. The research was framed in this way due to the highly mobile and perhaps situationally precarious mode of logistical subsistence and the need to acquire, manipulate, and propagate various forms of information. High logistical mobility coupled with a need for information with currency would demand some mechanism for human risk-management. The potential costs were likely too high simply to ignore risks and perils, and it was also suggested that opportunity for acquiring predictable, dependable surplus foodstuffs (as a form of 'profit') may have added additional imperatives for risk-pooling through prioritization and management of those surpluses. Finally, it was then suggested that a stochastic shortage of younger/prime caribou may have resulted in an *ad-hoc* episode of intensive geriatric caribou hunting to address a potential shortfall.

The faunal assemblage from VBC 202 Level II.22 differs in profound ways from VBC 190. II.22's much more fragmentary condition, as measured by a much lower NISP that is not attributable to a drastically lower MNI when compared to 190, indicate that it was formed by very different dynamics of behavior. Spatially, the II.22 fauna is clearly distributed according to and generally around (mainly to north, somewhat less to the south) the L8 hearth, in what roughly corresponds to drop and toss zones. This would tend to indicate that faunal processing and other behaviors (tool manufacture and repair, food consumption, took place around the L8 hearth, perhaps in some accordance with ethnoarchaeological analogs (Binford 1978). The repetitive accumulation of assemblages with similar age profiles as II.22 in Secteur 202, differing primarily, it would seem, only in terms of MNIs (a rough index of actual animal numbers taken per occupation), all skewing towards young/prime age cohorts, indicates either that different comparative prey valuations were in action in accumulating the II.22 assemblage or differing faunal demographics were in play. Any number of other factors could also condition the material. It is, however, interesting that during none of the 202 occupations was a similar, old-skewing caribou age profile assembled. It is clear that clarification of the occupational seasonality for both VBC 190 and VBC 202 II.22 could improve our understandings.

Suggestions for Future Research

Acquisition of reliable seasonal data are crucial to interpreting human occupations at Verberie. A thorough analysis of all VBC microfauna could help in this regard, as could a comprehensive review of all dental age profiles from the site. There may, across all VBC faunal assemblages, be enough examples of incompletely- to unfused long bone epiphyses to assist in clarifying the signal from dental crown height age profiles. Additionally, given the excellent results obtained from the GPR analysis, an obvious suggestion would be to employ another GPR survey at VBC, this time of the entirety of the Pleistocene terrace and point bar visible in aerial photos. Improvements in GPR, including higher-resolution antennae, improved software, more sophisticated analytical and interpretive techniques, and the development of method ant theory capable of using the technology to answer anthropological questions, have come to the fore since VBC was last surveyed. Finally, even in extant GPR imagery, some of which has been presented in this thesis, there are clearly remaining *in situ* archaeological materials at VBC. These await future diggers, who will perhaps be armed with even better cognitive and technological approaches. Given what this site has come to mean to me, over the course of four field seasons spent on it, and years of analysis, research, and writing devoted to it, I wish them the best of luck and all the success possible. Many people have depended on this extremely important site for their livelihoods.

Bibliography

Abbas, A. M., T. F. Abdallatif, et al. 2005 Archaeological investigation of the eastern extensions of the Karnak Temple using ground-penetrating radar and magnetic tools. *Geoarchaeology* 20(5): 537-554.

Abrams, P. 1982 Functional Responses of Optimal Foragers. *American Naturalist* 120:382-390.

Adler, D., G. Bar-Oz, A. Belfer-Cohen, and O. Bar-Yosef Ahead of the Game: Middle and Upper Paleolithic Hunting Behaviors in the Southern Caucasus. *Current Anthropology* 47:89-118.

Anderson, D. and J. Gillam Paleoindian Interaction and Mating Networks: Reply to Moore and Mosely. *American Antiquity* 66(3):530-535.

Andersson, M. 1981 On Optimal Predator Search. *Theoretical Population Biology* 19:58-86.

1978 Optimal Foraging Area: size and allocation of search effort. *Theoretical Population Biology* 13:397-409.

Andrews, B. 2006 Sediment Consolidation and Archaeological Site Formation. *Geoarchaeology* 21(5):461-478.

Andrews, P. 1995 Experiments in Taphonomy. *Journal of Archaeological Science* 22:147-153.

Anikovich, M. 1992 Early Upper Paleolithic Industries of Eastern Europe. *Journal of World Prehistory* 6(2):205-245.

Antoine, P., J. Coutard, P. Gibbard, B. Hallegouet, J. Lautridou, and J. Ozouf 2003 The Pleistocene Rivers of the English Channel Region. *Journal of Quaternary Science* 18(3-4):227-243.

Appadurai, A. 1996 *Modernity at Large: Cultural Dimensions of Globalization.* Minneapolis: U of M Press.

Arco, L., K. Adelsberger, L. Hung, and T. Kidder 2006 Alluvial Geoarchaeology of a Middle Archaic Mound Complex in the Lower Mississippi Valley, USA. *Geoarchaeology* 21(6):591-614.

Aronson, R. and T. Givnish 1983 Optimal Central-Place Foragers: A Comparison with Null Hyoptheses. *Ecology* 64:395-399.

Ashforth, B., G. Kreiner, M. Fugate 2000 All in a Day's Work: Boundaries and Micro Role Transitions. *Academy of Management Review* 25(3):472-491.

Ashley, G., Tactikos, J., and Owen, R. 2008 Hominin Use of Springs and Wetlands: Paleoclimate and Archaeological Records from Olduvai Gorge. *Palaeogeography.*

Atya, M. A., H. Kamei, et al. 2005 Complementary integrated geophysical investigation around Al-Zayyan temple, Kharga oasis, Al-Wadi Al-Jadeed (New Valley), Egypt. *Archaeological Prospection* 12(3): 177-189.

Audouze, F. 1987 The Paris Basin in Magdalenian Times. In, Olga Soffer (ed), *The Pleistocene Old World:* *Regional Perspectives.* New York: Plenum Press. pp. 183-200.

Audouze, F. and J.G. Enloe High Resolution Archaeology at Verberie: Limits and Interpretations. *World Archaeology* 29(2):195-207.

1991 Subsistence Strategies and Economy in the Magdalenian of the Paris Basin. In: RNC Barton, AJ Roberts, and DA Roe (eds), *The Late Glacial of Northwest Europe: Human Adaptation and Environmental Change at the End of the Pleistocene,* pp. 63-71. Council for British Archaeology Reports 77, London.

Aura, J., Y. Carrion, E. Estrelles, G. Jorda 2005 Plant Economy of Hunter-Gatherer Groups at the End of the Last Ice Age: Plant Macroremains from the Cave of Santa Malra (Alacant, Spain) ca. 12000-9000 BP. *Veget Hist Archaeobot* 14:542-550.

Autsi, E. 2004 Ground-penetrating Radar Time-slices from North Ballachulish Moss. *Archaeol. Prospect.* 11:65–75.

Babbill, D. and C. Merrill 2005 Real and Illusory Value Creation by Insurance Companies. *Journal of Risk and Insurance* 72(1):1-21.

Bailey, G. and A. Craighead 2003 Late Pleistocene and Holocene Coastal Paleoeconomies: A Reconsideration of the Molluscan Evidence from Northern Spain. *Geoarchaeology* (18)2:175-204.

Balek, C. 2002 Buried Artifacts in Stable Upland Sites and the Role of Bioturbation: A Review. *Geoarchaeology* 17(1):41-51.

Bamforth, D. 2002 Evidence and Metaphor in Evolutionary Archaeology. *American Antiquity* 67(3):435-452.

Bamforth, D. and N. Finlay Introduction: Archaeological Approaches to Lithic Production Skill and Craft Learning. *Journal of Archaeological Method and Theory* 15:1-27.

Baradello, L., J. M. Carcione, et al. 2004 Fast monostatic GPR modeling. *Geophysics* 69(2):466-471.

Barker, G. et al. 2007 The 'human revolution' in lowland tropical Southeast Asia: the antiquity and behavior of anatomically modern humans at Niah Cave (Sarawak, Borneo). *Journal of Human Evolution* 52:243-261.

Bar-Oz, G., A. Belfer-Cohen, T. Meshveliani, N. Djakeli, and O. Bar-Yosef 2008 Taphonomy and Zooarchaeology of the Upper Paleolithic Cave of Dzudzuana, Republic of Georgia. *International Journal of Osteoarchaeology* 18:131-151.

Barton, C., J. Bernebeu, E. Aura, and O. Garcia 1999 Land-use Dynamics and Socioecnomic Change: An Example from the Polop Alto Valley. *American Antiquity* (64)4:609-634.

Barton, R., R. Jacobi, D. Stapert, M. Street 2003 The Late-glacial Reoccupation of the British Isles and the Creswellian. *Journal of Quaternary Science* 18(7):631-643.

Bar-Yosef, O. 2004 Eat What is There: Hunting and Gathering in the World of Neanderthals and their Neighbors. *International Journal of Osteoarchaeology* 14:333-342.

Bar-Yosef, O. and S. Kuhn 1999 The Big Deal about Blades: Laminar Technologies and Human Evolution. *American Anthropologist* 101(2):322-338.

Baryshnikov, G. and J. Hoffecker 1994 Mousterian Hunters of the NW Caucasus: Preliminary Results of Recent Investigations. *Journal of Field Archaeology* 21(1):1-14.

Baxter, M. 2001 Methodological Issues in the Study of Assemblage Diversity. *American Antiquity* 66(4):715-725.

Beck, R., D. Bolender, J. Brown, and T. Earle 2007 Eventful Archaeology: the Place of Space in Structural Transformation. *Current Anthropology* 48(6):833-860.

Behrensmeyer, A. and D. Boaz The Recent Bones of Amboseli National Park, Kenya, in Relation to East African Paleoecology. In Behrensmeyer and Hill (eds) *Fossils in the Making: Vertebrate Taphonomy and Paleoecology*, pp. 72-92. University of Chicago Press.

Behrensmeyer, A., S. Kidwell, and R. Gastaldo 2000 Taphonomy and Paleobiology. *Paleobiology* 26(4):103-147.

Benet-Tygel, S. 1944 The Magdalenian Culture in Poland. *American Anthropologist* 46(4):479-499.

Benyshek, D. and J. Watson Exploring the Thrifty Genotype's Food-Shortage Assumptions: A Cross-Cultural Comparison of Ethnographic Accounts of Food Security Among Foraging and Agricultural Societies. *American Journal of Physical Anthropology* 131:120-126.

Berna, F., A. Matthews, and S. Weiner 2004 Solubilities of Bone Mineral from Archaeological Sites: the Recrystallization Window. *Journal of Archaeological Science* 31:867-882.

Bertran, P and J.-P. Texier 1994 Fabric Analysis: Application to Paleolithic Sites. *Journal of Archaeological Science* 22:521-535.

Betts, M. and T. Friesen 2004 Quantifying Hunter-Gatherer Intensification: A Zooarchaeological case Study from Arctic Canada. *Journal of Anthropological Archaeology* 23:357-384.

Bevan, B.W., and A.C. Roosevelt 2003 Geophysical exploration of Guajará, a prehistoric earth mound in Brazil. *Geoarchaeology* 18(3): 287-331.

Bicho, N., J. Haws, and B. Hockett 2006 Two Sides of the Same Coin-Rocks, Bones, and Site Function of Picareiro Cave, Central Portugal. *Journal of Anthropological Archaeology* 25:485-499.

Bignon, O., M. Baylac, J-D. Vigne, V. Eisenmann 2005 Geometric Morphmetrics and the Population Diversity of Late glacial Horses in Western Europe:

Phylogeographic and Anthropological Implications. *Journal of Archaeological Science* 32:375-391

Binford, L. 2001 Where Do Research Problems Come From? *American Antiquity* 66(4):669-678.

2001 Butchering, Sharing, and the Archaeological Record. *Journal of Anthropological Archaeology* 3:235-257.

1981 *Bones: Ancient Men and Modern Myths.* Academic Press.

1980 Willow Smoke and Dogs' Tails: Hunter-Gatherer Settlement Systems and Archaeological Site Formation. *American Antiquity* 45(1):4-20.

1980 Organization and Formation Processes: Looking at Curated Technologies. *Journal of Anthropological Research* 35(3):225-273.

1978a *Nunamiut Ethnoarchaeology.* Academic Press.

1978b Dimensional Analysis of Behavior and Site Structure: Learning from an Eskimo Hunting Stand. *American Antiquity* 43(3):330-361.

1977 Introduction. In *For Theory Building in Archaeology: Essays on Faunal Remains, Aquaic resources, Spatial Analysis, and Systemic Modeling.* L. Binford (ed) pp. 1-10. New York: Academic Press.

1968 Post-Pleistocene Adaptations. In *New Perspectives in Archaeology,* S.R. Binford and L.R. Binford (eds), 313-341. Chicago: Aldine.

1967 Smudge Pits and Hide Smoking: The Use of Analogy in Archaeological Reasoning. *American Antiquity* 32(1):1-12.

Binford, L. and S. Binford 1968 Variability and Change in the Near Eastern Mousterian of Levallois Facies. In New Perspectives in Archaeology, edited by S. Binford and L. Binford general editor. Aldine Publishing Company, Chicago.

1966 A Preliminary Analysis of Functional Variability in the Mousterian of Levallois Facies, in Recent Studies in Paleoanthropology (ed. by J.D. Clark and F.C. Howell). American Anthropologist. Vol. 68(No. 2):238-95.

Binford, L. and J. Bertram Bone Frequencies and Attritional Processes. In: Binford (ed) *For theory Building in Archaeology: Essays of Faunal Remains, Aquatic Resources, Spatial Analyses, and Systemic Modeling,* pp. 77-153. Academic Press.

Bird, R. and D. Bird 2008 Why Women Hunt: Risk and Cotemporary Foraging in a Western Desert Aboriginal Community. *Current Anthropology* 49(4):655-693.

1997 Delayed Reciprocity and Tolerated Theft: the Behavioral Ecology of Food-Sharing. *Current Anthropology* 38(1):49-78.

Bird, D. and J. O'Connell 2006 Behavioral Ecology and Archaeology. *Journal of Archaeological Research* 14:143-188.

Blades, B. 2003 End Scraper Reduction and Hunter-Gatherer Mobility. *American Antiquity* 68(1):141-156.

1999 Aurignacian Settlement Patterns in the Vezere Valley. *Current Anthropology* 40(5):712-719.

Bleed, P. 2006 Living in the human Niche. *Evolutionary Anthropology* 15:8-10

Blockley, S., S. Blockley, R. Donahue, C. Lane, J. Lowe, and A. Pollard 2006 The Chronology of Abrupt Climate Change and Late Upper Paleolithic Human Adaptation in Europe. *Journal of Quaternary Science* 21(5):575-584.

Blumenschine, R., C. Marean, and S. Capaldo 1996 Blind Tests of Inter-Analyst Correspondence and Accuracy in the Identification of Cutmarks, Percussion Marks, and Carnivore Tooth Marks on Bone Surfaces. *Journal of Archaeological Science* 23:493-507.

Bocquet-Appel, J-P. 2000 Population Kinetics in the Upper Paleolithic in Western Europe. *Journal of Archaeological Science* 27:551-570.

Bocquet-Appel, J., P. Demars, L. Noiret, and D. Dobrowsky 2005 Estimates of Upper-Paleolithic Meta-Population Size in Europe from Archaeological Data. *Journal of Archaeological Science* 32:1656-1668.

Bodu, P. 2010   Espaces et Habitats au Tardiglaciaire dans le Bassin Parisien: Une Illustration avec les Gisements Magdalenian de Pincevent et Azilien du Closeau. In *The Magdalenian Household: Unraveling Domesticity.* E. Zubrow, F. Audouze, J. Enloe (eds) SUNY Press. pp. 176-197.

Bond, A. 1980 Optimal Foraging in a Uniform Habitat: the Search Mechanism of the Green Lacewing. *Animal Behavior* 29:629-630.

Boniger, U. and J. Tronicke 2010   Improving   the Interpretability of 3D GPR Data Using Target-Specific Attributes: Applications to Tomb Detection. *Journal of Archaeological Science* 37(2):360-367.

Boone, J. 2002 Subsistence Strategies and Early Human Population History: An Evolutionary Ecological Perspective. *World Archaeology* 34(1):6-25.

Booth, A., N. Linford, R. Clark, and T. Murray 2008 Three-Dimensional, Multi-0ffset Ground-penetrating Radar Imaging of Archaeological Targets. *Archaeological Prospection* 15:93-112.

Bordes, F. 1971 Physical Evolution and Technological Evolution in Man: A Parallelism. *World Archaeology* 3(1):1-5.

1963 Reflections on typology and techniques in the Paleolithic. Arctic Anthropology 6(1):1-29.

1961 Mousterian Cultures in France. *Science* 134(3482):803-810.

Bordes, F. and D. de Sonneville-Bordes 1970 The Significance of Variability in Paleolithic Assemblages. *World Archaeology* 2(1):61-73.

Bordes, F. and J. Labrot 1967   La stratigraphie du gisement de roc de Combe (Lot) et ses implications. Bulletin de la Société Prehistoric Française 64:15-23.

Bourillet, J-F., J-Y. Reynaud, A, Baltzer, and S. Zaragosi 2003 The 'Fleuve Manche': the Submarine Sedimentary Features from the Outer Shelf to the Deep-Sea Fans. *Journal of Quaternary Science* 18(3-4):261-282.

Bourquin, S., J. Vairon, P. Le Strat 1997 Three-Dimensional Evolution of the Paris Basin Based on Detailed Isopach Maps of the Stratigraphic Cycles: Tectonic Influences. *Geology Rundsch* 86:670-685.

Bouzouggara, A., et al. 2007 82,000-year-old shell beads from North Africa and implications for the origins of modern human behavior. *Proceedings of the National Academy of Sciences of the United States of America* 104(24):9964-9969.

Borrerro, L. and R. Barbarena 2006 Hunter-Gatherer Home Ranges and Marine Resources. *Current Anthropology* 47(5):855-867.

Bos, J., S. Bohncke, C. Kasse, and J. Vandenberghe 2001 Vegetation and Climate during the Weichselian Early Glacial and Pleniglacial in the Niederlausitz, E. Germany: Macrofossil and Pollen Evidence. *Journal of Quaternary Science* 16(3):269-289.

Boyd, B. 2006 Sedentism in Non-Agricultural Societies. *World Archaeology* 38(2):164-178.

Boyle, K. 2000 Reconstructing Middle Paleolithic Subsistence Strategies in the South of France. *International Journal of Osteoarchaeology* 10:336-356.

1996 From Laugerie Basse to Jolivet: the Organization of Final Magdalenian Settlement in the Vezere Valley. *World Archaeology* 27(3):477-491.

Brace, C. Loring 2005   "Neutral Theory" and the Dynamics of the Evolution of "Modern" Human Morphology. *Human Evolution* 20(1):19-38.

1995 Bio-cultural interaction and the mechanism of mosaic evolution in the emergence of "modern" morphology. *American Anthropologist* 97(4):711 -721.

Brain, C.K. Some Criteria for the recognition of bone-collecting Agencies in African Caves. In Behrensmeyer and Hill (eds) *Fossils in the Making: Vertebrate Taphonomy and Paleoecology,* pp. 108-130. University of Chicago Press.

Brantingham, P. 2006 Measuring Forager Mobility. *Current Anthropology* 47(3):435-459.

Bratlund, B. 1996 Hunting Strategies in he Late Glacial of Northern Europe: A Survey of the Faunal Evidence. *World Prehistory* 10(1):1-48.

Brett, C. and G. Baird 1986 Comparative Taphonomy: A Key to Paleoenvironmental Interpretation based on Fossil Preservation. *Palaios* 1(3):207-227.

Bridgland, D., P. Antoine, N. Limondin-Lozouet, J. Santisteban, R. Westaway, and M. White 2006 The Paleolithic Occupation of Europe as Revealed by Evidence from the Rivers: Data from IGCP 449. *Journal of Quaternary Science* 21(5):437-455.

Briggs, D., W. Chaloner, R. Ambler, S. Macko, J. Bada, and J. Hubbard 1999 Molecular Taphonomy of Animal and Plant Cuticles: Selective Preservation and Diagenesis (and Discussion). *Philosophical Transactions: Biological Sciences* 354(1379), Molecular Information and Prehistory:7-17.

Bright, J., A. Ugan, and L. Hunsaker 2002 The Effect of Handling Time on Subsistence Technology. *World Archaeology* 34(1):164-181.

Brose, D. and M. Wolpoff 1971 Early Upper Paleolithic Man and Late Middle Paleolithic Tools. *American Anthropologist* 73(5):1156-1194.

Brumbach, H. and R. Jarvenpa 1997 Ethnoarchaeology of Subsistence Space and Gender: A Subarctic Dene case. *American Antiquity* 62(3):414-436.

Burgett, G. 1999 The Bones of the Beast: Actualistic Taphonomic Research and Its Role in Understanding Hominid Exploitation of Bison and Other Large Mammals. In Hofman and Enloe (eds) *Le bison: Gibier et Moyen de Subsistence du Paleolithique aux Paleoindiens des Grandes Plaines*, pp. 1-17. Editions APDCA, Antibes.

Burke, A. 2006 Introduction to the Special Issue: "Multidisciplinary Approaches to the Study of Site Function and Settlement Dynamics in Prehistory. *Journal of Anthropological Archaeology* 25:403-407.

Butler, V. and R. Lyman 1996 Taxonomic Identifications and Faunal Summaries: What Should We Be Including in Our Faunal Reports? *Society for American Archaeology Bulletin* 14 (1):22.

Byers, D. 2002 Taphonomic Analysis, Associational Integrity, and Depositional History of the Fetterman Mammoth, Eastern Wyoming, USA. *Geoarchaeology* 17(5):417-440.

Cachel, S., M. Otte, N. Rolland, L. Straus, and J. Svoboda 1997 Dietary Shifts and the European Upper Paleolithic Transition. *Current Anthropology* 38(4):579-603.

Cann, R, M. Stoneking, and A. Wilson Mitochondrial DNA and Human Evolution. *Nature* 325:31-36.

Canti, M. 2003 Earthworm Activity and Archaeological Stratigraphy: A Review of Products and Processes. *Journal of Archaeological Science* 30:135-148.

Carcione, J. M. 1996 Ground radar simulation for archaeological applications. *Geophysical Prospecting* 44(5): 871-888.

Carey, C., T. Brown, K. Challis, A. Howard, and L. Cooper 2006 Predictive Modeling of Multiperiod Geoarchaeological Resources at a River Confluence: A Case Study from the Trent-Soar, UK. *Archaeological Prospection* 13:241-250.

Carrozzo, M., G. Leucci, S. Negri, and L. Nuzzo 2003 GPR Survey to Understand the Stratigraphy of the Roman Ships Archaeological Site (Pisa, Italy). *Archaeological Prospection* 10:57-72.

Caspar, J. and M. De Bie 1996 Preparing for the Hunt in he Late Paleolithic Camp at Rekem, Belgium. *Journal of Field Archaeology* 23(4):437-460.

Cezar, G. et al. 2001 Two Brazilian archaeological sites investigated by GPR: Serrano and Morro Grande. *Journal of Applied Geophysics* 47(3-4): 227-240.

Chadwick, W.J., and J.A. Madsen 2000 The application of ground-penetrating radar to a coastal prehistoric archaeological site, Cape Henlopen, Delaware, USA. *Geoarchaeology* 15(8): 765-781.

Chaline, J., P. Brunet-Lecomte, and M. Campy 1995 The Last Glacial/Interglacial Record of Rodent Remains from the Gigny Karst Sequence in the French Jura Used for Paleoclimatic and Paleoecological Reconstructions. *Palaeogeography, Palaeoclimatology, Palaeoecology* 117:229-252.

Challis, K. and A. Howard 2006 A Review of Trends within Archaeological Remote Sensing in Alluvial Environments. *Archaeological Prospection* 13:231-240.

Champagne, F. and R. Espitalie 1981 Le Piage, Site Préhistorique du Lot. Mémoires de la Société Préhistorique Française Tome 15.

Chandler, D. and B. Hubbard 2008 Quantifying Sample Bias in Clast Fabric Analysis. *Sedimentology* 55:925-938.

Chang, C. 1988 Nauyalik Fish Camp: An Ethnoarchaeological Study in Activity-Area Formulation. *American Antiquity* 53(1):145-157.

Chapman, H., J. Adcock, and J. Gater 2009 An approach to mapping buried prehistoric palaeosols of the Atlantic seaboard in Northwest Europe using GPR, geoarchaeology and GIS and the implications for heritage management. *Journal of Archaeological Science* 36:2308-2313.

Charnov, E. 1976 Optimal Foraging: Attack Strategy of a Mantid. *Theoretical Population Biology* 9:129-136.

Chase, P. et al. 1994 Taphonomy and Zooarchaeology of a Mousterian Faunal Assemblage from La Quina, France. *Journal of Field Archaeology* 21:289-305.

Chazan, M. 1995 The Language Hypothesis for the Middle to Upper Paleolithic Transition: An Examination Based on a Multiregional Lithic Analysis. *Current Anthropology* 36(5):749-768.

Chianese, D., M. D'Emilio, S. Di Salvia, V. Lapenna, M. Ragosta and E. Rizzo 2004 Magnetic mapping, ground penetrating radar surveys and magnetic susceptibility measurements for the study of the archaeological site of Serra di Vaglio (southern Italy). *Journal of Archaeological Science* 31 (5):633-643.

Child, A. 1995 Microbial Taphonomy of Archaeological Bone. *Studies in Conservation* 40(1):19-30.

Chippindale, C. Capta and Data: On the True Nature of Archaeological Information. *American Antiquity* 65(4):605-612.

Churchill, S. and F. Smith 2000 Makers of the Early Aurignacian of Europe. *Yearbook of Physical Anthropology* 48:61-115.

Clark, J.D. et al. 2003 Stratigraphic, chronological and behavioral contexts of Pleistocene Homo sapiens from Middle Awash, Ethiopia. *Nature* 423:747-751

Clark, G. 1999 Highly Visible, Curiously Intangible. *Science* 283(5410):2029-2032.

1994 Migration as an Explanatory Concept in Paleolithic Archaeology. *Journal of Archaeological Method and Theory* 1(4):305-343.

Clark, G. and J. Lindly 1989 Modern Human Origins in the Levant and Western Asia: The Fossil and Archaeological Evidence. *American Anthropologist* 91(4):962-985.

Claassen, C. 2000 Quantifying Shell: Comments on Mason, Peterson, and Tiffany. *American Antiquity* 65(2):415-418.

Clevis, Q., G. Tucker, G. Lock, S. Lancaster, N. Gasparini, A. Desitter, and R. Bras 2006 Geoarchaeological Simulation of Meandering River Deposits and Settlement Distributions: A Three-Dimensional Approach. *Geoarchaeology* 21(8):843-874.

Cohen, V. and V. Stepanchuk 1999 Late Middle and Early Upper Paleolithic Evidence from the East European Plain and Caucasus: A New Look at Variability, Interactions, and Transitions. *Journal of World Prehistory* 13(3):265-319.

Coinman, N. 2005 Subsistence and Technology in the Late Levantine Upper Paleolithic. *Journal of the Israel Prehistoric Society* 35 pp. 159-177.

1998 The Upper Paleolithic of Jordan. In *The Prehistoric Archaeology of Jordan* D.O. Henry (ed), pp. 39-63. BAR International Series 705. Oxford: BAR Publishing.

1997 The Upper Paleolithic in Jordan: Evidence from the Wadi al-Hasa and South Jordan. In *Studies in the History and Archaeology of Jordan IV.* Amman: The Department of Antiquities of Jordan.

Comaroff, J. and J. Comaroff 1999 *Civil Society and the Political Imagination in Africa: Critical perspectives.* Chicago: U of Chicago Press.

Conard, N. and T. Prindiville 2000 Middle Paleolithic Hunting Economies in the Rhineland. *International Journal of Osteoarchaeology* 10:286-309.

Conard, N., S. Walker, and A. Kandel 2008 How Heating and Cooling and Wetting and Drying can Destroy Dense Faunal Elements and Lead to Differential Preservation. *Palaeogeography, Palaeoclimatology, Palaeoecology* 266:236-245.

Conkey, M. 1987 New Approaches in the Search for Meaning? A review of Research in "Paleolithic Art". *Journal of Field Archaeology* 14(4):413-430.

Conradt, L. and J. Roper 2003 Group Decision-Making in Animals. *Nature* 421:155-158.

Conyers, L. 2006 Innovative Ground-Penetrating Radar Methods for Archaeological Mapping. *Archaeological Prospection* 13:139-141.

2004 *Ground-penetrating Radar for Archaeology.* Walnut Creek: Alta Mira Press.

1995   The use of ground-penetrating radar to map the buried structures and landscape of the Ceren site, El Salvador. *Geoarchaeology* 10(4): 275-299.

Conyers, L. and C. Cameron 1998 Ground-Penetrating Radar Techniques and Three Dimensional Computer Mapping in the American Southwest. *Journal of Field Archaeology* 25(4):417-430.

Conyers, L., E. Ernenwein, M. Grealy, and K. Lowe 2008 Electromagnetic Conductivity Mapping for Site Prediction in Meandering River Floodplains. *Archaeological Prospection* 15:81-91.

Conyers, L. and D. Goodman 1997 *Ground-penetrating Radar: An Introduction for Archaeologists.* Altamira Press: London.

Coope, G. and S. Elias 1999 The Environment of Upper Paleolithic (Magdalenian and Azilian) Hunters at Hauterive-Champreveyres, Neuchatel, Switzerland,

Interpreted from Coleopteran Remains. *Journal of Quaternary Science* 15(2):157-175.

Cordier, S., D. Harmand, M. Frechen, and M. Beiner 2005 Fluvial system response to Middle and Upper Pleistocene climate change in the Meurthe and Moselle valleys (Eastern Paris Basin and Rhenish Massif). *Quaternary Science Reviews* 25:1460-1474.

Cosgrove, R. and A. Pike-Tay 2004 The Middle Paleolithic and Late Pleistocene Tasmania Hunting Behavior: A Reconsideration of the Attributes of Modern Human Behavior. *International Journal of Osteoarchaeology* 14:321-332.

Costamagno, S., M. Liliane, B. Cedric, V. Bernard, M. Bruno 2006 Les Pradelles (Marillac-le-Franc, france): A Mousterian Reindeer Hunting Camp? *Journal of Anthropological Archaeology* 25:466-484.

Cotter, J. 1981 The Upper Paleolithic. However it Got Here, It's Here (Can the Middle Paleolithic Be Far Behind?). *American Antiquity* 46(4):926-928.

Cowie, R. 1977 Optimal Foraging in the Great Tits (*Parus major*). *Nature* 268:137-139.

Cutler, A., A. Behrensmeyer, and R. Chapman 1999 Environmental Information in a Recent Bone Assemblage: Roles of Taphonomic Processes and Ecological Change. *Palaeogeography,Palaeoclimatology, Palaeoecology* 149:359-372.

Daniel, R. Stone Raw Material Availability and Early Archaic Settlement in the Southeastern US. *American Antiquity* 66(2):237-265.

David, F. and C. Farizy 1994 Les vestiges osseux: etude archaeozoologique. In Farizy, David, Jaubert (eds). *Hommes et Bisons du Paleolithique Moyen a Mauran (Haute-Garonne)*: pp. 177-134. Paris: CNRS Editions.

David, F, Vladimir D'Iatchenko, James G. Enloe, Michel Girard, Maurice Hardy Vincent Lhomme, Annie Roblin-Jouve, Anne-marie Tillier, and Clare Tolmie

2009   New Neandertal remains from the Grotte du Bison at Arcy-sur-Cure, France. Journal of Human Evolution 57:805–809.

Davidson, I. 2010 The Colonization of Australia and Its Adjacent Islands and the Evolution of Modern Cognition. *Current Anthropology* 51(S1):S177-S189.

Davies, C. 2005 Quaternary Paleoenvironments and Potential for Human Exploitation of the Jordan Plateau Desert Interior. *Geoarchaeology* 20(4):379-400.

Davies, N. 1977 Prey Selection and Social Behavior in Wagtails. *Journal of Animal Ecology.* 46:37-57.

Davis, L., M. Punke, R. Hall, M. Fillmore, and S. Willis 2004 A Late Pleistocene Occupation on the Southern Coast of Oregon. *Journal of Field Archaeology* 29(1/2):7-16.

Davis, R. 1998 The Enisei River of Central Siberia in the Late Pleistocene. *Journal of Archaeological Research* 6(2):169-194.

De Beaune, S. 2004 The Invention of Technology: Prehistory and Cognition. *Current Anthropology* 45(2):139-162.

Denton, G. 2000 Does an Asymmetric Thermohaline-Ice-Sheet Oscillatro Drive 100,000-yr Glacial Cycles? *Journal of Quaternary Science* 15(4):301-318.

D'Errico, F. 2003 Invisible Frontier: A Multiple Species Model for the Origin of Behavioral Modernity. *Evolutionary Anthropology* 12:188-202.

D'Errico, F., C. Henshilwood, G. Lawson, M. Vanhaeren, A. Tillier, M. Soressi, F. Bresson, B. Maureille, A. Nowell, J. Lakarra, L. Blackwell, and M. Julien 2003 Archaeological Evidence for the Emergence of Language, Symbolism, and Music-An Alternative Multidisciplinary Perspective. *Journal of World Prehistory* 17(1):1-70.

D'Errico, F., C. Henshilwood, P. Nilssen 2001 An engraved bone fragment from c. 70,000-year-old Middle Stone Age levels at Blombos Cave, South Africa: implications for the origin of symbolism and language. *Antiquity* 75(288):309-318.

De Sonneville-Bordes, D. 1963 Upper Paleolithic Cultures in Western Europe. *Science* 142(3590):347-355.

Dhaene, J. et al. a Coherent Risk Measure be Too Subadditive? *Journal of Risk and Insurance* 75(2):365-386.

Dibble, H., P. Chase, S. McPherron, and A. Tuffreau 1996 Testing the Reality of a "Living Floor" with Archaeological Data. *American Antiquity* 62(4):629-651.

Dibble, H. and S. McPherron 2006 The Missing Mousterian. *Current Anthropology* 47(5):777-803.

Di Clemente, D. and D. Hantula 2003 Optimal Foraging: Increasing Sensitivity to Delay. *Psychology and Marketing* 20(9):785-809.

Dobson, J. and G. Geelhoed 2001 On the Chatelperronian/Aurignacian Conundrum: One Culture, Multiple Human Morphologies? *Current Anthropology* 42(1):139-142.

Dogan, M. and S. Papamarinopoulos 2006 Exploration of the Hellenistic Fortification Complex at Asea Using a Multigeophysical Prospection Approach. *Archaeol. Prospect.* 13, 1–9.

Dominguez-Rodrigo, M. and T. Pickering 2003 Early Hominid Hunting and Scavenging: A Zooarchaeological Review. *Evolutionary Anthropology* 12:275-282.

Drucker, D. and H. Bocherens 2004 Carbon and Nitrogen Stable Isotopes as Tracers of Change in Diet Breadth during he Middle and Upper Paleolithic in Europe. *International Journal of Osteoarchaeology* 14:162-177.

2003 Carbon and Nitrogen Isotopic Composition of Red Deer Collagen as a Tool for Tracking Paleoenvironmental change during the Late-Glacial and Early Holocene in the Northern Jura (France). *Palaeogeography, Palaeoclimatology, Palaeoecology* 195:375-388.

Due Trier, O., S. Larsen, and R. Solberg 2009 Automatic Detection of Circular Structuresin High-resolution Satellite Images of Agricultural Land. *Archaeological Prospection* 16:1-15.

Elkin, D. 1995 Volume Density of South American Camelid Skeletal Parts. *International Journal of Osteoarchaeology* 5:29-37.

Ellwood, B., F. Harrold, S. Benoist, L. Straus, M. Morales, K. Petruso, N. Bicho, J. Zilhao, and N. Soler 2001 Paleoclimate and Intersite Correlations from Late Pleistocene/Holocene Cave Sites: Results from Southern Europe. *Geoarchaeology* 16(4):433-463.

Enloe, James 2010 Technology and Demographics: An Introduction. In *The Magdalenian Household: Unraveling Domesticity.* E. Zubrow, F. Audouze, J. Enloe (eds) SUNY Press. pp. 11-14.

2007 Ground Penetrating Radar in the Paleolithic: A Survey of an Open-air site at Verberie, France. Paper presented in session "Remote Sensing and Geophysical Techniques", at the 72nd annual meeting of the Society for American Archaeology, Austin, TX. 2007

2006 Geological Processes and Site Structure: Assessing Integrity at a Late Paleolithic Open-Air Site in Northern France. *Geoarchaeology* 21(6):523-540.

2004 Equifinality, Assemblage Integrity and Behavioral Inferences at Verberie. *Journal of Taphonomy* 2(3):147-165.

1999 Hunting Specialization: Single-Species Focus and Human Adaptation. In Brugal, David, Enloe, Jaubert (eds) *Le Bison: Gibier et Moyen de Subsistance des Hommes du Paleolithique aux Paleoindiens des Grandes Plaines.* Editions APDCA. pp. 501-509.

1997 Seasonality and Age Structure in Remains of *Rangifer tarandus* : Magdalenian Hunting Strategy at Verberie. *Anthropozoologica* 25-26:95-102.

1993 Subsistence Organization in the Early Upper Paleolithic: Reindeer Hunters of the Abri du Flageolet, Couche V. In *Before Lascaux: the Complex record of the Early Upper Paleolithic,* H Knecht, A. Pike-Tay, R. White (eds), pp. 101-115. CRC Press.

1983 Site Structure: A methodological approach to analysis. *Halliksa'i: UNM Contributions to Anthropology* (2):28-39.

Enloe, J. and F. Audouze 2010 The Magdalenian site of Verberie (Le Buisson Campin): An Overview. In *The Magdalenian Household: Unraveling Domesticity.* E. Zubrow, F. Audouze, J. Enloe (eds) SUNY Press. pp. 15-21.

Enloe, James and Francine David 1997 Rangifer herd behavior: Seasonality of hunting in the Magdalenian of the Paris Basin. In: LJ Jackson and P Thacker (eds), *Caribou and Reindeer Hunters of the Northern Hemisphere,* pp. 47-63, Avebury Press, Aldershot.

1992 Food Sharing in the Paleolithic: Carcass refitting at Pincevent. In JL Hofman and JG Enloe (eds), *Piecing Together the Past: Applications of refitting studies in Archaeology,* pp. 296-315, British Archaeological Reports International Series 578.

Enloe, J., F. David, and T. Hare 1994 Patterns of Faunal Processing ar Section 27 of Pincevent: The Use of Spatial Analysis and Ethnoarchaeological Data in the Interpretation of Archaeological Site Structure. *Journal of Anthropological Archaeology* 13:105-124.

Enloe, J. and E. Turner 2005 Methodological Problems and Biases in Age Determinations: A View from the Magdalenian. In: Ruscillo (ed) *Recent Advances in Aging and Sexing Animal bones: 9th ICAZ Conference, Durham 2002*, pp. 129-143. Oxbow Press.

Ervynck, A., W. Van Neer, H. Huster-Plogmann, and J. Schibler 2003 Beyond Affluence: The Zooarchaeology of Luxury. *World Archaeology* 34(3):428-441.

Faith, J. 2007 Changes in Reindeer Body Part Representation at Grotte XVI, Dordogne, France. *Journal of Archaeological Science* 34:2003-2011.

Faith, J. and A. Behrensmeyer 2006 Changing Patterns of Carnivore Modification in a Landscape Bone Assemblage, Amboseli Park, Kenya. *Journal of Archaeological Science* 33:1718-1733.

Fedele, F., B. Giaccio, R. Isaia, and G. Orsi 2002 Ecosystem Impact of the Camanian Ignimbrite Eruption in Late Pleistocene Europe. *Quaternary Research* 57:420-424.

Feurdean, A. and O. Bennike 2004 Late Quaternary Paleoecological and Paleoenvironmental Reconstruction in the Gutaiului Mountains, NW Romania. *Journal of Quaternary Research* 19(8):809-827.

Fisher, L. 2006 Blades and Microliths: Changing contexts of Tool production from Magdalenian to the Early Mesolithic in Southern Germany. *Journal of Anthropological Archaeology* 25:226-238.

Foley, R. and M. Lahr 2003 On Stony Ground: Lithic technology, Human Evolution, and the Emergence of Culture. *Evolutionary Anthropology* 12:109-122.

Fontana, L. 2003 le Renne, l'Aurochs et les Volcans: Hommes, gibiers et reconquête forestière en Limagne entre 12 300 BP et 7500 BP, *Paléo* 15, 87-104.

2000 Stratégies de subsistance au Badegoulien et au Magdalénien en Auvergne : nouvelles données, *in* G. Pion dir., *Le Paléolithique supérieur récent : nouvelles données sur le peuplement et l'environnement, Actes de la Table Ronde de Chambéry, 12 - 13 mars 1999*, Mémoire XXVIII, Société préhistorique française, Paris, p. 59-65.

1998 Mobilité et subsistance au Magdalénien supérieur et final en Auvergne, *in* J.-Ph. Brugal, L. Meignen, M. Patou-Mathis dir., *Économie préhistorique : les comportements de subsistance au Paléolithique, XVᵉ Rencontres internationales d'archéologie et d'Histoire d'Antibes*, Éditions ADPCA, Sophia Antipolis, p. 373-386.

Forte, E. and M. Pipan 2008 Integrated Seismic Tomography and GPR for the High-Resolution Study of Burial Mounds (tumuli). *Journal or Archaeological Science* 35(9):2614-2623.

Fowler, Donald 1992 Hermes Trismegistus in Eden: Praxis, Process, and Postmodern Archaeology. *Society for California Archaeology* 6:1-14.

Fowler, K.Greenfield, and L. van Schalwyk 2004 The Effects of Burrowing Activity on Archaeological Sites: Ndondondwane, South Africa. *Geoarchaeology* 19(5):441-470.

Frayer, D., M. Wolpoff, A. Thorne, F. Smith, and G. Pope 1993 Theories of Modern Human Origins: The Paleontological Test. *American Anthropologist* 95(1):14-50.

Frechen, M., B. van Vliet-Lanoe, P. van den Haute 2001 The Upper Pleistocene Loess Record at Harmignies/Belgium: High Resolution Terrestrial Archive of Climate Forcing. *Palaeogeography, Palaeoclimatology, Palaeoecology* 173:175-195.

Friesen, T. 2001 A Zooarchaeological Signature for Meat Storage: Re-thinking the Drying Utility Index. *American Antiquity* 66(2):315-331.

Frison, G. *The Casper Site: A Hell Gap Bison kill on the High Plains.* Academic Press.

Gabora, L. 2006 The Fate of Evolutionary Archaeology: Survival or Extinction? *World Archaeology* 38(4):690-696.

Gaffney, C., J. Gater, T. Saunders, J. Adcock D-Day: Geophysical Investigation of a World War II German Site in Normandy, France. *Archaeological Prospection* 11:121-128.

Gat, A. 2000 The Human Motivational Complex: Evolutionary Theory and the Causes of Hunter-Gatherer Fighting, Part II, Proximate, Subordinate, and Derivative Causes. *Anthropological Quarterly* 73(2):74-88.

Gilead, I. 1991 The Upper Paleolithic Period in the Levant. *Journal of World Prehistory* 5(2):105-154.

Gilead, I. and O. Bar-Yosef 1993 Early Upper Paleolithic Sites in the Qadesh Barnea Area, NE Sinai. *Journal of Field Archaeology* 20(3):265-280.

Gibbard, P. 1988 The History of the Great Northwest European Rivers during the Past Three Million Years. *Philosophical Transactions of the Royal Society of London* B 318:559-602.

Gifford, D. 1981 Taphonomy and Paleoecology: A Critical review of Archaeology's Sister Disciplines. In Schiffer (ed) *Advances in Archaeological Method and Theory* 4:365-438.

Gifford-Gonzalez, D. 1997 Gaps in the Zooarchaeological Analyses of Butchery: Is Gender an Issue? In: Hudson (ed) *Ethnoarchaeological and Experimental Contributions to the interpretation of Faunal Remains*, pp.. 181-199. Center for Archaeological Investigations, SIU at Carbondale, Occasional Paper No. 21.

1991 Examining and Refining the Quadratic Crown Height Method of Age Estimation. In: Stiner (ed) *Human Predators and Prey Mortality*, pp. 41-78. Westview Press.

Gizewski, Z., P. Wojtal, J.Csapo, J. Gizewski, Z. Jaczewski, and J. Csapo Jr. 2004 Remains of Late Pleistocene Reindeer from Chmielewo, NE Poland. *European Journal of Wildlife Resources* 50:207-212.

Gladfelter, B. 1977 Geoarcheology: The Geomorphologist and Archaeology. *American Antiquity* 42(4):519-538.

Golubin, A. 2006 Pareto-Optimal Insurance Policies in the Models with a Premium Based on the Actuarial Value. *Journal of Risk and Insurance* 73(3):469-487.

Goodman, D., Y. Nishimura, H. Hongo, and N. Higashi 2006 Correcting for Topography and the Tilt of GPR Antennae. *Archaeological Prospection* 13:157-161.

Goodman, D. and Nishimura, H. 1993 A Ground-Radar View of Japanese Burial Mounds. *Antiquity* 67(255): 349-354.

Goodman, D., S. Piro, et al. 2004 Discovery of a 1(st) century AD roman amphitheater and other structures at the forum novum by GPR." *Journal of Environmental and Engineering Geophysics* 9(1): 35-41.

Gould, S. and N. Eldredge 1977 Punctuated Equilbria: The Tempo and Mode of Evolution Reconsidered. *Paleobiology* 3:115-151.

Grant, A. 1982 The Use of Tooth Wear as a Guide to the Age of Domestic Animals. In Wilson, Grigson and Payne (eds) *Aging and Sexing Animal Bones from Archaeological Sites*, pp. 91-108. BAR Series 109.

Grasmueck, M., R. Weger and L. Hortsmeyer 2004 Three-Dimensional Ground-Penetrating Radar Imaging of Sedimentary Structures, Fractures, and Archaeological Features at Submeter Resolution. *Geology* 11/04 21(11):933-936.

Grayson, D. 1984 *Quantitative Zooarchaeology: Topics in the Analysis of Archaeological Faunas.* Academic Press.

Grayson, D. and F. Delpech 2003 Specialized Early Upper Paleolithic Hunters in Southwestern France? *Journal of Archaeological Science* 29:1439-1449.

1997 Changing Diet Breadth in the Early Upper Paleolithic of Southwestern France. *Journal of Archaeological Science* 25:1119-1129.

Grayson, D., F. Delpech, J-P. Rigaud, J. Simek 2001 Explaining the Devlopment of Dietary Dominance by a Single Ungulate Taxon at Grotte XVI, Dordogne, France. *Journal of Archaeological Science* 28:115-125.

Grayson, D. and D. Meltzer 2002 Clovis Hunting and Large Mammal Extinction: A Critical Rview of the Evidence. *Journal of World Prehistory* 16(4):313-359.

Grealy, M. 2006 Resolution of GPR Reflections at Differing Frequencies. *Archaeological Prospection* 13:142-146.

Grccn, R. E. et al. 2010 A draft sequence of the Neandertal genome. *Science* 328:710–722.

Grove, M. 2010 Logistical mobility reduces subsistence risk in hunting economies. *Journal of Archaeological Science* 37: 1913-1921.

Habgood, P. and N. Franklin 2008 The revolution that didn't arrive: a review of Pleistocene Sahul. *Journal of Human Evolution* 55:187-222.

Habermas, J. 1987 *The Theory of Communicative Action.* Cambridge: Polity Press

Hamada, M. and E. Valdez 2008 CAPM and Option Pricing with Elliptically Contoured Distributions. *Journal of Risk and Insurance* 75(2):387-409.

Hardy-Smith, T. and P. Edwards 2004 The Garbage Crisis in prehistory: artefact discard patterns at the Early Natufian site of Wadi Hammeh 27 and the origins of household refuse disposal strategies. *Journal of Anthropological Archaeology* 23:253–289.

Harrold, F. 2000 The Chatelperronian in Historical Context. *Journal of Anthropological Research* 56(1):59-75.

Hanson, B. 1980 Fluvial Taphonomic Processes: Models and Experiments. In Behrensmeyer and Hill (eds) *Fossils in the Making: Vertebrate Taphonomy and Paleoecology*, pp. 131-152. University of Chicago Press.

Hawkes, K., J. Altman, S. Beckerman, R. Grinker, H. Harpending, R. Jeske, N. Peterson, E. Smith, G. Wenzel, J. Yellen 1993 Why Hunter-Gatherers Work: An Ancient Version of the Problem of Public Goods. *Current Anthropology* 34(4):341-361.

Hawks, J. and M. Wolfpoff 2003 Sixty Years of Modern Human Origins in the American Anthropological Association. American Anthropologist 105(1):89-100.

Headland, T. 1997 Revisionism in Ecological Anthropology. *Current Anthropology* 38(4):605-630.

Heller, R. 1980 On Optimal Diet in a Patchy Environment. *Theoretical Population Biology* 17:201-214.

Henry, Donald 1995 *Prehistoric Cultural Ecology and Evolution: Insights from Southern Jordan.* New York: Plenum Press.

1994 Prehistoric Cultural Ecology in Southern Jordan. *Science* 265:336-341.

1992 Transhumance during the Late Levantine Mousterian. In *New Perspectives on the Middle Paleolithic: Adaptation, Behavior, and Variability*, H. Dibble and P. Mellars (eds) pp.143-162. Philadelphia: University of Pennsylvania.

1982 The Prehistory of Southern Jordan and Relationships to the Levant. *Journal of Field Archaeology* 9(4):417-444.

Henry, D., H. Hietala, A, Rosen, Y. Demidenko, V. Usik, T. Armagan 2004 Human Behavioral Organization in the Middle Paleolithic: Were Neanderthals Different? *American Anthropologist* 106(1):17-31.

Henshilwood, C., F. d'Errico, and I. Watts 2009 Engraved ochres from the Middle Stone Age levels at Blombos Cave, South Africa. *Journal of Human Evolution* 57:27-47.

Henshilwood, C ., F . d'Errico, M. vanHaeren, K . van Niekerk, and Z . Jacobs. 2004 Middle Stone Age shell beads from South Africa. *Science* 304:404.

Henshilwood, C. and C. Marean 2003 The Origin of Modern Human Behavior: Critique of the Models and Their Test Implications. *Current Anthropology* 44(5):627-651.

Hewlett, B., M. Lamb, B. Levendecker, and A. Scholmerich 2000 Internal Working Models, Trust, and Sharing among Foragers. *Current Anthropology* 41(2):287-297.

Hietala, H. and D. Stevens 1977 Spatial Analysis: Multiple Procedures in Pattern Recognition Studies. *American Antiquity* 42(4):539-559

Hildebrand, J., S. Wiggins, P. Henkart, and L. Conyers 2002 Comparison of Seismic reflection and GPR Imaging at the Controlled Archaeological Test Site, Champaign, Illinois. *Archaeological Prospection* 9:9-21.

Hill, A. 1980 Early Postmortem Damage to the Remains of Some Contemporary East African Mammals. In: Behrensmeyer and Hill (eds) *Fossils in the Making: Vertebrate Taphonomy and Paleoecology*, pp. 131-152. University of Chicago Press.

Hill, C. 2001 Geologic contexts of the Acheulean (Middle Pleistocene) in Eastern Sahara. *Geoarchaeology* 16(1):65-94.

Hindelang, M. and A. Maclean 1997 Bone Density Determination of Moose Skeletal Remains from Isle Royale National Park using Digital image Enhancement and Quantitative Computed Tomography (QCT). *International Journal of Osteoarchaeology* 7:193-201.

Hockett, B. and J. Haws 2002 Taphonomic and Methodological Perspectives of Leporid Hunting During the Upper Paleolithic of the Western Mediterranean Basin. *Journal of Archaeological Method and Theory* 9(3):269-302.

Hodder, I. 1979 Economic and Social Stress and Material Cultural Patterning. *American Antiquity* 44(3):446-454.

Hodges, C, 1981 Optimal Foraging in Bumblebees—Hunting by Expectation. *AnimalBehavior* 29:1166-1171.

Hoffecker, J. Innovation and Technical Knowledge in the Upper Paleolithic of Northern Eurasia. *Evolutionary Anthropology* 14:186-198.

1999 Neanderthals and Modern humans in Eastern Europe. *Evolutionary Anthropology*:129-141.

Holdaway, S. and P. Fanning 2008 Developing a Landscape History as Part of a Survey Strategy: A Critique of Current Settlement System Approaches based on Case Studies from Western New South Wales, Australia. *Journal of Archaeological Method and Theory* 15:167-189.

Houmark-Nielsen, M. and K. Kjaer 2003 Southwest Scandinavia, 40-15 kyr BP: Paleogeography and Environmental Change. *Journal of Quaternary Science* 18(8):769-786.

Iacumin, P., V. Nikolaev, M. Ramigni 2000 C and N Stable Isotope Measurements on Eurasian Fossil mammals, 40,000 to 10,000 Years BP: Herbivore Physiologies and Paleoenvironmental Reconstruction. *Palaeogeography, Palaeoclimatology, Palaeoecology* 163:33-47.

Ioannidou, E. 2003 Taphonomy of Animal Bones: Species, Age, and Breed Variability of Sheep, Cattle, and Pig Bone Density. *Journal of Archaeological Science* 30:355-365.

Isaac, G. 1981 Emergence of Human Behavior Patterns. Archaeological Tests of Alternative Models of Early Hominid Behavior: Excavation and Experiments. *Philosophical Transactions of the Royal Society of London* B 292:177-188.

Isarin, R. 1997 Permafrost Distribution and Temperatures in Europe during the Younger Dryas. *Permafrost and Periglacial Processes* 8:313-333.

Jackes, M., R. Sherburne, D. Lubell, C. Barker, and M. Wayman 2001 Destruction of Microstructure in Archaeological Bone: a Case Study from Portugal.

James, H. and M. Petraglia 2005 Modern Human Origins and the Evolution of Behavior in the Later Pleistocene Record of South Asia. *Current Anthropology* 46(Supplement):S3-S27.

Jans, M., C. Nielsen-Marsh, C. Smith, M. Collins, and H. Kars 2004 Characterization of Microbial Attack on Archaeological Bone. *Journal of Archaeological Science* 31:87-95.

Jaubert J, Lorblanchet M, Laville H, Slot-Moller R, Turq A, Brugal J-P. 1990 *Les Chasseurs d'Auroch de La Borde*. Editions de la Maison des Sciences de l'Homme: Paris.

Jensen, H. 1988 Functional Analysis of Prehistoric Flint Tools by High-Power Microscopy: A Review of West European Research. *Journal of World Prehistory* 2(1):53-88.

Jochim, M. Two Late Paleolithic Sites on the Federsee, Germany. *Journal of Field Archaeology* 22(3):263-273.

Jochim, M., C. Herhahn, and H. Starr 1999 The Magdalenian Colonization of Southern Germany. *American Anthropologist* 101(1):129-142.

Jones, E. 2006 Subsistence Change, Landscape Use, and Changing Site Elevation at the Pleistocene-Holocene Transition in the Dordogne of Southern France. *Journal of Archaeological Science* xx:1-10.

Jost, A., D. Lunt, M. Kageyama, A. Abe-Ouchi, O. Peyron, P. Valdes, and G. Ramstein High-Resolution Simulations of the Last Glacial maximum Climate over Europe: A Solution to Discrepancies with Continental Paleoclimatic Reconstructions? *Climate Dynamics* 24:577-590.

Kahn, J. 2001 Anthropology and Modernity. *Current Anthropology* 42(5):651-680.

Kasse, W. Hoek, J. Bohncke, M. Konert, J. Weijers, M. Cassee, and R. Van Der Zee 2005 Late Glacial Fluvial Response of the Niers-Rhine (Western Germany) to Climate and Vegetation Change. *Journal of Quaternary Science* 20(4):377-394.

Kaplan, H., Hill, K. 1985 Food sharing among Ache foragers: tests of explanatory hypotheses. *Current Anthropology* 26: 223-246.

Kaplan, H., Hill, K., Hurtado, A.M. 1990 Risk, foraging and food sharing among the Ache. In: Cashdan,E.A.(Ed.), *Risk and Uncertainty in Tribal and Peasant Economies*. Westview Press: Boulder. pp.107-143.

Kaufman, D. 1998 Measuring Archaeological Diversity: An Application of the Jackknife Technique. *American Antiquity* 63(1):73-85.

Keeley, L. 1991 *The Interpretation of Archaeological Spatial Patterning*. Plenum Publishing.

1987 Hafting and Retooling at Verberie. La Main et L'outil: Manches et Emmanchements Prehistorique. CNRS. pp. 89-96.

Keen, I. 2006 Constraints on the Development of Enduring Inequalities in Late Holocene Australia. *Current Anthropology* 47(1):7-38.

Kelly, Robert 1995 *The Foraging Spectrum: Diversity in Hunter-Gatherer Lifeways.* Washington, Smithsonian Institution.

Kelly, R. and L. Todd 1988 Coming into the Country: Early Paleoindian Hunting and Mobility. *American Antiquity* 53(2):231-244.

Kent, S. 1993 Variability in Faunal Assemblages: The Influence of Hunting skills, Sharing, Dogs, and Mode of Cooking on Faunal Remains at a Sedentary Kalahari Community. *Journam of Anthropological Archaeology* 12:323-385.

1992 Studying Variability in the Archaeological Record: An Ethnoarchaeological Model for Distinguishing Mobility Patterns. *American Antiquity* 57(4):635-660.

Kidder, L. and H. 1936 The Cave of Puy-de-Lacan: A Magdalenian Site in South-Central France. *American Anthropologist* 38(3):439-451.

Kidwell, S., T. Rothfus, and M. Best 2001 Sensitivity of Taphonomic Signatures to Sample Size, Sieve Size, Damage Scoring System, and Target Taxa. *Palaios* 16:26-52.

Kilberger, M. and J. Enloe 2005 Hunting *Rangifer* in the Late Upper Paleolithic: Developing methodologies for constructing mortality profiles from maxillary dentition. Poster presented at the tenth quadrennial International Congress of the International Council for ArchaeoZoology, Mexico City, August 23-28, 2006.

Kintigh, K. 1994 Contending with Contemporaneity in Settlement-Pattern Studies. *American Antiquity* 59(1):143-148.

Kintigh, K. and A. Ammerman 1982 Heuristic Approaches to Spatial Analysis in Archaeology. *American Antiquity* 47(1):31-63.

Klein, R. 2001 Southern Africa and modern human origins. *Journal of Anthropological Research* 57:1-16. Archaeology and the Evolution of Human Behavior. *Evolutionary Anthropology* pp. 17-36.

1999 The Human Career: Human Biological and Cultural Origins, second ed. University of Chicago Press, Chicago.

Anatomy, Behavior, and Modern Human Origins. *Journal of World Prehistory* 9(2):167-198.

1994 The problem of modern human origins. In: Nitecki, M.H., Nitecki, D.V. (Eds.), The Origins of Anatomically Modern Humans. Plenum Press, New York, pp. 3-17.

1989 Why Does Skeletal Part Representation Differ between Smaller and Larger Bovids at Klasies River Mouth and Other Archaeological Sites? *Journal of Archaeological Science* 6:363-381.

1978 Stone Age Predation on Large African Bovids. *Journal of Archaeological Science* 5:195-217.

Klein, R. and K. Cruz-Uribe 1984 *The Analysis of Animal Bones from Archaeological Sites.* University of Chicago Press.

Klein, R. et al. 1983 The Calculation and Interpretation of Ungulate Age Profiles from Dental Crown Heights. In: Bailey (ed) *Hunter-gatherer Economy in Prehistory: A European Perspective*, pp. 151-158. Cambridge University Press.

Klotz, S., U. Muller, V. Mosbrugger, J. de Beaulieu, and M. Reille 2004 Eemian to Wurmian Climate Dynamics: History and Pattern of Changes in Central Europe. *Palaeogeography, Palaeoclimatology, Palaeoecology* 211:107-126.

Kolb, M. and J. Snead 1997 It's A Small World after All: Comparative Analyses of Community Organization in Archaeology. *American Antiquity* 62(4):609-628.

Kooyman, B. 2006 Boundary Theory as a Means to Understanding Social Space in Archaeological Sites. *Journal of Anthropological Archaeology* 25:424-435.

Kowalewski, S. 2008 Regional Settlement Pattern Studies. *Journal of Archaeological Research* 16:225-285.

Kowalewski, M. and M. Labarbera 2004 Actualistic Taphonomy: Death, decay, and Disintegration in Contemporary Settings. *Palaios* 19:423-427.

Krebs, J. 1978 Optimal Foraging: Decision Rules for Predators. In *Behavioral Ecology: An Evolutionary Approach.* Krebs, Davies (eds) Oxford: Blackwell.

Krings, M., et al. 1997 Neandertal DNA Sequences and the Origin of Modern Humans. *Cell* 90:19-30.

Kuehn, S. 1998 New Evidence for Late Paleoindian-Early Archaic Subsistence Behavior in the Western great Lakes. *American Antiquity* 63(3):457-476.

Kuhn, S. and M. Stiner 2006 What's a Mother To Do? The Division of Labor among Neanderthals and Modern humans in Eurasia. *Current Anthropology* 47(6):953-980.

1998 The Earliest Aurignacian of Riparo Mochi (Liguria, Italy). *Current Anthropology* 39(2) Supplement: Special issue: the Neanderthal Problem and the Evolution of Human Behavior:S175-S189.

Kukla, G. and V. Cilek 1996 Plio-Pleistocene Megacycles: Record of Climate and Tectonics. *Palaeogeography, Palaeoclimatology, Palaeoecology* 120:171-194.

Kuznar, L. 2001 Risk Sensitivity and Value among Andean Pastoralists: Measures, Models, and Empirical Tests. *Current Anthropology* 42(3):432-440.

Lagarde, J., D. Amorese, M. Font, E. laville, and O. Dugue 2003 The Structural Evolution of the English Channel Area. *Journal of Quaternary Science* 18(3-4):201-213.

Lahr, M. and R. Foley 1998 Towards a Theory of Modern Human Origins: Geography, Demography, and Diversity in Recent Human Evolution. *Yearbook of Physical Anthropology* 41:137-176.

Laignel, B., F. Quesnel, C. Spencer, R. Meyer, and J-P. Lautridou Slope Clay-with-Flints (biefs a silex) as Indicators of Quaternary Periglacial Dynamics in the Western Part of the Paris Basin, France. *Journal of Quaternary Science* 18(3-4):295-299.

Lam, Y., X Chen, O. Pearson 2005 Bone Density Studies and the Interpretation of the Faunal Record. *Evolutionary Antrhopology* 14:99-108.

1999 Intertaxonomic Variability in Patterns of Bone Density and the Differential Representation of Bovid, Cervid, and Equid Elements in the Archaeological Record. *American Antiquity* 64(2):343-362.

Lam, Y., O. Pearson, C. Marean, and X. Chen 2003 Bone Density Studies in Zooarchaeology. *Journal of Archaeological Science* 30:1701-1708.

Laury, S. and M. McInnes 2003 The Impact of Insurance Prices on Decision Making Biases: An Experimental Analysis. *Journal of Risk and Insurance* 70(2):219-233.

Laville, H. and J-P. Rigaud 1973 The Perigordian V Industries in Perigord: Typological Variations, Stratigraphy and Relative Chronology. *World Archaeology* 4(3):330-338.

Lericolais, G., J-P. Aufret, and J-F. Bourillet 2003 The Quaternary Channel River: Seismic Stratigraphy of its Paleo-Valleys and Deeps. *Journal of Quaternary Science* 18(3-4):245-260.

Lebret, P. and J-P Lautridou 1991 The Loess of West Europe. *GeoJournal* 24(2):151-156.

Leckebusch, J. Precision Real-time Positioning for Fast Geophysical Prospection. *Archaeological Prospection* 12:199-202.

3D GPR: A Modern Three-Dimensional Prospection Method. *Archaeological Prospection* 10:213-240.

Leckebusch, J. and R. Peikert 2001 Investigating the True Resolution and Capabilities of Ground-Penetrating Radar in Archaeological Surveys: Measurements in a Sand Box. *Archaeological Prospection* 8:29-40.

Lee, Richard and I. De Vore 1968 *Man the Hunter.* Chicago: Aldine.

Lehman, J. 1976 The filter-feeder as an Optimal Forager, and the predicted shapes of Feeding Curves. *Limnology and Oceanography* 21:501-516.

Leonard, W. and M. Robertson 1992 Nutritional Requirements and Human Evolution: A Bioenergetics Model. *American Journal of Human Biology* 4:179-195.

Leopold, M. and J. Volkel 2004 Neolithic Flint Mines in Arnhofen, Southern Germany: A Ground penetrating Radar Survey. In *Archaeological Prospection* 11:57-64.

Lewin, J. and M. Macklin 2003 Preservation Potential for Late Quaternary River Alluvium. *Journal of Quaternary Science* 18(2):107-120.

Lewis, A. 1982 Patch use by Gray Squirrels and Optimal Foraging. *Ecology* 61:1371-1379.

Lewontin, R. 1979 Fitness, Survival, and Optimality. *Analysis of Ecological Systems*. Horn, Mitchell, Stairs (eds) Columbus: OSU Press.

Liebenberg, L. 2006 Persistence Hunting by Modern Hunter-Gatherers. *Current Anthropology* 47(6):1017-1025.

Limondin, N. 1995 Late-Glacial and Holocene Malacofaunas from Archaeological Sites in the Somme Valley (North France). *Journal of Archaeological Science* 22:683-698.

Lindly, J., G. Clark, O. Bar-Yosef, D. lieberman, J. Shea, H. Dibble, P. Chase, C. Gamble, R. Gargett, K. Jacobs, P. Mellars, A. Pike-Tay, Y. Smirnov, L. Straus, C. Stringer, E. Trinkaus, R. White 1990 Symbolism and Modern Human Origins. *Current Anthropology* 31(3):233-261.

Littleton, J. 2000 Taphonomic Effects of Erosion on Deliberately Buried Bodies. *Journal of Archaeological Science* 27:5-18.

Locock, M., C. Currie, and S. Gray 1992 Chemical Changes in Buried Animal Bone: Data from a Postmedieval Assemblage. *International Journal of Osteoarchaeology* 2:297-304.

Lorenzo, H . and P. Arias 2005 A Methodology for Rapid Archaeological Site Documentation Using Ground-Penetrating Radar and Terrestrial Photogrammetry. In *Geoarchaeology: An International Journal* 20:(5) 521-535.

Lorenzo, H., M. Hernandez, and V. Cuellar 2002 Select Radar Images of Man-made Underground Galleries. *Archaeological Prospection* 9:1-7.

Lourandos, H. 1993 Hunter-Gatherer Cultural Dynamics: Long- and Short-Term Trends in Australian Prehistory. *Journal of Archaeological Research* 1(1):67-88.

Lycett, N. and SJ Von Cramon-Taubadel 2008 Human cranial variation fits iterative founder effect model with African origin. *American Journal of Physical Anthropology* 136(1):108–113.

Lyman, R. 2006 Identifying Bilateral Pairs of Deer (*Odocoileus* sp.) Bones: How Symmetrical is Symmetrical Enough? *Journal of Archaeological Science* 33:1256-1265.

2002 Taphonomic Agents and Taphonomic Signatures. *American Antiquity* 67(2):361-365.

1996 Applied Zooarchaeology: The Relevance of Faunal Analysis to Wildlife Management. *World Archaeology* 28(1):110-125.

1985 Bone Frequencies, Differential Transport, In Situ Destruction, and the MGUI. *Journal of Archaeological Science* 12:221-236.

1984 Bone density and Differential Survivorship of Fossil Classes. *Journal of Anthropological Archaeology* 3:259-299.

Maat, G. 1993 Bone preservation, Decay, and its Related Conditions in Ancient Human Bones from Kuwait. *International Journal of Osteoarchaeology* 3:77-86.

MacDonald, D. and B. Hewlett 1999 Reproductive Interests and Forager Mobility. *Current Anthropology* 40(4):501-523.

Malainey, M., R. Przybylski, and B. Sherriff 2001 One Person's Food: How and Why Fish Avoidance May Affect the Settlement and Subsistence Patterns of Hunter-Gatherers. *American Antiquity* 66(1):161-161.

Mandel, R. and A. Simmons 2001 Prehistoric Occupation of Late Quaternary Landscapes near Kharga Oasis, Western Desert of Egypt. *Geoarchaeology* 16(1):95-117.

Mandryk, C. 1993 Hunter-Gatherer Social Costs and the Nonviolability of Submarginal Environments. *Journal of Anthropological Research* 49(1):39-71.

Mannino, M. and K. Thomas 2002 Depletion of a Resource? The Impact of Prehistoric Human Foraging on Intertidal Mollusc Communities and its Significance for Human Settlement, Mobility and Dispersal. *World Archaeology* 33(3):452-474.

Marean, C., Y. Abe, P. Nilssen, and E. Stone 2001 Estimating the Minimum Number of Skeletal Elements (MNE) in Zooarchaeology: A Review and a New Image-Analysis GIS Approach. *American Antiquity* 66(2):333-348.

Marean, C. and Z. Assefa 1999 Zooarchaeological Evidence for the Faunal Exploitation Behavior of Neanderthals and Early Modern Humans. *Evolutionary Anthropology*:22-37.

Marean, C. and C. Frey 1997 Animal Bones from Caves to Cities: Reverse Utility Curves as Methodological Artifacts. *American Antiquity* 62(4):698-711.

Marean, C. and L. Spencer 1991 Impact of Carnivore ravaging on Zooarchaeological Measure of Element Abundance. *American Antiquity* 56:645-658

Marks, A. 1983 The Middle to Upper Paleolithic Transition in the Levant. In *Advances in World Archaeology, Vol. 2*, pp. 51-98. Academic Press.

Marks, A. and D. Friedel 1977 Prehsitoric Settlement Patterns in the Avdat/Aqev Area. In *Prehistory and Paleoenvironments in the Central Negev, Israel, Vol. II*, pp. 131-158. Dallas: Southern Methodist University.

Marlowe, F. 2005 Hunter-Gatherers and Human Evolution. *Evolutionary Anthropology* 14:54-67.

Marshack, A. 1989 Evolution of the Human Capacity: the Symbolic Evidence. *Yearbook of Physical Antrhopology* 32:1-34.

Marshall, J., R. Jones, S. Crowley, F. Oldfield, S, Nash, A. Bedford 2002 A High Resolution Late-Glacial Isotopic Record from Hawes Water, Northwest England Climatic Oscillations: Calibration and Comparison of Paleotemperature Proxies. *Palaeogeography, Palaeoclimatology, Palaeoecology* 185:25-40.

Martinez, A. and O. Hamsici 2008 Who is LB1? Discriminant analysis for the classification of specimens. *Pattern Recognition* 41:3436 -- 3441

Mason, R., M. Peterson, and J. Tiffany 1998 Weighing vs. Counting: Measurement Reliability and the California School of Midden Analysis. *American Antiquity* 63(2):303-324.

McBrearty, S. and A. Brooks 2000 The revolution that wasn't: a new interpretation of the origin of modern human behavior. *Journal of Human Evolution* 39:453-563.

McCall, G. 2006 Multivariate perspectives on change and continuity in the Middle Stone Age lithics from Klasies River Mouth, South Africa. *Journal of Human Evolution* 51:429-439.

McCartney, P. and M. Glass 1990 Simulation Models and the Interpretation of Archaeological Diversity. *American Antiquity* 55(3):521-536.

McGowan, G. and J. Prangnell 2006 The Significance of Vivianite in Archaeological Settings. *Geoarchaeology* 21(1):93-111.

McNair, J. 1979 A Generalized Model of Optimal Diets. *Theoretical Population Biology* 15:159-170.

McNamara, J. 1982 Optimal Patch Use in a Stochastic Environment. *Theoretical Population Biology* 21:269-288.

McNamara, M., P. Orr, S. Kearns, L. Alcala, P. Anadon, and E. Penalver-Molla 2006 High-fidelity Organic Preservation of Bone Marrow in ca. 10 Ma Amphibians. *Geology* 34(8):641-644.

McNulty, A. Calkins, P. Ostrom, H. Gandhi, M. Gottfried, L. Martin, D. Gage Stable Isotope Values of Bone Organic Matter: Artificial Diagenesis Experiments and Paleoecology of Natural Trap Cave, Wyoming. *Palaios* 17:36-49.

Mellars, P. 2006 Why did modern human populations disperse from Africa *ca.* 60,000 years ago? A new model. *PNAS* 103(25):9381-9386.

2006 Archaeology and the Dispersal of Modern Humans in Europe: Deconstructing the Aurignacian. *Evolutonary Anthropology* 15:167-182.

2004 Neanderthals and the Modern Human Colonization of Europe. *Nature* 432:461-465

2005 The Impossible Coincidence. A Single-Species Model for the Origins of Modern Human Behavior in Europe. *Evolutionary Anthropology* 14:12-27.

2002 Reindeer Specialization in the Early Upper Paleolithic: the Evidence from Southwest France. *Journal of Archaeological Science* 31:613-617.

1999 The Neanderthal Problem Continued. *Current Anthropology* 40(3):341- 364.

1996 The Neanderthal Legacy: An Archaeological Perspective from Western Europe. Princeton University Press, Princeton.

1995 Symbolism, language, and the Neanderthal mind. In: Mellars, P., Gibson, K.R. (Eds.), Modeling the Human Mind. McDonald Institute Monographs, Cambridge, pp. 15-32.

1989 Major issues in the emergence of modern humans. *Current Anthropology* 30(3):349-385.

1973 The character of the middle-upper paleolithic transition in southwestern France. In The Explanation of Culture Change, edited by C. Renfrew, pp. 255-76 general editor. Duckworth, London.

1970 Some Comments on the Notion of 'Functional Variability' In Stone-Tool Assemblages. World Archaeology 2(1):74-89.

Meltzer, D. 1988 Late Pleistocene Human Adaptations in Eastern North America. *Journal of World Prehistory* 2(1):1-52.

Miller-Antonio, S., L. Scepartz, and D. Bakken 2001 New Directions in Paleolithic Archaeology: Asia and the Middle Pleistocene in Global Perspective. *Current Anthropology* 42(5):747-749.

Monahan, C. 1998 The Hadza Carcass Transport Debate Revisited and its Archaeological Implications. *Journal of Archaeological Science* 25:405-424.

Monnier, G. 2006 The Lower/Middle Paleolithic Periodization in Western Europe. *Current Anthropology* 47(5):709-744.

Moorman, B., S. Robinson and M. Burgess 2003 Imaging Periglacial Conditions with Ground-penetrating Radar. In *Permafrost and Periglacial Processes* 14:319-329.

Morin, E. 2007a Fat Composition and Nunamiut Decision-Making: A New Look at the Marrow and Bone Grease Indices. *Journal of Archaeological Science* 34:69-82.

2007b Beyond Stratigraphic Noise: Unraveling the Evolution of Stratified Assemblages in Faunalturbated Sites. *Geoarchaeology* 21(6):541-565.

Morin, E., T. Tsanova, N. Sirakov, W. Rendu, J-B. Mallye, and F. Leveque 2005 Bone Refits in Stratified Deposits: Testing the Chronological Grain at Saint-Cesaire. *Journal of Archaeological Science* 32:1083-1098.

Morozova, G. 2005 A Review of Holocene Avulsions of the Tigris and Euphrates Rivers and Possible Effects on the Evolution of Civilizations in Lower Mesopotamia. *Geoarchaeology* 20(4):401-423.

Morrison, D. 1978 On the Optimal Searching Strategy for Refuging Predators. *American Naturalist* 112:925-934.

Mortensen, P. 1972 Seasonal Camps and Early villages in the Zagros. In *Man, Settlement, and Urbanism*. Ucko, Tringham, Dimbleby (eds) pp. 293-297. London: Duckworth.

Movius, H. 1966 The Hearths of the Upper Periigordian and Aurignacian Horizons at the Abri Pataud, Les Eyzies (Dordogne) and Their Possible Significance. *American Anthropologist* 68(2):296–325.

Mulder, M., C. Nunn, and M. Towner 2006 Cultural Macroevolution and the Transmission of Traits. *Evolutionary Anthropology* 15:52-64.

Munro, N. 2004 Zooarchaeological Measures of Hunting Pressure and Occupation Intensity. *Current Anthropology* 45 Suplement:S5-S33.

Munson, P. and R. Garniewicz 2003 Age-Mediated Survivorship of ungulate Mandibles and Teeth in Canid-Ravaged Faunal Assemblages. *Journal of Archaeological Science* 30:405-416.

Munz, M. and W. Weidlich 1990 Settlement Formation Part II: Numerical Simulation. *Annals of Regional Science* 24:177-196.

Murton, J. and J-P. Lautridou 2003 Recent Advances in the Understanding of Quaternary Periglacial Features of the English Channel Coastlands. *Journal of Quaternary Science* 18(3-4):301-307.

Neal, A. and C. Roberts 2001 Internal Structure of a Trough Blowout, Determined from Migrated GPR Profiles. *Sedimentology* 48:791-810.

Nicholas, G. 1998 Wetlands and Hunter-Gatherers: A Global Perspective. *Current Anthropology* 39(5):720-731.

Nicholson, R. 1992 Bone Survival: the Effects of Sedimentary Abrasion and Trampling on Fresh and Cooked Bone. *International Journal of Osteoarchaeology* 2:79-90.

Norberg, R. 1977 An Ecological Theory on Foraging Time and Energetics and Choice of Optimal Food-Searching Method. *Journal of Animal Ecology* 46:511-529.

O'Connell, J. and J. Allen 1998 When Did Humans First Arrive in Greater Australia and Why Is It Important to Know? *Evolutionary Anthropology:*132-146.

O'Connor, T. 1996 A Critical Overview of Archaeological Animal Bone Studies. *World Archaeology* 28(1):5-19.

Odell, G. 1982 Some Additional Perspectives on Appropriate Models and Analogs for Hunter-Gatherer Populations. *American Antiquity* 47(1):192-198.

Ollason, J. 1980 Learning to Forage—Optimally? *Theoretical Population Biology* 18:44-56.

Olsen, S. 1964 *Mammal Remains from Archaeological Sites Part 1 – Southeastern and Southwestern united States.* Papers of the Peabody Museum of Archaeology and Ethnology, Harvard University, Cambridge. Volume 56, Number 1.

Olszewksi, D. and N. Coinman 1998 Settlement Patterning During the Late Pleistocene in the Wadi al-Hasa West Central Jordan. In *The Archaeology of the Wadi al-Hasa, West-Central Jordan, Volume 1: Surveys, Settlement Patterns and Paleoenvironments.* N. Coinman (ed), pp. 177-194. Tempe: Arizona State University.

Olszewski, T. 2004 Modeling the Influence of Taphonomic Destruction, Reworking, and Burial on Time-Averaging in Faunal Accumulations. *Palaios* 19:39-50.

Orlando, L. 2007 Georadar Data Collection, Anomaly Shape and Archaeological Interpretation - a Case Study from Central Italy. *Archaeological Prospection* 14:213-225.

Outram, A., C. Knusel, S. Knight, and A. Harding 2005 Understanding Complex Fragmented Assemblages of Human and Animal Remains: A Fully Integrated Approach. *Journal of Archaeological Science* 32:1699-1710.

Ozawa, K. 1990 Simulation studies of optical illusions based on a position dependent point-spread function. *Pattern Recognition* 23(12):1361-1306.

Ozdemir, C. and H. Ling 2006 An Experimental Investigation of Buried-Object Imaging in a Homogenous Medium Using Synthetic-Aperture Radar Concepts. *Microwave and Optical Technology Letters* 48(6):1209-1214.

Panagopoulou, E., P. Karkanas, G. Tsartsidou, E. Kotjabopoulou, K. Harvati, and M. Ntinou. 2002 Late Pleistocene Archaeological and Fossil human Evidence from Lakonis Cave, Southern Greece. *Journal of Field Archaeology* 29(3/4):323-349.

Pappu, S. 1999 A Study of Natural Site Formation Processes in the Kortallayar Basin, Tamil Nadu, South India. *Geoarchaeology* 14(2):127-150.

Passmore, D., C. Waddington, and T. van der Schriek 2006 Enhancing the Evaluation and Management of River Valley Archaeology; Geoarchaeology in the Till-Tweed Catchment, Northern England. *Archaeological Prospection* 13:269-281.

Pastre, J.F., N. Limondin-Lozouet, C, Leroyer, P. Ponel, and M. Fontugne 2002 River system evolution and environmental changes during the Late glacial in the

Paris Basin (France). *Quaternary Science Reviews* 22: 2177-2188.

Patch, S. and D. Gregory 2010 Refining Middle Woodland Site Structure: Ground Penetrating Radar Investigations at Site 40Mi70, Marion County, Tennessee. Paper presented in session "Anthropological Geophysics: Scale and configuration in the archaeological record at 74th Annual Society for American Archaeology Meeting. St. Louis. 2010.

Pearson, C. 1980 Rank-Size Distribution and the Analysis of Prehistoric Settlement Systems. *Journal of Anthropological Research* 36(4):453-462.

Peresani, M. 2008 A New Cultural Frontier for the Last Neanderthals: The Uluzzian in Northern Italy. *Current Anthropology* 49(4):725-731.

Pettitt, P. 2007 Trajectories before the transition, and revolutions that were or were not (book review). *Journal of Human Evolution* 53:755-759.

Pickering, T., C. Marean, M. Dominguez-Rodrigo 2002 Importance of Limb Bone Shaft Fragments in Zooarchaeology: A response to "On *in situ* Attrition and Vertebrate Body Part profiles" (2002), by M.C. Stiner. *Journal of Archaeological Science* 30:1469-1482.

Pike-Tay, A. 1995 Variability and Synchrony of Seasonal Indicators in Dental Cementum Microstructure of the Kaminuriak Caribou Population. *Archaeofauna* 4:273-284.

Pike-Tay, A. et al. 2000 Reconsidering the Quadratic Crown Height Method of Age Estimation for *Rangifer* from Archaeological Sites. *Archaeozoologica* XI:145-174.

Piro, S., P. Mauriello, F. Cammarano 2000 Quantitative Integration of Geophysical Methods for Archaeological Prospection. *Archaeological Prospection* 7:203-213.

Plog, S. and M. Hegmon 1993 The Sample Size-Richness Relation: The Relevance of Research Questions, Sampling Strategies, and Behavioral Variation. *American Antiquity* 58(3):489-496.

Pomfret, J. 2006 Ground-penetrating Radar Profile Spacing and Orientation for Subsurface Resolution of Linear Features. *Archaeol. Prospect.*13:151–153.

Ponel, P. 1995 Rissian, Eemian, and Wurmian Coleoptera Assemblages from la Grande Pile (Vosges, France). *Palaeogeography, Palaeoclimatology, Palaeoecology* 114:1-41.

Porter, C. and F. Marlowe 2007 How Marginal are Forager Habitats? *Journal of Archaeological Science* 34:59-68.

Prior, J. 1991 *Landforms of Iowa.* University of Iowa Press.

Prentiss, W. and J. Chatters 2003 Cultural Diversification in the Prehistoric Record. *Current Anthropology* 44(1):3-58.

Pulliam, H. 1974 On the Theory of Optimal Diets. *American Naturalist* 108:56-75.

Pyke, G. 1984 Optimal Foraging Theory: A Critical Review. *Annual Review of Ecological Systems* 15:523-575.

1982 Foraging in bumblebees: Rule of Departure from an Inflorescence. *Canadian Journal of Zooloogy* 60:417-428.

Raab, L. and A. Goodyear 1984 Middle-Range Theory in Archaeology: A Critical Review of Origins and Applications. *American Antiquity* 49(2):255-268.

Reich, D. et al. 2010 Genetic history of an archaic hominin group from Denisova Cave in Siberia. *Nature* 468:1053-1060.

Reille, M. and V. Andrieu 1994 The Late Pleistocene and Holocene in the Lourdes Basin, Western Pyrenees, France: New Pollen Analytical and Chronological Data. *Veget Hist Archaeobot* 4:1-21.

Renssen, H., C. Kasse, J. Vendenberghe, and S. Lorenz 2006 Weichselian Late Pleniglacial Surface Winds over Northwest and Central Europe: A Model-Data Comparison. *Journal of Quaternary Science* (in press).

Renssen, H. and P. Bogaart 2003 Atmospheric Variability over the ~14.7 kyr BP Stadial-Interstadial Transition in the North Atlantic Region as Simulated by an AGCM. *Climate Dynamics* 20:301-313.

Richards, L. 1983 Hunger and the Optimal Diet. *American Naturalist* 122:326-334.

Richards, M. and E. Trinkaus 2009 Isotopic evidence for the diets of European Neandertals and early modern humans. *Proceedings of the National Academy of Sciences USA* 106, 16034-16039.

Rick, T. 2002 Eolian Processes, Ground Cover, and the Archaeology of Coastal Dunes: A Taphonomic Case Study from San Miguel Island, California, USA. *Geoarchaeology* 17(8):811-833.

Rick, T., J. Erlandson, and R. Vellanoweth 2006 Taphonomy and Site Formation on California's Channel Islands. *Geoarchaeology* 21(6):567-589.

Roberts, M., J-P. Brevard, and H. Mol 1997 Radar Signatures and Structure of an Avulsed Channel: Rhone River, Aoste, France. *Journal of Quaternary Research* 12(1):35-42.

Rocek, T. 1988 The Behavioral and Material Correlates of Site Seasonality: Lessons from Navajo Ethnoarchaeology. *American Antiquity* 53(3):523-536.

Rodrigues, S., J. Porsani, V. Santos, P. DeBlasis, P. Giannini 2009 GPR and inductive electromagnetic *surveys* applied in three coastal sambaqui (shell mounds) archaeological sites in Santa Catarina state, South Brazil. *Journal of Archaeological Science* 36:2081-2088.

Roebroeks, W. 2006 The Human Colonization of Europe: Where Are We? *Journal of Quaternary Science* 21(5):425-435.

Rogers, A. a On Equifinality in Faunal Analysis. *American Antiquity* 65(4):709-723.

2000b Analysis of Bone Counts by Maximum Likelihood. *Journal of Archaeological Science* 27:111-125.

Rolland, N. and H. Dibble 1990 A New Synthesis of Middle Paleolithic Variability. *American Antiquity* 55:480-499.

Roscoe, P. 2002 The Hunters and gatherers of New Guinea. *Current Anthropology* 43(1):153-190.

Rose, L. and F. Marshall 1996 Meat Eating, Hominid Sociality, and Home Bases Revisited. *Current Anthropology* 37(2):307-338.

Rowlands, A. and A. Sarris 2007 Detection of Exposed and Subsurface Archaeological Remains using Multi-Sensor Remote Sensing. *Journal of Archaeological Science* 34(5):795-803.

Rowley-Conwy, P. 2004 How the West Was Lost. A Reconsideration of Agricultural Origins in Britain, Ireland, and Southern Scandinavia. *Current Anthropology* 45(supplement):S83-S113.

Ruffell, A. et al. 2004 Ground-penetrating Radar Facies as an aid to Sequence Stratigraphic Analysis: Applicationto the Archaeology of Clonmacnoise Castle, Ireland. *Archaeological Prospection* 11:247-262.

Runnels, C. and M. Ozdogan 2001 The Paleolithic of the Bosporus Region, NW Turkey. *Journal of Field Archaeology* 28(1/2):69-92.

Sackett, J. 1991 Straight Archaeology, French Style: the Phylogenetic Paradigm in Historic Perspective. In Clark (ed) *Perspectives on the Past: Theoretical Bases in Mediterranean Hunter-Gatherer Research.* pp. 109-139. University of Pennsylvania Press.

1986 Style, Function, and Assemblage Variability: A Reply to Binford. *American Antiquity* 51(3):628-634.

1977 The Meaning of Style in Archaeology: A General Model. *American Antiquity* 42(3):36-380.

Samuelson, P. 1942 The Stability of Equilibrium: Linear and Nonlinear Systems. *Econometrica* 10(1):1-25.

Schiegl, S., P. Goldberg, H-U. Pfretzschner, and N. Conard 2003 Paleolithic Burnt Bone Horizons from the Swabian Jura: Distinguishing Between In Situ Fireplaces and Dumping Areas. *Geoarchaeology* 18(5):541-565.

Schiffer, M. 1983 Toward the Identification of Formation Processes. *American Antiquity* 48(4):675-706.

Schild, R. and F. Wendorf 2004 Paleolithic Living Sites in Upper and Middle Egypt: A Review Article. *Journal of Field Archaeology* 29(3/4):447-461.

Schluter, D. 1982 Optimal Foraging in Bats: Some Comments. *American Naturalist* 119:121- 125.

Schmitt, D. and K. Lupo 1995 On Mammalian Taphonomy, Taxonomic Diversity, and Measuring Subsistence Data in Zooarchaeology. *American Antiquity* 60(3):496-514.

Schmider, B. 1982 The Magdalenian Culture of the Paris River-Basin and Its Relationship with the Nordic Cultures of the Late Old Stone Age. *World Archaeology* 14(2):259-269.

Scott, K. 1980 Two hunting episodes of Middle Paleolithic Age at La Cotte de St.-Brelade, Jersey (Channel Islands). *World Archaeology* 12(2):137-152.

Scultz, J. et al. 2006 Sequential Monitoring of Burials Containing Large Pig Cadavers Using Ground-Penetrating Radar. *J Forensic Sci*, May 2006, Vol. 51, No. 3.

Serrano, F., A. Guerra-Merchan, C. Lozano-Francisco, and J. Vera-Pelaez 1997 Multivariate Analysis of Remains of Molluscan Foods Consumed by Latest Pleistocene and Holocene Humans in Nerja Cave, Malaga, Spain. *Quaternary Research* 48:215-227.

Sharer R. and W. Ashmore 1993 *Archaeology: Discovering our Past.* Mayfield Publishing.

Shea, J. 2003a The Middle Paleolithic of the East Mediterranean Levant. *Journal of World Prehistory* 17(4):313-394.

2003b Neanderthals, Competition, and the Origin of Modern Human Behavior in the Levant. *Evolutionary Anthropology* 12:173-187.

Shennan, S. 2000 Population, Culture History, and the Dynamics of Culture Change. *Current Anthropology* 41(5):811-835.

Shennan, S. and K. Edinborough 2006 Prehistoric Population History: from the Late Glacial to the Late Neolithic in Central and Northern Europe. *Journal of Archaeological Science xx:*1-7.

Shoocongdej, R. 2000 Forager Mobility Organization in Seasonal Tropical Environments of Western Thailand. *World Archaeology* 32(1):14-40.

Smith, E. 1992 Human Behavioral Ecology: I. *Evolutionary Anthropology:*20-25.

Smith, M. 2007 Inconspicuous Consumption: Non-Display Goods and Identity Formation. *Journal of Archaeological Method And Theory* 14:412-438.

Smith, M., M. Brickley, and S. Leach 2007 Experimental Evidence for Lithic Projectile Injuries: Improving Identification of an Under-Recognized Phenomenon. *Journal of Archaeological Science* 34:540-553.

Soffer, O., J. Adovasio, D. Hyland 2000 Textiles, Basketry, Gender, and Status in the Upper Paleolithic. *Current Anthropology* 41(4):511-537.

South, Stanley 1978 Pattern Recognition in Historical Archaeology. *American Antiquity* 43(2):223-230.

Speth, J. 1991 Taphonomy and Early Hominid Behavior: Problems in Distinguishing Cultural and Non-Cultural Agents. In *Human Predators & Prey Mortality,* M. Stiner (ed), pp. 31-40. Boulder: Westview Press.

1983 *Bison Kills and Bone Counts: Decision Making by Ancient Hunters.* University of Chicago Press.

Speth, J. and K. Spielman 1983 Energy Source, Protein Metabolism, and Hunter-Gatherer Subsistence Strategies. *Journal of Anthropological Archaeology* 2(1):1-31.

Stahl, A. 1993 Concepts of Time and Approaches to Analogical Reasoning in Historical Perspective. *American Antiquity* 58(2):235-260.

Stallibrass, S. 1982 The Use of Cement Layers for Absolute Aging of Mammalian Teeth: A Selective Review of the Literature, with Suggestions for Further Studies and Alternative Applications. In: Wilson, Grigson, and Payne (eds) *Aging and Sexing Animal Bones from Archaeological Sites,* pp. 109-126. BAR Series 109.

Sterud, E., L. Straus, and K. Abramovitz 1981 Recent Developments in Old World Archaeology. *American Antiquity* 45(4):759-786.

Stettler, H. 2000 Upper Paleolithic Transitions: Evidence from Organic Artifacts of Cantabrian Spain. *Journal of Anthropological Research* 56(1):113-128.

Stewart, J. 2004 Neanderthal-Modern Competition? A Comparison between the Mammals Associated with Middle and Upper Paleolithic Industries in Europe during OIS 3. *International Journal of Osteoarchaeology* 14:178-189.

Stiner, M. 2002a Carnivory, Coevolution, and the Geographic Spread of the Genus *Homo. Journal of Archaeological Research* 10(1):1-63.

2002b On *in situ* Attrition and Vertebrate Body Part Profiles. *Journal of Archaeological Science* 29:979-991.

2001 Thirty Years on the "Broad Spectrum revolution" and Paleolithic Demography. *Proceedings of the National Academy of Sciences of the United States of America* 98(13):6993-6996.

1991a Food Procurement and Transport by Human and Non-Human Predators. *Journal of Archaeological Science* 18:455-482.

1991b *Human Predators and Prey Mortality.* Westview Press.

Stiner, M and S. Kuhn 2006 Changes in the Connectedness and Resilience of Paleolithic Societies in Mediterranean Ecosystems. *Human Ecology* 34:693-712.

Stiner, M., N. Munro, and T. Surovell 2000 The Tortoise and the Hare: Small-Game Use, the Broad-Spectrum revolution, and Paleolithic Demography. *Current Anthropology* 41(1):39-73.

Stojanowski, C. 2002 Hydrodynamic Sorting in a Coastal Marine Skeletal Assemblage. *International Journal of Osteoarchaeology* 12:259-278.

Stojanowski, C., R. Seidemann, and G. Doran 2002 Differential Skeletal Preservation at Windover Pond: Causes and Consequences. *American Journal of Physical Anthropology* 119:15-26.

Stoneking, M. and R. Cann 1989 African origin of human mitochondrial DNA. In: The Human Revolution: Behavioural and Biological Perspectives on the Origins of Modern Humans, P. Mellars and C. Stringer (eds.), Edinburgh University Press, Edinburgh, pp. 17-30.

Storey, G. R., and W. E. Whittaker 2005a Ground-Penetrating Radar Survey of the Efficy Mounds National Monument Sny Magill Mound Group (13CT18), Clayton County. Contract Completion Report 1233. Office of the State Archaeologist, Iowa City. 2005.

2005b Ground-Penetrating Radar Survey of the Possible 13AM446, Effigy Mounds National Monument, Allamakee County, Iowa. Completion Report 1234. Office of the State Archaeologist, Iowa City. 2005.

2005c Ground Penetrating Radar Survey of the Sny Magill Mound Group, Effigy Mounds National Monument, Iowa. Under review for *American Antiquity*.

2004a Ground-Penetrating Radar Survey for Primary Roads Project NH5-151-4(84)--3H-53 of Portions of the Bowen's Prairie Cemetery (13JN152), Section 6, T86N-R2W, Jones County, Iowa. Contract Completion Report 1110. Office of the State Archaeologist, University of Iowa, Iowa City.

2004b Ground-Penetrating Radar Survey of the Herbert Hoover Boyhood Home (13CD134), West Branch, Cedar County, Iowa (with William E. Whittaker). Contract Completion Report 1123. Office of the State Archaeologist, Iowa City.

Straight, W. and D. Eberth 2002 Testing the Utility of Vertebrate Remains in Recognizing Patterns in Fluvial Deposits: An Example from the Lower horseshoe Canyon Formation, Alberta. *Palaios* 17:472-490.

Straus, L. 2006 Of Stones and Bones: Interpreting Site Function in the Upper Paleolithic and Mesolithic of Western Europe. *Journal of Anthropological Archaeology* 25:500-509.

2005 The Upper Paleolithic of Cantabrian Spain. *Evolutionary Anthropology* 14:145-158.

2000 Solutrean Settlement of North America? A Review of Reality. *American Antiquity* 65(2):219-226.

1999 Iberia: Bridge or Cul-de-Sac? Implications of the Iberian Record for the Debate on the Middle to Upper Paleolithic Transition. *Human Evolution* 14(1-2):139-149.

1995 The Upper Paleolithic of Europe: An Overview. *Evolutionary Anthropology* 4-16.

1994 The Pace of Change in the Paleolithic. *American Anthropologist* 96(3):713-716.

1991a Southwestern Europe at the Last Glacial Maximum. *Current Anthropology* 32(2):189-199.

1991b Human Geography of the Late Upper Paleolithic in Western Europe: Present State of the Question. *American Antiquity* 47(2):259-278.

Straus, L., D. Meltzer, and T. Goebel 2005 Ice Age Atlantis? Exploring the Solutrean-Clovis "Connection". *World Archaeology* 37(4):507-532.

Sturm, J. 2010 Using Ground-Penetrating Radar to Study a Historic Denver Neighborhood. . Paper presented in session "Anthropological Geophysics: Scale and configuration in the archaeological record at 74th Annual Society for American Archaeology Meeting. St. Louis. 2010.

Sullivan, A. 1992 Investigating the Archaeological Consequences of Short-Duration Occupations. *American Antiquity* 57(1):99-115.

Sutton, M. 1995 Archaeological Aspects of Insect Use. *Journal of Archaeological Method and Theory* 2(3):253-298.

Svoboda, J. 1994a The Pavlov Site, Czech Republic: Lithic Evidence from the Upper Paleolithic. *Journal of Field Archaeology* 21(1):69-81.

1994b Predmosti after 110 Years. *Journal of Field Archaeology* 21(4):457-472.

Symens, N. 1986 A Functional Analysis of Selected Stone Artifacts from the Magdalenian Site at Verberie, France. *Journal of Field Archaeology* 13(2):213-222.

Taghon, G. 1981 Beyond Selection: Optimal Ingestion Rate as a Function of Food Value. *American Naturalist* 118:202-214.

Takamiya, H. 2006 An Unusual Case? Hunter-Gatherer Adaptations to an Island Environment: A Case Study from Okinawa, Japan. *Journal of Island & Coastal Archaeology* 1:49-66.

Tang, G. and T. Huang 1980 Using the Creation Machine to Locate airplanes on aerial photos. *Pattern Recognition* 12:431-442.

Tattersall, I. Once we were not alone. *Scientific American* 282(1):56-62. 1995 *The Fossil Trail: How We Know What We Think We Know About Human Evolution.* Oxford University Press.

Tebbens, L., A. Veldkamp, W. Westerhoff, and S. Kroonenberg 1999 Fluvial Incision and Channel Downcutting as a Response to Late-Glacial and Early Holocene Climate Change: the Lower Reach of the River Meuse (Maas), The Netherlands. *Journal of Quaternary Research* 14(1):59-75.

Templeton, Alan R. 1993 The "Eve" Hypothesis: A Genetic Critique and Reanalysis. *American Anthropologist* 95(l):51-72.

Thieme, H. 1996 Altpalaolithische Wurfspeere aus Schoningen, Niedersachsen—ein Vorbericht. *Archaologisches Korrespondenzblatt* 26:377–393.

Thomas, K. 1996 Zooarchaeology: Past, Present and Future. *World Archaeology* 28(1):1-4.

Thompson, V., P. Arnold, T. Pluckhahn, and A. VanDerwarker 2010 Anthropological Archaeology, Remote Sensing, and the Analysis of Persistent Places. Paper presented in session "Anthropological Geophysics: Scale and configuration in the archaeological record at 74th Annual Society for American Archaeology Meeting. St. Louis. 2010.

Thompson, J. 2012 The allegory of the hammer and the nail gun and other unstable orthodoxies of 'modernity': possible pitfalls of 'behavioural modernity'. *AURA Newsletter* 29(2):3-12.

Thompson, J. and G. Storey 2010 Ground-Penetrating Radar and Imaging of Complex Subsurface Archaeological Materials. Paper presented in session "Anthropological Geophysics: Scale and configuration in the archaeological record at 74th Annual Society for American Archaeology Meeting. St. Louis. 2010.

Trivers, R. 1971 The Evolution of Reciprocal Altruism. *The Quarterly Review of Biology* 46(1): 35-57.

Turner, A.1982 Optimal Foraging by the Swallow—Prey size Selection. *Animal Behavior* 30:862-872.

Turner-Waller, G., C. Nielsen-Marsh, U. Syversen, H. Kars, and M. Collins 2002 Sub-Micron Spongiform Porosity is the Major Ultra-Structural Alteration Occurring in Archaeological Bone. *International Journal of Osteoarchaeology* 12:407-414.

Uerpmann, H. 1973 Animal Bone Finds and Economic Archaeology: A Critical Study of 'Osteo-Archaeological' Method. *World Archaeology* 4:307-322.

Ulijaszek, S. 2001 Potential Seasonal Ecological Challenge of Heat Strain among Australian Aboriginal People Practicing Traditional Subsistence Methods: A Computer Simulation. *American Journal of Physical Anthropology* 116:236-245.

Vafidis, A., N. Economou, Y. Ganiatsos, M. Manakou, G. Poulioudis, G. Sourlas, E. Vrontaki, A. Sarris, M. Guy and Th. Kalpaxis 2005 Integrated geophysical studies at ancient Itanos (Greece). *Journal of Archaeological Science* 32(7):1023-1036.

Valensi, P. 2000 The Archaeology of Lazaret Cave (Nice, France). *International Journal of Osteoarchaeology* 10:357-367.

Vanhaeren, M. and F. d'Errico 2005 Grave Goods from the Saint-Germain-la-Riviere Burial: Evidence for Social Inequality in the Upper Paleolithic. *Journal of Anthropological Archaeology* 24:117-134.

Van Huissteden, K., J. Vandenberghe, and D. Pollard 2003 Paleotemperature Reconstructions of the European Permafrost Zone during Marine Oxygen Isotope Stage 3 Compared with Climate Model Results. *Journal of Quaternary Science* 18(5):453-464.

Vishnyatsky, L. 1999 The Paleolithic of Central Asia. *Journal of World Prehistory* 13(1):69-122.

Voorrips, A. and J. O'Shea 1987 Conditional Patterning: Beyond the Nearest Neighbor. *American Antiquity* 52(3):500-521.

Waters, M. and D. Kuehn 1996 The Geoarchaeology of Place: The Effect of Geological Processes on the Preservation and Interpretation of the Archaeological Record. *American Antiquity* 61(3):483-497.

Weaver, W. 2006 Ground-penetrating Radar Mapping in Clay: Success from South Carolina, USA. *Archaeoogical Prospection* 13:147–150.

Weaver, T. and K. Steudel-Numbers 2005 Does Climate or Mobility Explain the Differences in Body Proportions Between Neanderthals and Their Upper Paleolithic Successors? *Evolutionary Anthropology* 14:218-223.

Weidlich, W. and M. Munz 1989 Settlement Formation Part I: A Dynamic Theory. *Annals of Regional Science* 24:83-106.

Weniger, G. 1989 The Magdalenian in West-Central Europe: Settlement Pattern and Regionality. *Journal of World Prehistory* 3(3):323-372.

Whallon, R. 2006 Social Networks and Information: Nonutilitarian Mobility among Hunter-Gatherers. *Journal of Anthropological Archaeology* 25:259-270.

White, T. et al. 2003 Pleistocene Homo sapiens from Middle Awash, Ethiopia. *Nature* 423:742-747.

Wiessner, P. 1982a Risk, Reciprocity, and Social Influences on !Kung San Economics. In *Politics and History in Band Societies,* E. Leacock and R.B. Lee (eds), pp. 61-84. Cambridge: Cambridge University Press.

1982b Beyond Willow Smoke and Dogs' tails: A Comment on Binford's Analysis of Hunter-Gatherer Settlement Systems. *American Antiquity* 47(1):171-178.

1974 A Functional Estimate of Population from Floor Size. *American Antiquity* 39(2):343-350.

Winterhalder, B. 1997 Social Foraging and the Behavioral Ecology of Intragroup Resource Transfers. *Evolutionary Anthropology:*46-57.

Winterhalder, B. and E. Smith 2000 Analyzing Adaptive Strategies: Human Behavioral Ecology at Twenty-Five. *Evolutionary Anthropology:*51-72.

Wobst, H. 1978 The Archaeo-Ethnology of Hunter-Gatherers or the Tyranny of the Ethnographic Record in Archaeology. *American Antiquity* 43(2):303-309.

Wolpoff, M. and R. Caspari 1997 *Race and Human Evolution*. New York: Simon and Schuster.

1996 The Modernity Mess. *Journal of Human Evolution* 30(2):167-172.

Wood, J.1978 Optimal Location in Settlement Space: A Model for Describing Location Strategies. *American Antiquity* 43(2):258-270.

Wood, W. R. and D. L. Johnson 1978 A Survey of Disturbance Processes in Archaeological Site Formation. In *Advances in Archaeological Method and Theory, Vol. 1.* M. Schiffer (ed) pp. 315-381. New York: Academic Press.

Wrangham, R., J. Jones, G. Laden, D. Pilbeam, and N. Conklin-Brittain 1999 The Raw and the Stolen: Cooking and the Ecology of Human Origins. *Current Anthropology* 40(5):567-594.

Yalciner, C. et al. 2009 New Temple Discovery at the Archaeological Site of Nysa (Western Turkey) using GPR Method. *Journal of Archaeological Science* 36(8):1680-1689.

Yellen, J. 1977 Cultural Patterning in Faunal Remains: Evidence from the !Kung Bushmen. In: Ingersoll and Yellen (eds) *Experimental Archaeology*, pp. 271-331. Columbia University Press.

Zhou, H. and M. Sato 2001 Archaeological investigation in Sendai Castle using ground-penetrating radar. *Archaeological Prospection* 8: 1-11.

Zilhao, J. 2006 Neanderthals and Moderns Mixed, and it Matters. *Evolutionary Anthropology* 15:183-195.

Zilhao, J. and F. d'Errico Chronology and Taphonomy of the Earliest Aurignacian and Its Implications for the Understanding of Neanderthal Extinction. *Journal of World Prehistory* 13(1):1-68.

Zilhao, J., F. d'Errico, J-G. Bordes, A. Lenoble, J-P. Texier, and J-P. Rigaud 2006 Analysis of Aurignacian interstratification at the Châtelperronian-type site and implications for the behavioral modernity of Neandertals. *Proceedings of the National Academy of Sciences* 103(33):12643-12648.

www.ingramcontent.com/pod-product-compliance
Lightning Source LLC
Chambersburg PA
CBHW061008030426

42334CB00033B/3407